Anarchy, State and Public Choice

Advanced Studies in Political Economy

Series Editors: Virgil Henry Storr and Stefanie Haeffele

The Advanced Studies in Political Economy series consists of republished as well as newly commissioned work that seeks to understand the underpinnings of a free society through the foundations of the Austrian, Virginia, and Bloomington schools of political economy. Through this series, the Mercatus Center at George Mason University aims to further the exploration of and discussion on the dynamics of social change by making this research available to students and scholars.

Anarchy, State and Public Choice

Edited by

Edward Stringham

Foreword by

Peter J. Boettke and Rosolino A. Candela

MERCATUS CENTER
George Mason University

Arlington, Virginia

About the Mercatus Center at George Mason University

The Mercatus Center at George Mason University is the world's premier university source for market-oriented ideas—bridging the gap between academic ideas and real-world problems.

A university-based research center, Mercatus advances knowledge about how markets work to improve people's lives by training graduate students, conducting research, and applying economics to offer solutions to society's most pressing problems.

Our mission is to generate knowledge and understanding of the institutions that affect the freedom to prosper and to find sustainable solutions that overcome the barriers preventing individuals from living free, prosperous, and peaceful lives.

Since 1980, the Mercatus Center has been part of George Mason University, located on the Arlington and Fairfax campuses.

Originally published in 2005 by Edward Elgar Publishing as *Anarchy, State and Public Choice*. © 2005 Edward Stringham. This edition published with permission.
Foreword © 2018 Peter J. Boettke, Rosolino A. Candela, and the Mercatus Center at George Mason University.
All rights reserved. Printed in the United States of America.

ISBN 978-1-942951-40-7

Mercatus Center at George Mason University
3434 Washington Blvd., 4th Floor
Arlington, Virginia 22201
www.mercatus.org

Cover design by Joanna Andreasson
Typesetting services by Robin Black of Inspirio Design

Contents

Foreword to the Mercatus Center Edition

The development of Virginia Political Economy (VPE)[1] throughout the 20th century played a crucial role in changing economists' presumptions about the economic role of the state.[2] Beginning in the 1950s and 1960s, economists in the VPE tradition first emphasized the various government failures that plague policy attempts to address the existence of market failures. As James M. Buchanan, Gordon Tullock, and others pointed out, special interest groups, short-sighted policy bias, and regulatory capture all may undermine the execution of policies intended to provide public goods, erode monopoly power, and eliminate externalities. Although imperfections in the market process may exist, VPE economists argued that government interventions to address such market failures will not necessarily be any better. Market failures, the government failure presumption suggests, may simply be failures to appreciate not only the costs of government intervention, but also the benefits of private solutions to overcoming problems of facilitating social order.

Anarchy, State and Public Choice marked a transition in VPE by taking the government failure presumption one step further to develop a presumption of anarchy in political economy, which claims that no solution exists to resolve the paradox of government, namely to empower and then constrain the state to a limited economic role of enforcing private property rights. Whereas economists of the VPE tradition share a presumption of government failure, Edward Stringham's *Anarchy, State and Public Choice* provides contending perspectives regarding how optimistic or pessimistic political economists can be toward the presumption of anarchy in political economy. The publication of *Anarchy, State and Public Choice*[3] marked a critical transition in the study of anarchy in the tradition of VPE, from a presumption of pessimistic anarchism to one of optimistic anarchism.

Originally published in 2005 by Edward Elgar, *Anarchy, State and Public Choice* revived interest in a previous generation of scholars who had provided an economic analysis of anarchy.[4] Both generations of scholars shared a common research question: how can self-interested individuals establish norms and rules that foster the conditions for social cooperation under the division of labor? However, each generation arrived at different conclusions to that research question.

vii

THE GENERATION OF PESSIMISTIC ANARCHISM

Inspired by the civil unrest during the Vietnam War and the civil rights movement (chapter 15, page 191), Buchanan, Tullock, and Winston Bush undertook a radical reexamination of alternative institutional arrangements for governing society at Virginia Polytechnic Institute and State University (then known as VPI) in Blacksburg.[5] As Bush (chapter 2, page 10) put it, "It is not surprising that 'anarchy' and 'anarchism' have re-emerged as topics for discussion in the 1960s and the 1970s, as tentacles of government progressively invade private lives and as the alleged objectives of such invasions recede yet further from attainment."

Beginning with the publication of *Explorations in the Theory of Anarchy*[6] and *Further Explorations in the Theory of Anarchy*,[7] this first group of scholars, "stimulated more or less directly by Winston Bush" (Buchanan, chapter 15, page 191), was defined by a presumption of pessimistic anarchism. Anarchy, as it was understood in these two early volumes, referred to a "state in society characterized by the absence of law coupled with anonymity" (Hogarty, chapter 10, page 99). "The anarchists of the 1960s," according to Buchanan (chapter 15, page 192), "were enemies of order, rather than proponents of any alternative organizational structure." Therefore, the common assumption held by these pessimistic anarchists was an identification of government with law (see chapter 17), failing to distinguish between "*the law as government-enforced prohibitions* from *the law as social order*" (Storr, chapter 11, page 114, emphasis in original).

It is understandable, given the historical context in which they were writing, that Buchanan, Bush, and the other contributors regarded anarchism with skepticism. However, the basis of their skepticism was that anarchy as a viable alternative of governance presumes either that individuals would have to be already persuaded by the merits of anarchy (see chapter 16), or that it "tends to presume the behavior necessary to produce the results intended" for anarchy to succeed (Samuels, chapter 13, page 163). Without conceiving of an alternative structure of governance, these pessimistic anarchists claimed that anarchy would require a benevolent transformation of human nature, because anarchy, as they viewed it, would be unbound by any rules to constrain violent and opportunistic behavior (see chapter 15). It was this critique of anarchy to which the contributors of *Anarchy, State and Public Choice* would later respond.

THE GENERATION OF OPTIMISTIC ANARCHISM

Stringham, like his predecessor Bush, was a "principal instigator"[8] in promoting a research interest in the economic analysis of anarchy. While he was still a graduate student at George Mason University (GMU), not only did Stringham foster a climate of critical inquiry to advance research in anarchy, but he also organized the publication of *Anarchy, State and Public Choice* and inspired a new generation of young graduate students to make contributions to this research program. Each of these graduate student papers was written in response to contributions in *Explorations in the Theory of Anarchy* and *Further Explorations in the Theory of Anarchy.*[9]

This second generation of scholars working in the VPE tradition can be characterized by a presumption of optimistic anarchism. For them, anarchy, "simply put, means a society without government," yet not necessarily with disorder (Storr, chapter 11, page 113). They challenged the pessimism of the previous generation on both theoretical as well as empirical grounds. Although radical in their conclusions, the premises of their argument follow logically out of the VPE paradigm.

In an ironic generational twist, the theoretical challenge of the optimistic anarchists was to assume behavioral symmetry in both market as well as nonmarket settings. "Ironically, in 'Before Public Choice,' and in *The Limits of Liberty*," Benjamin Powell (chapter 9, page 91) argues, "Buchanan does not analyze government with the same assumptions he makes about people in anarchy." If individuals are modeled to act opportunistically in anarchy, then the same assumptions must be used to model individuals in government. Moreover, in response to Tullock's "The Edge of the Jungle," Christopher Coyne (chapter 5) points out that limitations to the discipline of repeated dealings, which Tullock claims will hamper the protection of property rights under anarchy, must also apply to his theory of government. Tullock had assumed that government officials would be constrained from predation by the discipline of repeated dealings with their subjects. "Underlying Tullock's oversight," Coyne (chapter 5, page 56) argues, "is his characterization of the rulers as monetary income maximizers." However, like any other individual, rulers must be assumed to be maximizing psychic income, which includes both monetary and nonmonetary forms of income. If so, "[r]ulers may gain (psychic) income by holding and wielding power even though they may not maximize monetary revenue by doing so. And, if they do so, their actions may conflict with the ruled group's interests far more than Tullock's analysis suggests" (chapter 5, page 56). In short, the optimistic anarchists challenged the pessimistic presumption of anarchy—namely, by undermining the optimistic presumption that government is a viable provider of governance. This challenge was not only theoretical but also empirical.

Whereas the pessimistic anarchists saw the gains from trade and innovation being limited by the extent to which governments secured property rights and enforced contracts, the empirical challenge of this new and optimistic generation of graduate students was to perceive the existence of such potential gains from trade and innovation as an entrepreneurial profit opportunity for the endogenous formation of norms and rules. On empirical grounds, both generations of anarchist scholars had argued not only that the relative performance of anarchy "would vary by time and place, by historical experience, etc." (Hogarty, chapter 10, page 101), but also that "[t]here is nothing inherent in the service of coercive third-party enforcement that would exclude the possibility of its private provision *a priori*" (Leeson, chapter 7, page 73, emphasis in original). The task of exploring the possibility and relative performance of anarchy is regarded by both generations as an empirical one, which merits detailed historical case study.

However, as Virgil Storr (chapter 11, page 120) argues, using brown rats, children on a desert island, or prisoners as case studies of anarchy does "little to convince us that anarchy is unworkable or undesirable." That is not to say, as Warren Samuels (chapter 13) rightly argues, that the use of power or coercion among bad men would be absent under a state of anarchy. However, this misses the fundamental point. Given that power and coercion is ubiquitous under any institutional arrangement, the fundamental question, as Scott Beaulier (chapter 14) points out, is of a comparative institutional nature: under which institutional system can bad men do least harm? Conceived in this manner, the question that analytical anarchism is trying to answer is "*the fundamental question* in all of political economy" (chapter 14, page 188, emphasis in original).[10]

In attempting to answer this question, both generations of scholars were employing methodological individualism, consistent with the public choice paradigm. However, whereas the earlier VPI generation was more Hobbesian, the GMU generation of anarchists was more Smithian in orientation. As Jason Osborne (chapter 3, page 34) concludes his chapter, although anarchy is not "in all cases strictly superior to government in terms of maximizing individuals' wealth, it is hoped that it demonstrates that we can expect much more cooperation than Winston Bush had in mind." For example, in response to J. Patrick Gunning (chapter 6), who argued for the emergence of government on the basis of its specialized ability to enforce contracts, Peter Leeson (chapter 7) counters with both experimental and historical evidence to argue that noncoercive private mechanisms have emerged to enforce contracts. "Ostracism, injured reputation, refusal of future interaction or general boycott, for example, would all be considered indirect means of 'punishment' under a non-coercive enforcement mechanism" (chapter 7, page 68).

The central message of *Anarchy, State and Public Choice* is not that the amount of social cooperation under anarchy is always and everywhere greater than under government, but rather that the level of cooperation among self-interested individuals is greater than we might imagine. Seen from this perspective, it should be viewed as a complement, rather than a substitute, to the volumes to which it was responding. *Explorations in the Theory of Anarchy* and *Further Explorations in the Theory of Anarchy* convincingly demonstrate that lawlessness is undesirable and that the study of analytical anarchism cannot be devoid of economic content. However, its contributors were overly pessimistic about the prospects of anarchy and overly optimistic about the ability of government to deliver law and social order. To complement this narrative, the contributors of *Anarchy, State and Public Choice*, using the tools of public choice analysis, argue that we must "assume anarchy" to be a viable alternative for governance. As Raghuram Rajan has argued, "at least in the developing world, the complete markets model is too far distanced from reality to be useful."[11] The standard neoclassical model populated by fully informed and homogenous agents, in which governments provide well-defined and well-enforced property rights, is unreliable to understanding the developing world, precisely because the situation is one in which individuals are heterogeneous, have imperfect information, and exhibit high discount rates. Moreover, governments in the developing world also provide poor enforcement of property rights or are outright predatory. Therefore, collective action problems that may exist under anarchy may prove to be even worse under a dysfunctional government. Moreover, specific events, such as the collapse of communism in Eastern and Central Europe, ethnic and religious fractionalization in the Balkans and the Middle East, and the exportation of liberal democracy to failed and weak states in the developing world, have demonstrated that governance requires the endogenous formation of rules, rather than their exogenous imposition.[12]

THE FUTURE OF VPE AND ANARCHY

Anarchy, State and Public Choice is a novel contribution in the grand tradition of VPE. A testament to its importance is the new generation of young and optimistic anarchists, among them the contributors to this volume,[13] whose work has continued beyond the pages of this book. Since the publication of *Anarchy, State and Public Choice*, experimental evidence has revealed not only higher levels of cooperation under anarchy than otherwise imagined,[14] but also historical case studies across place and time demonstrating alternative institutional mechanisms to facilitate social order outside the shadow of the state. From the medieval Scottish borderlands[15] to contemporary Somalia[16] or from 17th- and 18th-century pirates to modern-day prison gangs, anarchy works better than we think.[17] The capacity for anarchy to provide governance consists of various mechanisms to exclude and sort uncooperative or otherwise untrustworthy individuals from potential trading partners,[18] but also inclusionary sorting mechanisms that signal commitment and trustworthiness on different margins among heterogeneous trading partners.[19] Rather than engaging in a normative assessment of anarchy, what has followed from *Anarchy, State and Public Choice* is the positive analysis of self-governance and the vast array of mechanisms used to enforce property rights and contracts outside the shadow of the state. *Anarchy, State and Public Choice* has proved to be a watershed moment not only in the study of VPE, but also to the study of analytical anarchism as a progressive research program.

Peter J. Boettke
Department of Economics
George Mason University

Rosolino A. Candela
Political Theory Project
Department of Political Science
Brown University

NOTES

1.   We use the term *Virginia Political Economy* to focus on that strand of public choice that first emerged at the Thomas Jefferson Center for Studies in Political Economy (1956–1968) at the University of Virginia, which was later reorganized as the Center for Study of Public Choice (1969–1983) at Virginia Polytechnic Institute and State University and then moved to George Mason University in 1983. Other strands of public choice have developed at the University of Chicago by George Stigler, Sam Peltzman, and Gary Becker; at the University of Rochester by William Riker; and at the University of Indiana by Vincent and Elinor Ostrom. See William C. Mitchell, "Virginia, Rochester, and Bloomington: Twenty-Five Years of Public Choice and Political Science," *Public Choice* 56, no. 2 (1988): 101–19; also see Peter J. Boettke and Ennio E. Piano, "Libertarianism and Public Choice," in *Oxford Handbook of Public Choice,* ed. Roger D. Congleton, Bernard Grofman, and Stefan Voigt (New York: Oxford University Press, forthcoming).
2.   See Peter J. Boettke and Peter T. Leeson, "Introduction," in *The Economic Role of the State,* ed. Peter J. Boettke and Peter T. Leeson (Northampton, MA: Edward Elgar, 2015).
3.   Edward P. Stringham, ed., *Anarchy, State and Public Choice* (Cheltenham, UK: Edward Elgar, 2005). Republished by the Mercatus Center in 2018.
4.   What is interesting to note is how the citation pattern of the forerunners to this volume has changed since its publication. Before the publication of *Anarchy, State and Public Choice,* citations to Gordon Tullock's *Explorations in the Theory of Anarchy* (Blacksburg, VA: Center for the Study of Public Choice, Virginia Polytechnic Institute and State University, 1972) and *Further Explorations in the Theory of Anarchy* (Blacksburg, VA: University Publications, 1974) numbered 36 and 16, respectively. As of December 2017, the number of citations to *Explorations in the Theory of Anarchy* has more than doubled from 36 in 2005 to 91, and the number of citations to *Further Explorations in the Theory of Anarchy* has also more than doubled from 16 to 47.

5. It was also the rise of the welfare state and Vietnam War statism during the 1960s and 1970s that provided the historical context within which not only Murray Rothbard, but also David Friedman, who was also later a faculty member of VPI (1976–1980), explored anarchism as a viable alternative to the skepticism of Buchanan, Tullock, and Bush.

6. Tullock, *Explorations in the Theory of Anarchy.*

7. Tullock, *Further Explorations in the Theory of Anarchy.*

8. This term was used by Peter Leeson, a fellow graduate student at George Mason University, to describe Stringham's role in reviving an active environment of research among graduate students not just in the economic analysis of anarchy, but also more broadly in the field of Austrian economics, from which Stringham takes his broader interest in the spontaneous emergence of rules for self-governance. For more on this topic, see http://austrianeconomists.typepad.com/weblog/2008/07/ed-stringham-an.html.

9. The exception to this is chapter 12 by Laurence Moss.

10. As Buchanan argued this point, "The economist should not be content with postulating models and then working within such models. His task includes the derivation of the institutional order itself from the set of elementary behavioral hypotheses with which he commences. In this manner, genuine institutional economics becomes a significant and an important part of fundamental economic theory." See James M. Buchanan, *The Collected Works of James M. Buchanan Volume 5: The Demand and Supply of Public Goods* (Indianapolis: Liberty Fund, [1968] 1999), 5.

11. Raghuram Rajan, "Assume Anarchy," *Finance and Development* 41, no. 3 (2004): 56.

12. See Peter J. Boettke and Peter T. Leeson, "Is the Transition to the Market Too Important to be Left to the Market?," *Economic Affairs* 23, no. 1 (2003): 33–39; Peter J. Boettke, "An Anarchist's Reflection on the Political Economy of Everyday Life," *Review of Austrian Economics* 25, no. 1 (2012): 1–8; Peter J. Boettke, "Anarchism and Austrian Economics," *New Perspectives on Political Economy* 7, no. 1 (2012): 125–40; Christopher J. Coyne, *After War: The Political Economy of Exporting Democracy* (Stanford, CA: Stanford University Press, 2008); Peter T. Leeson, "Endogenizing Fractionalization," *Journal of Institutional Economics* 1, no. 1 (2005): 75–98.

13. See Benjamin Powell and Edward P. Stringham, "Public Choice and the Economic Analysis of Anarchy: A Survey," *Public Choice* 140, no. 3/4 (2009): 503–38.

14. Benjamin Powell and Bart J. Wilson, "An Empirical Investigation of Hobbesian Jungles," *Journal of Economic Behavior & Organization* 66, no. 3 (2008): 669–86.

15. Peter T. Leeson, "The Laws of Lawlessness," *Journal of Legal Studies* 38, no. 2 (2009): 471–503.

16. Peter T. Leeson, "Better Off Stateless: Somalia before and after Government Collapse," *Journal of Comparative Economics* 35, no. 4 (2007): 689–710; Peter T. Leeson and Claudia Williamson, "Anarchy and Development: An Application of the Theory of Second Best," *Law and Development Review* 2, no. 1 (2009): 77–96; Benjamin Powell, Ryan Ford, and Alex Nowrasteh, "Somalia after State Collapse: Chaos or Improvement?" *Journal of Economic Behavior & Organization* 67, no. 3/4 (2008): 657–70.

17. Peter T. Leeson, "An-arrgh-chy: The Law and Economics of Pirate Organizations," *Journal of Political Economy* 115, no. 6 (2007): 1049–94; Peter T. Leeson, *Anarchy Unbound: Why Self-Governance Works Better Than You Think* (Cambridge, UK: Cambridge University Press, 2014); David Skarbek, "Covenants without the Sword? Comparing Prison Self-Governance Globally," *American Political Science Review* 110, no. 4 (2016): 845–62; David Skarbek, "Governance and Prison Gangs," *American Political Science Review* 105, no. 4 (2011): 702–16.

18. Edward P. Stringham, "The Extralegal Development of Securities Trading in Seventeenth Century Amsterdam," *Quarterly Review of Economics and Finance* 43, no. 2 (2003):

321–44; Edward P. Stringham, *Private Governance: Creating Order in Economic and Social Life* (Oxford, UK: Oxford University Press, 2015).

19.   See, for example, Peter T. Leeson, "Efficient Anarchy," *Public Choice* 130, no. 1/2 (2007): 41–53; Peter T. Leeson, "Trading with Bandits," *Journal of Law and Economics* 50, no. 2 (2007): 303–21; Peter T. Leeson, "Social Distance and Self-Enforcing Exchange," *Journal of Legal Studies* 37, no. 1 (2008): 161–88.

Acknowledgments to the first edition

I am thankful to the late Winston Bush, who persuaded public choice economists to study anarchy three decades ago. Their initial work at the Center for the Study of Public Choice is the impetus for this volume. I was fortunate enough to take classes from James Buchanan and Gordon Tullock at George Mason University. On many occasions I heard how rewarding their collaborative project on anarchism had been, so I decided that the younger economists at George Mason University should take up the issue once more.

Thanks go to these six contributors at George Mason University for doing such a great job. It has been a pleasure working with them, and I learned a lot. I also thank Buchanan, Tullock, Jeffrey Rogers Hummel and Peter Boettke for writing comments. At various dates in 2002 the articles were presented at George Mason University, the Association for Private Enterprise Education Conference, the Austrian Scholars Conference, and a symposium on the topic at the Mercatus Center, so thanks go to those who gave comments there, including Bryan Caplan and Tyler Cowen.

I appreciate Jeffrey Tucker for advising me to move forward at the initial stage of this project, and I appreciate Alan Sturmer, Tara Gorvine, Caroline Cornish and those at Edward Elgar Publishing for their work at latter stages. I also thank Tullock for allowing us to reprint the original essays. Tullock is a great professor who never misses an opportunity to deride anarchism, but he has been very encouraging in his unique way.

Most of all, I thank Peter Boettke for all his encouragement and support. All the young contributors to the volume wrote their dissertation under Peter Boettke, and we are grateful for that. Without Boettke, none of this would have been possible. This book is dedicated to him.

Edward Stringham, 2005

List of contributors

Scott Beaulier, Dean, College of Business, North Dakota State University

Peter J. Boettke, University Professor of Economics and Philosophy, George Mason University; Director, F. A. Hayek Program for Advanced Study in Philosophy, Politics, and Economics, Mercatus Center at George Mason University

James M. Buchanan, formerly Distinguished Professor Emeritus of Economics, George Mason University; formerly General Director, Center for Study of Public Choice, George Mason University

Winston Bush, formerly Professor of Economics, Virginia Polytechnic Institute

Christopher J. Coyne, Associate Professor of Economics, George Mason University; Associate Director, F. A. Hayek Program for Advanced Study in Philosophy, Politics, and Economics, Mercatus Center at George Mason University

J. Patrick Gunning, formerly Professor of Economics, Feng Chia University

Thomas Hogarty, formerly Professor of Economics, Virginia Polytechnic Institute

Jeffrey Rogers Hummel, Professor of Economics, San Jose State University

Peter T. Leeson, Duncan Black Professor of Economics and Law, George Mason University; Senior Fellow, F. A. Hayek Program for Advanced Study in Philosophy, Politics, and Economics, Mercatus Center at George Mason University

Laurence Moss, formerly Professor of Economics and Law, Babson College

Jason Osborne, Chief Operating Officer, Credit Adjustments, Inc.

Benjamin Powell, Professor of Economics, Rawls College of Business at Texas Tech University; Director, Free Market Institute at Texas Tech University

Warren Samuels, formerly Professor of Economics, Michigan State University

Virgil Henry Storr, Research Associate Professor of Economics, George Mason University; Don C. Lavoie Senior Fellow, F. A. Hayek Program for Advanced Study in Philosophy, Politics, and Economics, Mercatus Center at George Mason University

Edward Stringham, Davis Professor of Economic Organizations and Innovation, Trinity College; President, American Institute for Economic Research

Gordon Tullock, formerly Professor Emeritus of Law and Economics, George Mason University

1. Introduction

Edward Stringham

It is high time to shift out of the pragmatic mind-set that has been our national characteristic. The grand alternatives for social organization must be reconsidered. The loss of faith in the socialist dream has not, and probably will not, restore faith in laissez-faire. But what are the effective alternatives? Does anarchism deserve a hearing, and, if so, what sort of anarchism?

James M. Buchanan[1]
1986 Nobel Laureate in Economic Science

Most people do not even consider the idea that society can be organized without a state. Anarchism is simply too idealistic or too different from the current world. But does that prove that a stateless society is unworkable or that it should not be pursued? Or does that prove that most social order depends on the state? Throughout history, political structures have varied vastly over time, and just because a system was uncommon at one point in time does not mean that it can never come about. Tribalism, monarchism, socialism and democracy have all been tried. Why not anarchism? Perhaps civil society can be attained without government. Without considering all potential methods to organize society, one cannot determine the best system. Anarchists want their vision considered.

Whereas Thomas Hobbes believed that a war of all against all characterizes anarchy, anarchists believe the opposite. Government is near-ubiquitous today, yet in the past century millions of people have been murdered by their own governments (Rummel, 1994). Perhaps government does not create order and instead does the opposite. Could it be the case that cooperation does not depend on government? Could it be the case that more cooperation would occur without a state? Although most people agree with Hobbes that some form of government is necessary, until recently the issue was merely an assumption that had never been analyzed from an economic point of view. This changed in the early 1970s when members of the Center for the Study of Public Choice became the first group of economists to engage in a systematic study of these questions. *Explorations in the Theory of Anarchy* and *Further Explorations in the Theory of Anarchy*, published in 1972 and 1974 (Tullock, 1972 and 1974a), contained contributions by economists who became extremely influential in the following decades: James Buchanan, Winston

Bush, Thomas Hogarty, J. Patrick Gunning, Laurence Moss, Warren Samuels, William Craig Stubblebine and Gordon Tullock.

These authors decided to ask the big questions rather than debating small changes in public policy. In his autobiography, James Buchanan describes the project:

> Winston Bush galvanized our interests in the theory of anarchy, an organizational alternative that had never seriously been analyzed. What were the descriptive features of Hobbesian anarchy? Could something like an anarchistic equilibrium be defined?
>
> Bush was instrumental in organizing a series of weekly workshops in 1972 during which each participant in turn presented papers on differing aspects of the theory of anarchy. As revised, these papers were published in *Explorations in the Theory of Anarchy*. Those weeks were exciting because never before or since have I participated so fully in a genuinely multiparty ongoing research effort, one that we knew to be relevant in some ultimate sense . . . For me this brief period of research activity was important because it gave me a new focus on my whole enterprise. (1992: 116)

From a Nobel Laureate, this says a lot. James Buchanan dedicated his 1975 *The Limits of Liberty* to Winston Bush, and from reading subsequent scholarship in public choice one can see how significant *Explorations in the Theory of Anarchy* was. Considering the impact of Buchanan's *The Limits of Liberty* and Tullock's *The Social Dilemma* on the profession, it is not difficult to conclude that *Explorations in the Theory of Anarchy* is too important to be ignored.

As Winston Bush (1972: 5) wrote, 'Anarchy as an organizing principle for society must appeal to anyone who places individual freedom high on his scale of values.' With the exception of Moss (1974), however, none of the contributors to the original volumes believed anarchism was a viable alternative. They believed that when government is lacking, people will be unable to engage in contracts, and their property rights will be insecure. The lesson that most readers take from the original volumes is that government is necessary for social cooperation.

But did these public choice economists prove the necessity of the state? Maybe not. James Buchanan seems less sure today than he was three decades ago. In a recent publication, Buchanan (2004: 268) wrote, 'As I now reflect on that burst of interest in the theory of anarchy, I now realize that we were perhaps too influenced by the Bush–Tullock presumption to the effect that the behavioral hypotheses used were necessarily empirically grounded.' The Hobbesian beliefs about human behavior might not always hold. Buchanan (ibid.) wrote that their pessimistic assumptions 'led us to neglect at that time any effort to work out just what an ordered anarchy would look like. What would be the results if persons should behave so as to internalize all of the relevant externalities in their dealings among themselves?'

Shortly after the publication of *Explorations in the Theory of Anarchy*, other free-market economists began defending the idea that the state is unnecessary (Anderson and Hill, 1979; Cuzan, 1979; Friedman, 1973, 1979; Peden, 1977; Rothbard, 1973, 1977a; Sneed, 1977). To these authors, society can have law, order and private property without government at all. In fact, they argued that government law enforcement is antithetical to the market system. When Nozick's (1974) *Anarchy, State, and Utopia* appeared, arguing that ordered anarchy is impossible, many authors voiced their disagreement (Barnett, 1977; Childs, 1977; Davidson, 1977; Paul, 1977; Rothbard, 1977b; Sanders, 1977). *Explorations in the Theory of Anarchy*, however, has not received the same attention until now.[2]

This volume contains seven responses to the essays in *Explorations in the Theory of Anarchy*, as well as reprints of seven original articles and new rejoinders by James Buchanan, Gordon Tullock, Jeffrey Rogers Hummel and Peter Boettke. The younger generation has noticeably less faith in government than their predecessors. They question whether markets are as fragile as the public choice economists believed and question whether government can be relied on as a solution.

Let us consider the arguments. Winston Bush wrote the pioneering article, 'Individual welfare in anarchy'. His work, a later version of which was published in the *Journal of Economic Theory* (Bush and Mayer, 1974), provides a mathematical model of social interaction without a state. When people interact, they can choose to respect the other's property or to engage in predation. Bush argues that in a state of anarchy, individuals expend too many resources on predation, making both parties worse off. After the distribution of property rights under Hobbesian anarchy is established, agreeing on a common set of rules will be mutually beneficial. Although he favors society without rules, Bush believes that predation would prevail. When Robinson Crusoe and Friday first meet, they know little of each other, might never interact again, and have no ability to rely on external enforcement, so we might expect the results of the standard prisoner's dilemma to hold. Bush might be considered one of the first pessimistic anarchists.

Jason Osborne, on the other hand, contends that even in these circumstances, people will engage in less cheating than the Winston Bush model foretells. Drawing from work of Ronald Heiner, Osborne argues that individuals can adopt a strategy known as contingent cooperation. This model postulates that even in one-shot games, individuals can communicate before interacting, thereby enabling them to detect signals about the likelihood that the other party will cooperate. Even in one-shot games, humans have more knowledge about other people than the prisoner's dilemma assumes. Even if signal detection is far from perfect, we will see less predation than standard assumptions predict.

Gordon Tullock's 'The edge of the jungle' advances the Winston Bush hypothesis and argues that cooperation would be limited under anarchy. Without government enforcement, long-term contracting and many other beneficial trades would not occur. People would spend too many resources engaging in opportunistic behavior, which would eventually lead to anarchy's demise. Tullock maintains that those with a comparative advantage in the use of force will overpower the weak and impose government. Although government could be used to redistribute resources, Tullock argues that creating this external enforcer could benefit all members of society. The government apparatus still uses power to enforce the law, but it eliminates the use of force by others. The ensuing reduction of conflict creates incentives for production rather than predation.

Christopher Coyne responds by describing how private law enforcement may solve the problems in Hobbesian anarchy. Yes, society may need law enforcement, but it need not be public. Coyne argues that Tullock has a narrow view of anarchy: anarchy means lack of government, not lack of rules. Could it be that public choice economists would embrace an anarchy composed of privately generated rules? Coyne's response describes the many types of private rule-enforcing bodies that exist and discusses how customary law, arbitration and systems of private security have created and enforced rules independently of the state. The possibility of private property anarchy is a real one.

J. Patrick Gunning does not rule out ordered anarchy, but he believes that anarchy can only function at a primitive level. He believes that more advanced relations involving trade require external enforcement. In Gunning's words, 'Even if trades are expected to be infinitely recurring, there may be no trade.' He gives an example of a pygmy and a giant who would be unable to make contracts unless a third party, a super-giant, entered the picture. The super-giant is an analogy for the government that prevents cheating. In this view, the government is potentially beneficial to all because it enables people to engage in contracts.

Peter Leeson responds by arguing that many contracts do in fact take place without external enforcement. Perhaps Gunning's assumption that parties necessarily cheat is nothing more than an assumption. Leeson cites evidence from experimental economics to show that even in one-shot games without external enforcement, people are less likely to cheat than Hobbesian theory predicts. We cannot rely on law in the vast majority of social interactions, but the market still creates incentives for cooperation. For example, businesses provide good service not because of rules but because they want future business. In addition to cases without third-party enforcement, Leeson provides examples of third-party enforcement that do not use force. He describes how multilateral reputation mechanisms can induce contractual compliance even though compulsion is not involved.

Engaging in contracts without government is only one issue; having property rights without government is another. James Buchanan analyzes the situation of Hobbesian anarchy as a prisoner's dilemma in 'Before public choice'. Buchanan believes that people will act opportunistically when given the incentive, and although they would be better off following common rules, they have no way to commit. Buchanan uses this to derive a contract theory of the state. By implementing an external enforcer, the prisoner's dilemma can be solved.

Benjamin Powell, in contrast, takes the assumptions of Buchanan's model and asks whether government can bring an improvement. Where Buchanan concludes that people will engage in opportunistic behavior when external enforcement is lacking, Powell does not question the result. Instead, he uses the same assumptions as Buchanan to analyze the situation after we implement government. Powell argues that the idea that government can solve the prisoner's dilemma only holds if we assume the state to be an external force not constituted of humans. Once we recognize that government is necessarily composed of flesh and blood, the same results do not hold. If all people are Hobbesian egoists, why would we not expect government to act opportunistically? No theory or evidence suggests that people will become better once they join government. Even if we accept the pessimistic assumptions, anarchy cannot be ruled inferior.

Thomas Hogarty tries to rule anarchy inferior on empirical grounds. He provides three case studies to support why we should have government. As his first example of anarchy, Hogarty points out that brown rats do not have government, and, in fact, often bite each other. As his second example, Hogarty discusses how the children in *Lord of the Flies* did not have government and engaged in many malicious acts. As his final example, Hogarty argues that a prisoner-of-war camp during the American Civil War provides an example of individual interaction without a state. Rather than acting cooperatively, the prisoners engaged in aggressive behavior. All three case studies lack cooperation, so Hogarty concludes we need government.

In response, Virgil Storr questions whether Hogarty's examples justify government. Yes, Storr agrees, brown rats removed from their familiar packs and placed among rats from different localities do in fact bite each other, but he questions how much this experiment can tell us about human cooperation. Storr also questions the extent to which a children's novel, a work of fiction, can be used to draw inferences about interaction under anarchy. Finally, Storr takes issue with the treatment of an overcrowded POW camp as a case study in anarchy. When government imprisons a group of people and controls their supplies, we should not be surprised if conflict arises. To Storr, none of these examples provides evidence of deficiencies in anarchy.

Not only may anarchy be possible, but Laurence Moss argues that the idea has a long history in American thinking. Although anarchist theory has been developed further in recent years, the idea that markets can function without government was popular in eighteenth-century America as well. Moss argues that eighteenth-century anarchists such as Josiah Warren, Lysander Spooner and Benjamin Tucker were simply defending the ideals of the Declaration of Independence. Moss then discusses how this tradition has been picked up by Murray Rothbard and other modern free-market economists. Even though most people consider anarchism to be radical, Moss concludes, 'Property anarchism is as American as apple pie!'

Warren Samuels dislikes this apple pie and worries about a pure market economy. He believes that power relations will be present under private property anarchism, or any form of markets for that matter. He sympathizes with the anarchist goals of freedom, order and markets, while sharing a suspicion of the state, but he questions whether anarchism will deliver those ends. Samuels maintains that agencies enforcing libertarian law would be nominally private but equivalent to government. Samuels criticizes Murray Rothbard for simply wanting to replace one type of coercion with another. To Samuels, the theory of anarchism fails to resolve the problem of power relations and thus should not be considered a superior alternative to government.

Not so, says Scott Beaulier, who takes issue with the argument that private law enforcement is just as coercive as government. He points out that Samuels's notion of power is so broad that any exercise of choice is an exercise of power. Beaulier argues this cannot be used as a criticism against anarcho-capitalism, so the question is, what type of power relations do we want? Public law enforcement involves a coercive monopoly on power, whereas private law enforcement gives individuals a choice. Because political power gives people no choice, it is often misused. Politics simply replaces voluntary market relations with involuntary ones.

How does Buchanan respond to the new works herein? Does he take issue with the authors who reject the necessity of Leviathan? Surprisingly, Buchanan does not defend government against its critics. Instead, he argues that the arguments miss their mark. Buchanan maintains, 'The seminar papers, as published in the small volumes edited by Gordon Tullock, as well as Tullock's book, *The Social Dilemma* (1974b) and my own book, *The Limits of Liberty* (1975), should, at least in part, be interpreted as reactions to the times.' He argues they were a response to the encroaching disorder on many university campuses in the late 1960s and early 1970s. This alternative explanation that *Explorations in the Theory of Anarchy* was less concerned with establishment of government but more with the establishment of rules is welcome. Could these rules be privately produced according to Buchanan's (1965) theory of clubs? Buchanan does not answer this question, but we hope future public choice economists will.

One such economist is Gordon Tullock. Tullock takes on libertarian anarchist arguments in his response. He maintains that although modern examples of private law enforcement are quite common, they all take place in the shadow of the state. He argues that private police companies, detectives, mediators and arbitrators depend on government. Reputation and boycott can work against untrustworthy businessmen but cannot work against those who use force. Tullock argues that we need government to impede such banditry. Those who are unable to protect themselves will be conquered or destroyed. A professional military will nearly always be more successful than a band of disorganized militiamen; hence the need, or the inevitability, of a national armed force. Finally, Tullock brings up a number of other problems he sees with anarchy, such as traveling over private roads, quarantine and fire protection. Although he recognizes that private communities do provide these services, Tullock attempts to blur the line between proprietary communities and local governments.

Jeffrey Rogers Hummel objects. Tullock is wrong, Hummel argues, to conflate rules with government. Just because condominiums undertake certain activities that governments also undertake does not make them governments. Hummel further states, 'Just as government is not a necessary condition for rule of law, it is equally obvious that government is not a sufficient condition for effective defense against invasion.' He points out that nations are often overtaken by others, so the simple existence of government does not solve the world's problems. To Hummel the solution lies not in government but in persuading enough people to support liberty. The use of force by any entity cannot persist if the public remains in opposition.

Peter Boettke concludes the volume by discussing the evolutionary potential of anarchy as a research program. Boettke outlines how analytical anarchism is more than a normative endeavor. The world has many puzzles that cannot be explained by theories that assume the dependence of markets on government. In many cases contracts are enforceable, yet trade takes place. By documenting how private parties find ways to eliminate opportunism, the anarchist research program provides a more accurate picture of the market process. Even under conditions of large group settings and near-anonymity, market participants find ways to cooperate rather than cheat. The endogenous creation and enforcement of rules is part of the market process. Boettke concludes, 'Work along these lines is not only valuable at a fundamental theoretical level, but also of practical significance as well as we attempt to wrestle with the great social transformations of our era.'

Although the younger authors believe the public choice economists of the 1970s offered a promising start, they believe that their analysis was incomplete. Is social interaction without the state as bad as Hobbes and these public choice economists believe? Much of the recent analysis suggests otherwise. But maybe it is true that humans are inherently prone to conflict. Perhaps the Hobbesian dilemma is a real threat. Whatever the case may be, government does not seem to offer a solution. Either Leviathan is part of the problem or Leviathan is superfluous. Under either scenario, anarchy might be the best choice after all. We are glad that public choice economists started studying this topic three decades ago, and we hope to see a resurgence in explorations in the theory of anarchy.

NOTES

1. Buchanan, James (1974), 'Review of *The Machinery of Freedom: Guide to a Radical Capitalism*', *Journal of Economic Literature*, **12**: 914–15.
2. Jackson (1974) reviewed *Explorations in the Theory of Anarchy*, and Ireland (1976) reviewed *Further Explorations in the Theory of Anarchy*. Except for brief mentions by Anderson and Hill (1979), Moss (1974), and Friedman (1976, 1980), however, libertarian anarchists did not seem to comment on the project in the 1970s. Recent works that cite Winston Bush's theory of anarchy include Carter and Anderton (2001), Grossman (2001) and Hirshleifer (2001).

REFERENCES

Anderson, T.L. and Hill, P.J. (1979), 'An American Experiment in Anarcho-Capitalism: The Not So Wild, Wild West', *Journal of Libertarian Studies*, **3**: 9–29.

Barnett, Randy (1977), 'Whither Anarchy? Has Robert Nozick Justified the State?', *Journal of Libertarian Studies*, **1**: 15–21.

Buchanan, James (1965), 'An Economic Theory of Clubs', *Economica*, **32**: 1–14.

Buchanan, James (1974), 'Review of *The Machinery of Freedom: Guide to a Radical Capitalism*', *Journal of Economic Literature*, **12**: 914–15.

Buchanan, James (1975), *The Limits of Liberty: Between Anarchy and Leviathan*, Chicago: University of Chicago.

Buchanan, J.M. (1992), *Better Than Plowing and Other Personal Essays*, Chicago: University of Chicago Press.

Buchanan, J.M. (2004), 'Heraclitian Vespers', in J. Pitt, D. Salehi-Isfahami and D. Echel (eds), *The Production and Diffusion of Public Choice Policy Economy*, Malden, MA: Blackwell Publishing, pp. 263–71.

Bush, Winston (1972), 'Individual Welfare in Anarchy', in G. Tullock (ed.), *Explorations in the Theory of Anarchy*, The Public Choice Society Book and Monograph Series, Blacksburg, VA: Center for the Study of Public Choice, pp. 5–18; see also Chapter 2, this volume.

Bush, Winston and Mayer, Lawrence (1974), 'Some Implications of Anarchy for the Distribution of Property', *Journal of Economic Theory*, **8**: 401–12.

Carter, John and Anderton, Charles (2001), 'An Experimental Test of a Predator–Prey Model of Appropriation', *Journal of Economic Behavior and Organization*, **45**: 83–97.

Childs, Roy (1977), 'The Invisible Hand Strikes Back', *Journal of Libertarian Studies*, **1**: 23–33.

Cuzan, Alfred (1979), 'Do We Ever Really Get Out of Anarchy?', *Journal of Libertarian Studies*, **3**: 151–8.

Davidson, James Dale (1977), 'Note on *Anarchy, State, and Utopia*', *Journal of Libertarian Studies*, **1**: 341–8.

Friedman, David (1973/1989), *The Machinery of Freedom, Guide to Radical Capitalism*, 2nd edn, La Salle, IL: Open Court.

Friedman, David (1976), 'Review of *Further Explorations in the Theory of Anarchy* edited by Gordon Tullock', *Public Choice*, **16** (1): 101–4.

Friedman, David (1979), 'Private Creation and Enforcement of Law – A Historical Case', *Journal of Legal Studies*, **8**: 399–415.

Friedman, David (1980), 'Many, Few, One: Social Harmony and the Shrunken Choice Set', *American Economic Review*, **70**: 225–32.

Grossman, Herschel (2001), 'The Creation of Effective Property Rights', *American Economic Review*, **91**: 347–52.

Hirshleifer, Jack (2001), *The Dark Side of the Force: Economic Foundations of Conflict Theory*, New York: Cambridge University Press.

Ireland, Thomas (1976), 'Review of *Further Explorations in the Theory of Anarchy* edited by Gordon Tullock', *Atlantic Economic Journal*, **4**: 80.

Jackson, M.W. (1974), 'Review of *Explorations in the Theory of Anarchy* edited by Gordon Tullock', *Western Political Quarterly*, **27**: 757–8.

Moss, Laurence (1974), 'Private Property Anarchism: An American Variant', in G. Tullock (ed.), *Further Explorations in the Theory of Anarchy*, The Public Choice Society Book and Monograph Series, Blacksburg, VA: University Publications, pp. 1–31; see also Chapter 12, this volume.

Nozick, Robert (1974), *Anarchy, State, and Utopia*, New York: Basic Books.

Paul, Jeffrey (1977), 'Nozick, Anarchism and Procedural Rights', *Journal of Libertarian Studies*, 1: 337–40.

Peden, Joseph (1977), 'Property Right in Celtic Irish Law', *Journal of Libertarian Studies*, **1**: 81–95.

Rothbard, Murray (1973/1996), *For a New Liberty: Libertarian Manifesto*, San Francisco: Fox and Wilkes.

Rothbard, Murray (1977a), *Power and Market: Government and the Economy*, 2nd edn, Kansas City: Sheed, Andrews and McMeel.

Rothbard, Murray (1977b), 'Robert Nozick and the Immaculate Conception of the State', *Journal of Libertarian Studies*, **1**: 45–57.

Rummel, R.J. (1994), *Death By Government*, New Brunswick, NJ: Transaction Publishers.

Sanders, John (1977), 'The Free Market Model Versus Government: A Reply to Nozick', *Journal of Libertarian Studies*, **1**: 35–44.

Sneed, John (1977), 'Order Without Law: Where Will Anarchists Keep the Madmen?', *Journal of Libertarian Studies*, **1**: 117–24.

Tullock, Gordon (ed.) (1972), *Explorations in the Theory of Anarchy*, Blacksburg, VA: Center for the Study of Public Choice.

Tullock, Gordon (ed.) (1974a), *Further Explorations in the Theory of Anarchy*, Blacksburg, VA: University Publications.

Tullock, Gordon (1974b), *The Social Dilemma: The Economics of War and Revolution*, Blacksburg, VA: University Publications.

2. Individual welfare in anarchy*

Winston Bush

Anarchy as an organizing principle for society must appeal to anyone who places individual freedom high on his scale of values. In a basic sense, everyone is anarchist, in that he views all socially imposed restrictions on his own freedom of action as 'bads,' even if he may recognize these, or some of these, to be necessary costs of social harmony. It is not surprising that 'anarchy' and 'anarchism' have re-emerged as topics for discussion in the 1960s and the 1970s, as tentacles of government progressively invade private lives and as the alleged objectives of such invasions recede yet further from attainment. Social scientists must acknowledge the widespread current appeal of radical organizational alternatives, and they must cut through the excesses of revolutionary rhetoric and try to identify the common concern that much of it expresses. For this reason, if for no other, anarchy deserves to be seriously discussed, neither in romantic advocacy nor in pejorative attack, but with the most powerful tools of modern social analysis. Perhaps precisely because of the emotional overtones, the tools of modern economic analysis have not, to our knowledge, been applied to explain or to depict the general characteristics of an economy without laws or property rights.[1]

There are two quite different conceptions or models of individual behavior in genuine anarchy, that hypothetical state where no societal controls exist. We may label these as Hobbesian and Proudhonian. In Hobbes' natural state, the absence of authority presents the individual with a choice of using his labor to produce goods or to take by force those goods produced by others. There is nothing in human nature, as such, that insures that *all* members of the community will opt for the first alternative. The well-being of a person depends on his relative ability to produce, to take from others, and to protect his own. There is no demonstrable tendency toward equality of shares in this world of gross inefficiency and human suffering where life is surely 'nasty, brutish, and short.' The logical bases of such descriptive models cause social philosophers to search for optimal or efficient sets of rules within which individual behavior may be

* This paper was first published in *Explorations in the Theory of Anarchy*, edited by Gordon Tullock, The Public Choice Society Book and Monograph Series, Center for the Study of Public Choice, Blacksburg, VA, USA, 1972, pp. 5–18.

constrained so as to eliminate or to reduce the sheer resource waste that the absence of order generates.

The Proudhonian conception is based on the faith that, once freed from the constraints of social rules, individuals will develop their natural talents and live in harmony one with another. To our knowledge, there is little or no behavioral analysis, hypothetical or empirical, to support this model. Among anarchist philosophers there has been a surprising absence of critical examination of just how the whole system works. There has been a naive extension from a rule-free, constraint-free model of individual bliss to a model of social interaction. But if we introduce even a second person, what is to happen when free-ranging desires come into conflict? The anarchists have not offered satisfactory answers.

This does not imply, however, that the Hobbesian model, which points up the necessity for the imposition of constraints on individual behavior, does not also leave major unanswered questions. If rules exist, these must be enforced, and how is the enforcer himself to be controlled? Once the State is established, how can it be limited? Honesty compels us to acknowledge that the debate between the anarchist and the collectivist has not been and probably will never be resolved.

The analysis of this paper represents a first step toward answering a more elementary question. In terms of a very simple model, based on extremely restrictive assumptions, the conditions of an equilibrium income distribution under Hobbesian anarchy are described. Once this step is taken, the analysis lends itself readily to extensions and elaborations in several respects, only a few of which will be noted in this paper.

The analysis introduces some positive content into the sometimes vague and ambiguous concepts of anarchy. In an elementary but rigorous sense, the initial leap from the Hobbesian jungle is shown to represent a Pareto shift, although the distributional effects of such a shift are not clearly defined. More importantly, perhaps, the analysis offers a foundation for explaining those areas of everyday human interaction which have long been and which will, hopefully, remain essentially anarchistic.[2]

I. THE MODEL

Given any initial distribution of income and no institutional or ethical barriers that prevent one individual or group from stealing or forceably taking income from another individual or group, a redistribution of income may arise producing a new and modified distribution of income. I shall call this modified distribution the *natural* distribution of income. This distribution depends on the initial distribution of income and the preference and the ability of individuals.

Whereas the marginal utility of income transferred among individuals is assumed to be positive to all individuals involved, the physical effort expended in stealing, producing a coercive transfer, etc., is assumed to be an unpleasant commodity. This last assumption means that once the natural distribution is established, a Pareto redistribution of income relative to the natural distribution is possible. An individual would be willing to give up some of his share of the natural distribution to his rivals if a transfer scheme which involved less effort than stealing, physical force, etc., could be agreed upon.

In order to simplify the problem, assume a world in which only two individuals exist. Each day each individual is allocated some arbitrary quantity of an all-purpose consumer good, X. Although the initial daily allocation never changes, the quantity given one individual may be different than the quantity given to the other. This is the initial distribution of income. Given the initial income of each individual, along with his taste, and his ability, the natural distribution can be determined.

Definition of Symbols

^iX – The initial income of individual i.

X_i – Individual i's natural income. It is equal to his initial income plus or minus the amount transferred to or from him through interaction with individual j.

$$X - \equiv \sum_{i=1}^{2} {}^iX$$

E_i – The total level of effort expended by individual i in taking income from individual j and protecting his own income from individual j.

a_i – The ability of individual i or the effectiveness of E_i and $a_i > 0$.
     $(i, j = 1, 2; i \neq j)$

The term a_i is assumed to be a positive constant. This means that the effectiveness of the method used by i in either appropriating income from individual j or protecting his income from individual j is the same and proportional to the level of effort he expends.

The preferences of individual i are represented by a utility function of the form

$$U_i = U_i (X_i, E_i), (i = 1, 2) \tag{2.1}$$

and

$$U_{X_i} > 0, U_{E_i} < 0,$$

where U_{X_i} and U_{E_i} are the partial derivatives of U_i with respect to X_i and E_i. The constraint facing individual i is

$$X_i = {}^iX + a_iE_i - a_jE_j, \ (i, j = 1, 2; i \neq j) \tag{2.2}$$

and $X_i \geqq 0, 0 \leqq E_i \leqq T$, where T is the maximum level of effort i can expend per day. Assuming utility maximizing behavior, the first-order conditions for an internal solution for individual i are

$$\frac{U_{E_i}}{U_{X_i}} = -a_i \qquad (i = 1, 2). \tag{2.3}$$

The marginal rate of substitution of effort for income must equal the rate at which effort can be used to generate income. Assuming further that U_i is strictly quasi-concave, the second-order conditions for a utility maximization are insured.

Using the information contained in the above paragraph, X_i and E_i can be written as a function of ${}^iX$, E_j, a_i and a_j.

$$X_i = X_i({}^iX, E_j, a_i, a_j), \ (i, j = 1, 2; i \neq j) \tag{2.4}$$

$$E_i = E_i({}^iX, E_j, a_i, a_j), \ (i, j = 1, 2; i \neq j) \tag{2.5}$$

In Figure 2.1, the equilibrium levels of natural income and effort of individual 1, $\hat{X}_1$ and $\hat{E}$, are shown for given values of his initial income and ability, ${}^1X$ and a_1, and for given values of the ability and effort of individual 2, a_2 and E_2. The curve originating at T and passing through the point $(\hat{X}_1 \ \hat{E}_2)$ is called the income–effort curve. For a given value of a_1, this curve traces out all of the equilibrium points of $(X_1 \ E_1)$ as ${}^1X - a_2E_2$ is varied along the vertical axis. In drawing the income–effort curve in Figure 2.1, the following additional assumptions concerning U_i, which will be used frequently below, were used.

$$\frac{dX_i}{d^iX}\bigg|^{E_j}_{a_i \ a_j} > 0 \qquad \frac{dE_i}{d^iX}\bigg|^{E_j}_{a_i \ a_j} < 0 \qquad (i, j = 1, 2; i \neq j) \tag{2.AI}$$

when an internal solution exists and

$$E_i = T \text{ at } X_i \geqq \underline{X}_i, \tag{2.AII}$$

where $\underline{X}_i$ is the minimum subsistence level of X_i.

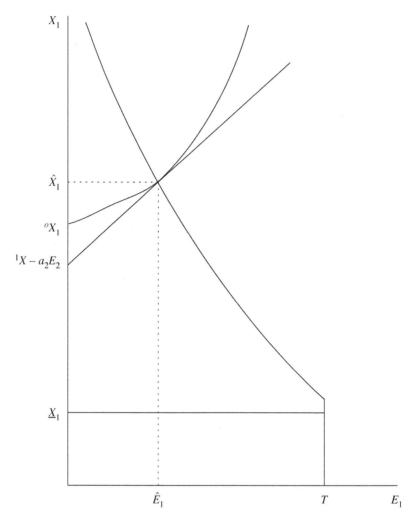

Figure 2.1   Income–effort curve

Assumption 2.AI implies that X_i is a normal good but that E_i is a normal bad. The interpretation of 2.AII is that an individual would rather exert the maximum level of effort, T, in obtaining X than starve to death.

The natural equilibrium levels of effort, E_i^*, for both individuals in the anarchistic community can be derived using the relationships described in (2.5).[3] These relationships can be looked upon as reaction functions. Once E_i^* is determined, the natural equilibrium levels of income, X_i^*, can be obtained

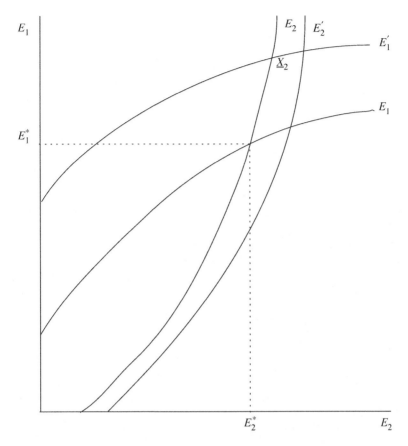

Figure 2.2   Reaction curves

directly from the relationships shown in (2.2) since utility maximizing behavior implies that both individuals are on their budget constraints.

Reaction curves for individuals 1 and 2 are shown in Figure 2.2 for given values of initial income and ability for both individuals. These curves show the desired level of effort in generating income of one individual for different levels of effort of the other individual. Natural equilibrium occurs at the point where the two curves cross. More formally, this means that, using the equations in (2.5), E_i^* can be written as a function of $^iX, {}^jX, a_i$, and a_j.[4]

$$E_i^* = E_i^*(^iX, {}^jX, a_i, a_j), (i, j = 1, 2; i \neq j). \quad (2.6)$$

Using (2.2), X_i^* can be written as

$$X_i^* = {}^iX + a_iE_i^* - a_jE_j^*, \, (i, j = 1, 2; i \neq j) \tag{2.7a}$$

or

$$X_i^* = X_i^* \, ({}^iX, {}^jX, a_i, a_j), \, (i, j = 1, 2; i \neq j). \tag{2.7b}$$

Reaction curves E_1 and E_2 in Figure 2.2 illustrate the case in which a stable natural equilibrium exists and $E_i^* > 0$, $X_i^* > \underline{X}_i$.[5] In addition to the assumptions made above, conditions sufficient to insure that a state such as the one illustrated in Figure 2.2 exists are:

2.AIII   no corner solution exists in which $E_i = 0$ which implies

$$a_i > \frac{U_{E_i}}{U_{X_i}}$$

at the point where

$$E_i = 0 \text{ and } {}^iX - a_jE_j = {}^iX, \, (i, j = 1, 2; i \neq j);$$

2.AIV   with reference to the relationships in (2.5)

$$\frac{\partial E_i}{\partial E_j} \, \frac{\partial E_j}{\partial E_i} < 1, \, (1, j = 1, 2; i \neq j); \text{ and}$$

2.AV   impossibility of dominance

$$\frac{{}^iX - \underline{X}_i}{T} > | \, a_i - a_j \, |, \, (i, j = 1, 2; i \neq j).$$

When assumptions 2A.I through 2.AV hold, the community is in the state Hobbes [4, Ch. 13] described as 'that during the time men live without a common power to keep them all in awe, they are in the condition which is called warre; and such a warre, as is of every man, against every man.'

From assumptions 2.AI and 2.AII we know that the reaction curves in Figure 2.2 will have a positive or zero slope. They have a positive slope when an internal solution exists for an individual and zero slope when E_i is at its maximum, T. Note that if $a_1 = a_2$, ${}^1X$ and ${}^2X$ and preferences of both individuals are the same, the reaction curves in Figure 2.2 would be minor images of each other and cross along a 45° line originating from the origin. In this case $E_1^* = E_2^*$ and $X_1^* = X_2^* = {}^1X = {}^2X$.

Assumption 2.AIII insures that the reaction curves in Figure 2.2 will have positive intercepts. Given his initial income and zero effort by the other individual, an individual will always exert positive effort in appropriating income from the other individual. A quasi-utopian situation would occur if initial income were so great that a corner solution occurred for both individuals in which effort was zero.[6] In such a situation there would never be any conflict even if the ability of both were positive. This seems to be the situation envisioned by Godwin [3] and other writers on anarchy who felt that minimal conflict would occur in an anarchistic state.

Given 2.AI through 2.AIII, assumption 2.AIV contains sufficient conditions for the existence of an equilibrium, although this equilibrium may not be unique. Assuming a cobweb type adjustment mechanism, 2.AIV is also sufficient to ensure that a stable equilibrium exists.

Although assumptions 2.AI through 2.AIV insure that a stable equilibrium exists in which $E_i^* > 0$, X_i^* may be less than the survival level. As an example, if $X_2 = \underline{X}_2$ at the point denoted as such on individual 2's reaction curve in Figure 2.2 and individual 1's reaction curve was E_1', then individual 1 would dominate individual 2 since he could starve 2 to death. If assumption 2.AV holds, this situation would be impossible. 2.AV also implies that if both individuals have the same ability and the initial income of both is greater than survival level, then $X_i^* \geqq \underline{X}_i$. Assumptions 2.AI through 2.AV together imply that even if one individual has no ability and the other positive ability, both will survive.

Adding the following assumption, 2.AVI, to assumptions 2.AI through 2.AV will make the comparative statics of changes in initial income and ability with respect to the natural equilibrium levels effort and income determinate.

2.AVI   The substitution effect of a change in ability with respect to effort outweighs the income effect, which implies for (2.5)

$$\frac{dE_i}{da_i}\bigg|_{\substack{i_X \\ a_j \\ E_j}} < 0, \ (i, j = 1, 2; i \neq j).$$

The comparative static relationships of the equations in (2.6) under assumptions 2.AI through 2.AVI are:

$$\frac{dE_i^*}{d^iX}\bigg|_{\substack{j_X \\ a_i \\ a_j}} = \frac{\dfrac{\partial E_i}{\partial^1 X}}{1 - \dfrac{\partial E_i}{\partial E_j}\dfrac{\partial E_j}{\partial E_i}} \leqq 0, \ (i, j = 1, 2; i \neq j); \tag{2.8}$$

$$\frac{dE_i^*}{d^jX}\bigg|_{\substack{i_X \\ a_i \\ a_j}} = \frac{\dfrac{\partial E_i}{\partial E_j}\dfrac{\partial E_j}{\partial^j X}}{1 - \dfrac{\partial E_i}{\partial E_j}\dfrac{\partial E_j}{\partial E_i}} \lesseqgtr 0;$$

$$\frac{dE_i^*}{da_i}\bigg|_{\substack{i_X \\ j_X \\ a_j}} = \frac{\dfrac{\partial E_i}{\partial E_j}\dfrac{\partial E_j}{\partial a_i} + \dfrac{\partial E_i}{\partial a_i}}{1 - \dfrac{\partial E_i}{\partial E_j}\dfrac{\partial E_j}{\partial E_i}} \gtreqqless 0;$$

and

$$\frac{dE_i^*}{da_j}\bigg|_{\substack{i_X \\ j_X \\ a_i}} = \frac{\dfrac{\partial E_i}{\partial E_j}\dfrac{\partial E_j}{\partial a_j} + \dfrac{\partial E_i}{\partial a_j}}{1 - \dfrac{\partial E_i}{\partial E_j}\dfrac{\partial E_j}{\partial E_i}} \gtreqqless 0.$$

In terms of Figure 2.2, an increase in the initial income of, say, individual 2 will shift his reaction curve from a position such as E_2' to E_2 decreasing (or leaving unchanged the natural equilibrium level of effort of one or both) the natural equilibrium effort of both individuals. An increase in the ability coefficient of individual 2 will shift his reaction curve from a position such as E_2 to E_2' increasing (or leaving unchanged one or both) the natural equilibrium levels of effort of both individuals.

II.   ANARCHY VS RULES: A PARETO REDISTRIBUTION OF INCOME

The above model can be used to illustrate why the natural distribution may not be the final distribution of income although it is an important determinant of the final distribution. Since effort is an unpleasant commodity for both individuals, they would be willing to give up some of their natural income if they could simultaneously decrease their levels of effort. In fact, when $E_i^* > 0$, an $^oX_i < X_i^*$ can be found such that

$$U^*(X_i^*, E_i^*) = U(^oX_i, 0), \ (i = 1, 2). \tag{2.9}$$

Therefore, a Pareto superior move can be accomplished if both individuals agree to discontinue their effort to take income away from each other and share X in such a way that

$$^oX_i \leqq X_i^F \leqq X - {}^oX_j \qquad (i, j = 1, 2; i \neq j) \qquad (2.10)$$

and

$$X_j^F = X - X_i^F, \qquad (2.11)$$

where X_i^F and X_j^F are the final levels of income.

As an example of the Pareto superior move discussed in the above paragraph, consider the situation depicted by Figure 2.1 as the equilibrium levels of natural income and effort for individual 1. In this situation individual 1 would be indifferent between the point $(\hat{X}_1, \hat{E}_1)$ on the income–effort curve and income $^oX_1$ and zero effort.

The movement to the Pareto optimal state was what Hobbes [4, Ch. 17] called the 'final design' of men. 'The final Cause, End, or Design of men, . . ., in the introduction of that restraint upon themselves . . ., is the foresight of their own preservation, and of a more contented life thereby. . . .' This implication of the model for property rights is interesting. For a world of anarchy, a set of rules defining property rights can be developed and applied which will increase the total utility of both individuals. In this sense rules concerning property rights are better than anarchy and, therefore, should tend to develop.

As in the traditional bilateral exchange problem, the final distribution of income cannot be determined. All that can be said is that a Pareto redistribution *relative to the natural equilibrium* is possible and that the optimal redistributive rule would be one in which E_i is zero and the final income levels fall within the range given by the relationships of (2.10) and (2.11).

The above analysis was presented as if the two individuals always expended effort to determine the natural distribution of income before the move to the final distribution was made. Of course, this need not happen if both individuals are aware of the other's preferences, ability and initial income. If both have this information, they might move directly from the initial distribution to the final distribution.

In a world of only two individuals no enforcement costs of Pareto optimal property rights should be necessary since both individuals know that the inferior anarchistic state will result if they do not abide by the rules. For a larger number of individuals some may find it beneficial to 'cheat' and some schemes for enforcement would be necessary.[7]

The initial levels of income with $E_i = 0$ will be a possible final state only if ^iX falls within the range given for X_i^F in (2.10). If ^iX does not fall within this range, a set of property rights should emerge which redistributes income relative to the initial level of income. In the past, arguments for optimal redistribution of income have relied on such questionable assumptions as interdependent preferences, the incorporation of some 'distributional' argument itself in the utility function, diminishing marginal utility of income, or the use of interpersonal comparisons of utility functions [2, 5, 7, 10]. Note that none of these assumptions are used here. A person agrees to an income redistribution in which he loses part of his initial income because (1) in the absence of property rights he does not have the ability and the desire to expend the effort that is necessary to retain his initial level and (2) since effort is an unpleasant commodity, he is better off agreeing to property rights as described above that define income level than expending effort to determine these levels.

III.   AN EXAMPLE

As an example of the above analysis, consider the situation in which a sailor in a lifeboat from a wrecked ship lands on a small island inhabited by only one person. The initial situation is that the sailor brings the lifeboat and its contents as his initial wealth, ^sX, ashore and the native has initially the island and everything on it which is denoted ^NX. Once both individuals recognize the initial situation, the problem facing the community of two is to determine the natural equilibrium values X_s^*, X_N^*, E_s^* and E_N^*.

Assume that the preferences of the two individuals are represented by utility functions of the form

$$U_s = X_s^{\alpha_s}(C - E_s)^{\beta_s}; \; \alpha_s, \; \beta_s > 0, \tag{2.12}$$

$$U_N = X_N^{\alpha_N}(C - E_N)^{\beta_N}; \; \alpha_N, \; \beta_N > 0, \tag{2.13}$$

and $C > T$. The budget constraints facing the two individuals are

$$X_s = {}^sX + a_sE_s - a_NE_N \tag{2.14}$$

$$X_N = {}^NX + a_NE_N - a_sE_s. \tag{2.15}$$

The first-order conditions for utility maximization are

$$\frac{\beta_sX_s}{\alpha_s(C - E_s)} = a_s \tag{2.16}$$

$$\frac{\beta_NX_N}{\alpha_N(C - E_N)} = a_N. \tag{2.17}$$

The reaction functions for the two individuals would be

$$E_s = \frac{\beta_s a_N E_N + a_s \alpha_s c - \beta_s{}^s X}{a_s(\alpha_s + \beta_s)} \tag{2.18}$$

$$E_N = \frac{\beta_N a_s E_s + a_N \alpha_N C - \beta_N{}^N X}{a_N(\alpha_N + \beta_N)} \tag{2.19}$$

Using (2.14) through (2.19), expressions for the equilibrium levels of natural income and effort can be derived in terms of the parameters of the model, the ability coefficients and initial income.

$$E_s^* = \frac{(\alpha_N + \beta_N)[a_s \alpha_s C - \beta_s{}^s X] + \beta_s[\alpha_N a_N C - \beta_N{}^N X]}{a_s[\alpha_s \alpha_N + a_s \beta_N + \alpha_N \beta_s]} \tag{2.20}$$

$$E_N^* = \frac{(\alpha_s + \beta_s)[\alpha_N a_N C - \beta_N{}^N X] + \beta_N[\alpha_s a_s C - \beta_s{}^s X]}{a_N[\alpha_s \alpha_N + \alpha_s \beta_N + \alpha_N \beta_s]} \tag{2.21}$$

$$X_s^* = \frac{\alpha_s[(\alpha_N + \beta_N)^s X + \beta_N{}^N X + \alpha_N C(a_s - a_N)]}{\alpha_s \alpha_N + \alpha_s \beta_N + \alpha_N \beta_s} \tag{2.22}$$

and

$$X_N^* = \frac{\alpha_N[(\alpha_s + \beta_s)^N X + \beta_s{}^s X + \alpha_s C(a_N - a_s)]}{\alpha_s \alpha_N + \alpha_s \beta_N + \alpha_N \beta_s} \tag{2.23}$$

Using the assumption that an individual can survive if he receives at least X, the conditions needed for the existence of an equilibrium in which both the sailor and native survive are

$$|a_s - a_N| < \min \begin{cases} \dfrac{(\alpha_s + \beta_s)^N X + \beta_s{}^s X}{\alpha_s \alpha_N C} + \underline{X} \\[2ex] \dfrac{(\alpha_N + \beta_N)^s X + \beta_N{}^N X}{\alpha_s \alpha_N C} + \underline{X}. \end{cases} \tag{2.24}$$

Once the sailor and native determine the natural equilibrium, the sailor should recognize that he would be just as well off with

$$^{o}X_{s} = \left(\frac{U_{N}^{*}}{C^{\beta}N}\right) 1/\alpha_{s} \tag{2.25}$$

of X and $E_{s} = o$ as X_{s}^{*} and E_{s}^{*} and the native should recognize that he would be just as well off with

$$^{o}X_{N} = \left(\frac{U_{N}^{*}}{C^{\beta}N}\right) 1/\alpha_{N} \tag{2.26}$$

of X and $E_{N} = 0$ as X_{N}^{*} and E_{N}^{*}. Both realizing the gains from defining property rights, they would redistribute wealth in such a way that X_{s}^{F} and X_{N}^{F} fall into the range

$$^{o}X_{s} \leqq X_{s}^{F} \leqq X - {^{o}X_{N}} \tag{2.27}$$

and

$$X_{N}^{F} = X - X_{s}^{F}. \tag{2.28}$$

IV.   CONCLUSIONS

In the two previous sections of the paper it was shown that the determinants of income distribution in anarchy are individuals' preferences, ability, and initial income-wealth. The properties of the equilibrium natural distribution of income were discussed. Conditions needed for survival in an anarchistic state were also given. The analysis of the paper implies that rules defining property rights should emerge in such a state since an agreement is possible in which both individuals could discontinue expending unpleasant effort. But property rights do not emerge to justify and preserve the initial distribution, as so much careless discussion appears to suggest. As shown in Section II, only under very restrictive conditions will the initial distribution tend not to be modified under the set of property assignments forthcoming. These assignments, and consequent distribution, depend on the natural distribution of income which may be quite different from the initial distribution.

There are several real-world implications stemming from this analysis that remain to be developed. Only one need be mentioned here. A necessary condition for socio-political stability is that existing claims to income shares (the existing distribution as determined by property rights) fall within those limits defined by the equilibrium natural distribution.

NOTES

1. A partial exception is the work of Tullock, notably [9, Ch. 1]. Kolm [6] also discusses briefly an economy without laws or property rights.
2. For a paper that stresses the significance of these areas, see R.N. McKean [8].
3. An asterisk is used to denote natural equilibrium values.
4. Note that when ability is introduced a determinant solution is obtained (instead of a set of points) to the usual bilateral exchange problem.
5. The existence of a natural equilibrium suggests an interesting question that the model is not equipped to answer. If either X_1^* or X_2^* is below survival level, should the dominating person let the other person starve to death or enslave him? (In Tullock's [9, Ch. 1] terms, should he be a bandit or a tax collector?) Only by introducing time preference into the individual's utility function can the problem be adequately treated. In the present model, the individual will be starved to death.
6. In other words, the marginal rate of substitution of error for income is greater than the ability coefficient at $E_i = 0$.
7. For an excellent discussion of the relevance of numbers for the choice that individuals will make regarding alternative rules see Buchanan [1].

REFERENCES

1. James M. Buchanan, 'Ethical Rules, Expected Values, and Large Numbers,' *Ethics*, October 1965, LXXVI, 1–13.
2. W. Breit and W.P. Culbertson, Jr, 'Distributional Equality and Aggregate Utility: Comment,' *American Economic Review*, June 1970, LX, 435–41.
3. William Godwin, *Political Justice: A Reprint of the Essays on Property*. Edited by H.S. Salt. Allen and Unwin, 1970.
4. Thomas Hobbes, *Leviathan*. Everyman, 1943.
5. H.H. Hochman and J.D. Rogers, 'Pareto Optimal Redistribution,' *American Economic Review*, September 1969, LIX, 542–57.
6. Serge-Christophe Kolm, 'Possibilités et Difficultés de la Regulation des Problèmes d'Environnement et de Nuisance par Entente Spontanée entre les Intéressés.' Mimeograph, CEPREMAP, Paris, 1972.
7. A.P. Lerner, *The Economics of Control*. New York: Macmillan Co., 1947.
8. R.N. McKean, 'Economics of Trust, Altruism, and Corporate Responsibility.' Paper prepared for Russell Sage Foundation Conference on Altruism and Economic Theory, March 1972.
9. Gordon Tullock, *The Social Dilemma*. Unpublished monograph, The Center for Public Choice, Virginia Polytechnic Institute and State University, Blacksburg, Virginia, 1972.
10. G.M. von Furstenberg and Dennis C. Mueller, 'The Pareto Optimal Approach to Income Redistribution: A Fiscal Approach,' *American Economic Review*, September 1971, LXI, 628–38.

3. Jungle or just Bush? Anarchy and the evolution of cooperation

Jason Osborne

[W]hen people cooperate, it is generally a conspiracy for aggression against others (or, at least, is a response to such aggression).

Jack Hirshleifer (1994: 3–4)

Hirshleifer expresses a point of view that permeates most of the analysis of anarchy in economic literature. The only interactions between individuals involve attempts to acquire each other's wealth, or prevent this redistribution. Evidently, the only exception to this rule is the alignment of goals between or among individuals for the purpose of pillaging those outside of the conspiracy.

Addressing this issue, this chapter will focus on Winston Bush's view of Hobbesian anarchy, and compare it to a different vision of human interaction. The first section will demonstrate the inadequacy of government to solve conflict, given that a government could even be possible given the assumptions of the Bush model. The second part will provide a new analysis of anarchy in an evolutionary setting, derived from the recent work of Ronald Heiner (2002). This chapter will, it is hoped, reveal that the assumptions of these traditional conflict models are at best ridiculous, and that modeling individuals according to experimentally verified behavior yields a much higher level of cooperation than economists would have us believe.

1. DIVING INTO THE BUSH

In his article 'Individual welfare in anarchy', Winston Bush creates a model outlining the optimization problem facing two individuals in anarchy. Each has an endowment of wealth and must choose an amount of effort to expend both protecting his endowment and stealing from the other. Bush shows that the two will indeed steal from each other, but would be better off if they did not. He concludes that in order to solve this prisoner's dilemma, they could agree to a system of property rights, and in the case of more individuals, must form a government.

At the core of Bush's analysis is this Hobbesian belief that under anarchy 'The well-being of a person depends on his relative ability to produce, to take from others, and to protect his own' (1972: 5). He sees the only alternative to this approach to be the Proudhonian notion that men under anarchy live in some sort of harmonious wonderland, for which Bush sees 'little or no behavioral analysis, hypothetical or empirical, to support'.

So driving Bush's result is the fact that two individuals under anarchy would never be able to learn how to pool their labor for production purposes, nor trade one's product for the other's. Bush, however, claims that somehow these individuals will, in fact, institute a system of property rights once they realize they will be better off. How our two friends will be able to confer with each other regarding the need for property rights, when they cannot even trade an apple for an orange, must be left to the imagination. Though man is driven by wishing to maximize his own well-being, he is also able to employ his logical mind toward this end, and surely will be able to uncover the great mysteries of trade without having this knowledge levied upon him by some authority figure.

At any rate, with Hobbesian assumptions in hand, we shall turn to the model.

Bush's Model

Individual i, hence referred to as Ivan, possesses an initial amount of wealth ^{i}x, and chooses to expend some amount of effort E_i in the protection of ^{i}x as well as the theft of some portion of ^{j}x. He maximizes his utility $U_i = U(x_i, E_i)$, subject to $x_i = {^{i}x} + a_i E_i - a_j E_j$, where a_i is some positive constant indicating individual i's effectiveness at protecting and pillaging. Individual j, whom we shall call Joe, faces a symmetric problem. Bush (1972: 7–10) derives first-order conditions and the reaction functions of individuals i and j, and demonstrates that an equilibrium exists where $E_i, E_j > 0$. While even Bush realizes that Ivan and Joe will not require external enforcement of their new-found property rights, he does believe it will be necessary as more individuals enter this property-based society. I would like to show that government, i.e. external enforcement, does not necessarily help the situation at all.

External Enforcement

So suppose Ivan and Joe, rather than agreeing merely to respect each other's property, choose instead to erect an external enforcement agent, which we will assume does perform its desired intention of enforcing property rights and does efficiently allocate its revenues toward this end. Notice this does not prevent them from exerting effort toward stealing from each other, but instead merely reduces the effectiveness of their efforts. Ivan, and similarly Joe, must maximize the following:

$$U(x_i, E_i) \quad \text{s.t.} \quad x_i = {}^i x - T + f(T)^*(a_i E_i - a_j E_j), \qquad (3.1)$$

where T, bounded between 0 and $\min({}^i x, {}^j x)$, is the amount of payment required by the enforcer; and $f(T)$, bounded between 1 and 0, is the factor by which the effectiveness of aggressive behavior is reduced. Note that the problem is identical to that faced by Ivan and Joe before the existence of the enforcer, the only difference being likened to a simultaneous reduction in their endowments and pillaging effectiveness.

Referring to Bush's comparative-static relationships (1972: 13), the payment of the tax will increase the equilibrium effort spent by both toward theft, while the decrease in effort effectiveness will tend to reduce the amount of effort spent by both. So which effect will win out over the other? We will modify Bush's example (1972: 15–17), in order to answer this question.

We will assume the same utility functions for Ivan and Joe from Bush:

$$\begin{aligned} U_i &= x_i^{\alpha_i{}^*}(C - E_i)^{\beta_i} \\ U_j &= x_j^{\alpha_j{}^*}(C - E_j)^{\beta_j} \\ \alpha_i, \alpha_j, \beta_i, \beta_j &> 0, \end{aligned} \qquad (3.2)$$

where C is a constant greater than the maximum possible level of effort.

What we are changing is the constraints facing each:

$$\begin{aligned} x_i &= {}^i x - T + s^T(a_i E_i - a_j E_j) \\ x_j &= {}^j x - T + s^T(a_j E_j - a_i E_i) \\ 0 &< s < 1. \end{aligned} \qquad (3.3)$$

The first-order conditions for Ivan and Joe are:

$$a_i s^T = \frac{x_i b_i}{(C - E_i)a_i}$$

$$a_j s^T = \frac{x_j b_j}{(C - E_j)a_j}. \qquad (3.4)$$

Their reaction functions are:

$$E_i = \frac{b_i a_j E_j s^T + a_i a_j c s^T - b_i(^i x - T)}{a_i(a_i + b_i)s^T}$$

$$E_j = \frac{b_j a_i E_i s^T + a_j a_j c s^T - b_j(^j x - T)}{a_j(a_j + b_j)s^T} .$$

(3.5)

Solving for the equilibrium levels of effort:

$$E_i^* = \frac{(\alpha_j + \beta_j)(a_i \alpha_i c \sigma^T - \beta_i(^i x - T)) + \beta_i(a_j \alpha_j c \sigma^T - \beta_j(^j x - T))}{a_i \sigma^T(\alpha_i \alpha_j + \alpha_i \beta_j + \alpha_j \beta_j)}$$

$$E_j^* = \frac{(\alpha_i + \beta_i)(a_j \alpha_j c \sigma^T - \beta_j(^j x - T)) + \beta_j(a_i \alpha_i c \sigma^T - \beta_i(^i x - T))}{a_j \sigma^T(\alpha_j \alpha_i + \alpha_j \beta_i + \alpha_i \beta_i)} .$$

(3.6)

Performing some simple algebra on equations (3.6), we find that the equilibrium level of effort exerted by Ivan is greater than that before the enforcer came to town if and only if $T > {}^i x(1 - \sigma^\wedge T)$. The same is true for Joe if and only if $T > {}^j x(1 - \sigma^\wedge T)$. So until the threshold level of T, at $T/(1 - \sigma^\wedge T) = {}^i x$ for Ivan and ${}^j x$ for Joe, they will reduce their respective level of effort as the tax rate increases. After the threshold has been reached, they will begin to increase their efforts again.

So now we will answer the question we have been waiting for. Are Ivan and Joe better off? The equilibrium levels of wealth are:

$$x_i^* = \frac{\alpha_i[(\alpha_j + \beta_j)(^i x - T) + \beta_j(_j x - T) + \alpha_j C \sigma^T(a_i - a_j)]}{\alpha_j \alpha_i + \alpha_j \beta_i + \alpha_i \beta_j}$$

$$x_j^* = \frac{\alpha_j[(\alpha_i + \beta_i)(^j x - T) + \beta_i(_i x - T) + \alpha_i C \sigma^T(a_j - a_i)]}{\alpha_j \alpha_i + \alpha_j \beta_i + \alpha_i \beta_j} .$$

(3.7)

Solving (3.7) for the values of final wealth when the parameters are the same for both individuals, we have that $x_i^* = {}^i x$ and $x_j^* = {}^j x$ without government. With government, $x_i^* = {}^i x - T$ and $x_j^* = {}^j x - T$. With some asymmetry in the parameters, however, we have a different result.

Referring to (3.7): the first two terms in the numerator clearly indicate that government is reducing wealth. The third term, however, is much more interesting. Since $0 < \sigma^\wedge T < 1$, multiplying a term by it reduces its absolute value.

So, whichever of Ivan and Joe is relatively better at plundering the other is unambiguously made worse off by government. The underdog in this simple model, however, is made better off by government up to a certain point. Suppose $a_j > a_i$, then Ivan is better off with the government until T reaches the threshold where

$$\frac{T}{1 - \sigma^\wedge T} = \frac{\alpha_j C \mid a_i - a_j \mid}{\alpha_i + 2\beta_i} \,. \tag{3.8}$$

Let us ask a different question: does the amount that Ivan is made better off, in terms of final income, exceed the amount that Joe is made worse off? That is, could a simple redistribution of income yield a result leaving them both better off? Performing some more algebra, we find that up to a threshold level of T where

$$(1 - \sigma^\wedge T) = \frac{\alpha_i + \alpha_j + 2\beta_i + 2\beta_j}{C(\alpha_j - \alpha_i)(a_j - a_i)} \,, \tag{3.9}$$

Ivan is, in fact, more better off than Joe is worse off.

We have seen that government, as an enforcement agency, can to a limited extent make some people better off under certain conditions, including asymmetry of coercive abilities. In particular, those who would be exploited under anarchy are better off, but those who would be exploiters are now not able to plunder as much as they would have. We are, however, missing a crucial portion of this problem. That is, what is the government's utility-maximizing behavior? In real life, this enforcement agency is not external, but instead comprises a subset of those who are being enforced. It is a simple mental exercise to imagine that those who would be more effective at plundering under anarchy would be more effective at using government to plunder as well. Put another way, Hirshleifer's (1995) conflict success game under anarchy becomes Tullock's (1967) rent-seeking game under government. Unfortunately for those involved, these games produce the exact same results.

2.   EVOLUTIONARY COOPERATION

For this section we will reformulate Ivan and Joe's problem into a prisoner's dilemma (PD) game. Exerting effort to acquire the other's wealth will be characterized as noncooperative behavior, and expending zero effort as cooperative behavior. Note that we are not expanding the decision space to include other kinds of actions that we would consider cooperative in everyday life. Ivan and Joe, for example, still do not have the capacity to pool their resources in a mutually beneficial investment project of some kind. In other words, this is not the loving, peaceful, anarchic utopian dream world. Ivan and Joe are each still choosing to either engage in banditry against the other, or just leave the other alone. This is all that is required to prove the stability of cooperative behavior.

Because of the definition of the decision space, there is no option not to play this game. That is, 'cooperation' within the game is defined simply as the absence of aggression. In his recent work, Ronald Heiner has shown that in the one-shot prisoner's dilemma game, there is an evolutionary tendency toward 'contingent cooperation', as long as the sum of 'greed' and 'cooperation' payoff differences exceeds the 'fear' payoff difference. It should not be difficult to believe that this condition would hold in our case.[1]

Signal Detection

Heiner's analysis is derived from the signal detection literature of behavioral psychology. Consider an event Y, and a correlated signal x. Figure 3.1 illustrates the relationship between the probability of detecting x given that Y has occurred to the probability of detecting x given that Y has not occurred. With the 45 degree line representing pure chance (x and Y are uncorrelated), the bowed curve, referred to in the literature as ROC (receiver operating characteristic), represents under a particular signal detection technology the possible combination of probabilities. The greater the signal technology, the further out the curve bows.

Many years of behavioral experiments have shown that humans (and even dogs and rats) make trade-offs between these probabilities given certain parameters, such as payoffs. In particular, subjects can locate themselves on any part of their ROC curve. Put another way, one may increase the probability of x rightly indicating Y by exercising less caution in interpreting the signal, but at the expense of increasing the probability that x wrongly indicating Y has occurred (Heiner, 2002: 3–4). These ROC curves also can be used to explain precisely the so-called irrational behavior that exists in prisoner's dilemma and trust game experiments and has baffled game theorists over the years (ibid.: 15).

Contingent Cooperation

Using this idea of signal detection, Heiner creates a new type of prisoner's dilemma player, called the contingent cooperator. This player chooses his

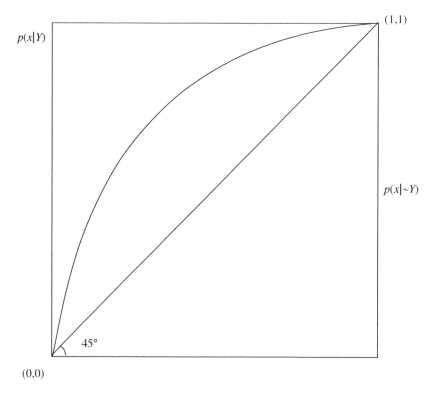

Figure 3.1   Signal detection and the receiver operating characteristic curve

action based upon a signal received from the player against whom he is matched. That is, he cooperates if he receives the *x* signal, and defects otherwise. This type of player is able to shift along his ROC curve, adjusting the probabilities of rightly and wrongly detecting the signal, based upon the payoffs and population makeup. In doing so, he is always able to maintain a performance advantage over the other player types, thereby securing the takeover of the population by contingent cooperation through replicator dynamics.[2]

While the equilibrium proposed by Bush, and in the entirety of one-shot prisoner's dilemma literature, is one of mutual defection, Heiner's equilibrium is characterized by a great deal more cooperation. Cooperation is not, however, universal. The amount of cooperation achieved in equilibrium depends upon the payoffs and the signal detection capability, since the players must be ready to defend against perturbations of other player types.

Role of Government

Heiner has done the heavy lifting to demonstrate the evolutionary equilibrium of contingent cooperation, and 40 years of experimentation have proved that humans detect signals and modify their detection probabilities according to the parameters of the decisions facing them. Now we will ask whether there is a role for government in facilitating even more cooperation than is achieved without.

Ivan/Joe	Cooperate	Defect
Cooperate	R, R	S, T
Defect	T, S	P, P

Figure 3.2   Prisoner's dilemma payoff matrix

Let us refer to the temptation, reward, penalty and succor's payoffs respectively as T, R, P and S, with $T > R > P > S$ (see Figure 3.2). We will also denote $r = p(x|Y)$ and $w = p(x|{\sim}Y)$, as does Heiner. Now the expected payoff for the contingent cooperator in equilibrium is:

$$P + r[(T - P) - (P - S)] + r^2[(P - S) - (T - R)]. \tag{3.10}$$

An invading defecting type player would have the following expected payoff:[3]

$$P + w(T - P). \tag{3.11}$$

Note that if the contingent cooperators set their r and w probabilities equal to one, their expected payoff would be equal to R, and that of the defector would be T, resulting in a successful invasion of the population by defection behavior. Thus, the contingent cooperator must set his probabilities sufficiently low in order to maintain a performance advantage. More precisely, he must choose r and w such that:

$$P + r[(T - P) - (P - S)] + r^2[(P - S) - (T - R)] = P + w(T - P). \tag{3.12}$$

Supposing that $T - R = P - S$, we can express the equality as:[4]

$$\frac{r}{w} = \frac{T-P}{(T-P)-(P-S)}. \qquad (3.13)$$

Let us imagine, as in section 1, an external enforcement agency. Further suppose that this agency decides to punish defection with a penalty we will refer to as ρ.[5] Thus, the new T and P payoffs are $T - \rho$ and $P - \rho$, respectively. It is important to note the following:

$$[(T - \rho) - R] = (T - R) - \rho = (P - S) - \rho = [(P - \rho) - S]. \qquad (3.14)$$

That is, the equality of greed and fear payoff differences still holds. If this were not the case, we would need to replace the squared term of the payoff function.

In light of the change in payoffs, the contingent cooperator must now choose his new r and w probabilities such that:

$$\frac{r'}{w'} = \frac{T-P}{(T-P)-(P-S)+\rho}. \qquad (3.15)$$

Since ρ shows up only as an additive term in the denominator, $r'/w' < r/w$. In other words, there is now more cooperation than before, as illustrated in Figure 3.3. The ratio, r/w, is represented by the slope of the ray extending from the origin to the point (r,w) on the ROC curve. As shown, a lower ratio of r and w equates to a higher r probability. That is, the probability of detecting the x signal increases, resulting in more cooperation.

Now we need to check whether individuals are better off under this new punishment regime. The contingent cooperator's expected payoff is now given by:

$$V = P - \rho + r[(T - P) - (P - S) + \rho]. \qquad (3.16)$$

Differentiating with respect to ρ:

$$\frac{dV}{d\rho} = -1 + r + \frac{dr}{d\rho}[(T-P)-(P-S)+\rho]$$

$$= r - 1 - r\frac{(T-P)-(P-S)+\rho}{[(T-P)-(P-S)+\rho]-w'(r)(T-P)}, \qquad (3.17)$$

with $dr/d\rho$ derived from the implicit function given by (3.15).

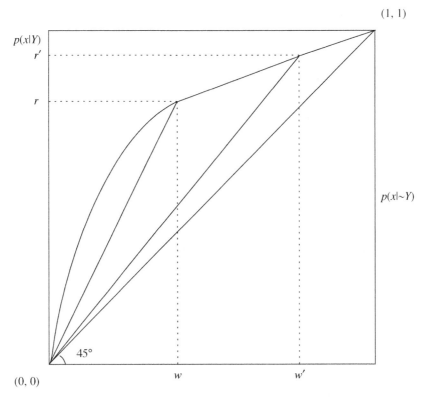

Figure 3.3 Outcomes under different punishment regimes:
$$r'/w' < r/w \Rightarrow r' > r$$

Rearranging to perhaps make more sense of this, $dV/d\rho < 0$ if

$$(r - 1) + (r + 1) [(T - P) - (P - S) + \rho] < w'(r)(T - P). \qquad (3.18)$$

There is clearly a threshold level of r below which individuals are better off and above which are worse off under the punishment regime. If the agency of enforcement were to additionally require a tax to be paid by individuals in return for their services, the r threshold would be lowered further. Suppose a flat tax is levied on each individual in the amount of τ. The T, R, P and S payoffs are all reduced by τ. The selected r and w probabilities will not be affected, since the τs all cancel each other in the r,w ratio equation. So the only thing that changes is a τ subtracted from the expected payoff function, and thus, the left side of the inequality above. Again, as the left side decreases, so does the minimum threshold r probability, and likewise the minimum required level of cooperation.

3. CONCLUSIONS, COMMENTS AND SUGGESTIONS FOR FURTHER WORK

The signal detection and evolutionary analysis found in Heiner's work represents an important step in economists' conception of human behavior. We have long been bewildered by phenomena observed in the world and in the laboratory which do not conform to our assumptions of hyper-rationality or self-interest. Attempts to explain these anomalies away using notions of altruism or reputation range from unsatisfactory to downright lame. Why do you not steal money from an old lady walking down the street? Is it because you care so much for others' well-being? Is it because you believe that you will harm your reputation? Is it because you made a calculation in your mind that by leaving the old lady alone, you will be causing others to leave you alone? Or is it simply because, through a process of evolution, we have been conditioned to cooperate with each other in order to ensure our survival?

While the analysis presented in this chapter does not achieve the author's life goal of demonstrating the superiority of anarchy, it should serve as a springboard to engage other related problems within the same framework. In particular, it would be interesting to flesh out the issues of power and wealth asymmetries in this model. As presented, all individuals face the same payoff functions. What happens when the payoffs vary among individuals? Is there a stronger argument for external enforcement of cooperation, as in the Bush model?

Another topic of interest which may involve more laboratory work is that of spatial equilibrium. The model is based on individuals randomly bumping into each other and engaging in one-shot games. People, however, do not engage exclusively in random one-shot games. They seem to locate themselves generally in such a way that they can interact with other individuals of their own type, and from whom they can more easily detect signals. How would subjects in an experiment behave if they were able to locate themselves in a particular space where the probability of interacting with a particular individual is a function of the distance between them? Would there develop a clustering of cooperation? Would these clusters be less susceptible to invasion?

In conclusion, while this chapter may not prove that anarchy is in all cases strictly superior to government in terms of maximizing individuals' wealth, it is hoped that it demonstrates that we can expect much more cooperation than Winston Bush had in mind. Furthermore, we have seen that government seems only to be able to produce some good if there exists an asymmetry of power. But then, will not government simply become the new exploiter?

NOTES

1. Suppose Ivan and Joe are identical, and Ivan aggresses against Joe without contest. By putting up a fight, Joe will not have been able to retain more than the amount acquired by Ivan, given that aggressive abilities are symmetric. For the purposes of this chapter, we will focus on symmetric abilities, although the asymmetries are much more interesting and will be the topic of future work.
2. For more on replicator dynamics, see Weibull (1995) or any evolutionary game theory text.
3. Heiner (2002), Table 1.
4. Is the payoff difference to be gained by defecting against a cooperator equal to that gained by defecting against a defector? While one would not be able to acquire as much from a defector, one would be able to prevent the other from acquiring as much for himself. The effects surely work against each other, though perhaps not canceling each other out. For ease of analysis, we will assume the equality.
5. Consider ρ the expected penalty of defection, for simplicity. That is, ρ is the actual penalty levied multiplied by the probability of being caught.

REFERENCES

Bush, Winston (1972), 'Individual Welfare in Anarchy', in G. Tullock (ed.), *Explorations in the Theory of Anarchy*, The Public Choice Society Book and Monograph Series, Blacksburg, VA: Center for the Study of Public Choice, pp. 5–18.

Heiner, Ronald A. (2002), 'Robust Evolution of Contingent Cooperation in Pure One-Shot Prisoners' Dilemmas', Working Paper, Department of Economics, George Mason University, VA, USA.

Hirshleifer, Jack (1994), 'The Dark Side of the Force', *Economic Inquiry*, **32**, 1–10.

Hirshleifer, Jack (1995), 'Anarchy and Its Breakdown', *Journal of Political Economy*, **103** (1), 26–52.

Tullock, G. (1967), 'The Welfare Costs of Tariffs, Monopolies and Theft', *Western Economic Journal*, **5**, 224–32.

Weibull, Joergen W. (1995), *Evolutionary Game Theory*, Cambridge: MIT Press.

4. The edge of the jungle*

Gordon Tullock

The existence of large, elaborate social structures among human beings is hard to explain on instinctive grounds. The point of this series is to look into the foundations of property rights and attempt to explain these foundations on the basis of assumptions of individual maximization. In general, we have been using the Bush model of natural distribution in which we follow 'the old way, the simple plan; let him take who is able, let him keep who can.' It is the purpose of this paper to add on to this model another rule of individual maximization which can, I think, be regarded as the foundation of all interhuman cooperation.

Let me begin, however, by making two modest modifications of Bush's basic model. Firstly, cooperative organizations may exist, even in a Bush state of nature. A pride of lions operates internally in terms of strength and combativeness of the individual members of the pride. Nevertheless, it is more efficient in its hunting so that a low-ranking member of the pride will normally eat more than he would if he attempted to hunt on his own. Similarly, we might expect groups organized on the Bush plan engaging in conflict, or in efforts to control or enslave other individual human beings or other groups. I take it that this is not a vital modification, but it does provide for an elementary construction of groups which gets us out of Hobbes' problem that man must sleep. A group of ten could organize among themselves according to the pure Bush–Hobbesian model; but with respect to another group of 100 slaves, they might be able to exert a great deal more control than any individual within the ruling elite can exert over the remainder of the elite.

My next modification is a bit more serious, and is an effort to deal with what I think is a weakness in the Bush model. There is no serious reason for trading to proceed between members when the stronger can seize anything he wishes. This is particularly true if one assumes an organized group exploiting a larger group of subjects. I think that we can, by a little reasoning about evolution and biology, deduce something about human beings which is

* This paper was first published in *Explorations in the Theory of Anarchy*, edited by Gordon Tullock, The Public Choice Society Book and Monograph Series, Center for the Study of Public Choice, Blacksburg, VA, USA, 1972, pp. 65–75.

observably correct and which explains the need for trade in addition to, or supplementing, straightforward, pure use of coercion.

Consider a pride of lions. Granted the Malthusian nature of the world, there must be periods of time in which the amount of food taken is not great enough so that the highest ranking members of the pride can completely satiate themselves, while leaving enough to keep the lower ranking members in good health. Under these circumstances, some reduction in the food consumption by the strongest members will not greatly affect their health, but will very significantly benefit the weaker members. There is, however, no way in which evolution could directly work for restraint on the part of the stronger members. Surely such restraint, if it were built in as a hereditary part of their constitution, would mean that they are less likely to survive than other, equally strong lions who do not have such restraint. The gene pool would always move toward eating food to full satiation. It would, of course, prevent the lion from eating enough food to reduce its physical efficiency by becoming fat.

If we observe lions, dogs, and human beings when they are confronted with something which they want and which is not present in large enough quantities for satiety, we see a good deal of threatening behavior among them and sometimes fighting. On one level, this would appear to be foolish from the standpoint of the weaker. Suppose that there is a quantity of meat and two lions, one larger than the other, who want it. If they fight, the larger has a very good chance of winning and the smaller, therefore, will not only get nothing to eat but will probably be quite severely injured.[1] Nevertheless, we do observe occasional fights and a great deal of behavior which can only be described as threatening of fights under such circumstances. Further, on occasion the larger lion will give way.

Granted the larger lion does occasionally give way, the behavior of the smaller lion becomes rational. In essence, the smaller lion is rationally designed to engage in irrational behavior. The smaller lion imposes upon the larger lion the prospects of physical injury, even though the prospects of physical injury for the smaller lion are much greater; hence he reduces the attractiveness of the combination of food plus fight to the larger lion below what it would be if it were simply the food, with the smaller lion withdrawing. There should be some level of belligerence for the smaller lion which maximizes its evolutionary success. Note, however, that this requires that the smaller lion sometimes fight and fight hard. Since at the moment the fight begins, the odds are heavily against the smaller lion, it must again behave irrationally under these circumstances if it is to have much chance of survival.

The mechanism which makes this possible, I believe, is 'loss of temper.' Individuals make threatening noises about things that they want for rational calculations. The actual serious fighting by the smaller of the animals or, as we shall see in a moment, by the larger of the animals, however, requires temporarily behaving in what is an irrational way. You threaten your opponent with irrational behavior on your part and the threat is indeed rational. Therefore a built-in, hereditary reaction pattern such that you will, on occasion, behave irrationally may be quite rational in the long run.

The existence of this type of loss of temper then automatically produces a bargaining range. Assume, once again, a large and a small lion growling at each other over a piece of meat. Assume that evolution has designed their behavior in such a way that it is basically rational. The larger lion would get some particular gain from each unit of food. Further, each unit of food he takes increases the likelihood that the smaller lion will lose his temper and there will be a fight in which the smaller lion will be killed, but the larger lion will suffer injury probably greater than the value of that unit of food. The larger lion, of course, is running down his demand curve for food as he eats. The smaller lion, on the other hand, is going up his demand curve as the larger lion eats each mouthful. Presumably there is some point at which the survival probability of the smaller lion is higher if he takes his chances in attacking the lion than if he remains without eating; but the built-in apparatus which made the smaller lion fight at an earlier stage would probably, over a large number of cases, increase the survival potential of that particular gene. In any event, if the fight occurs, the net result is a decline in life expectancy for both animals. Further, the potential of the fight is a continuously rising cost imposed on both animals. Under the circumstances, some kind of a bargain in which the danger of the fighting is reduced to zero would be desirable.

We do not observe this kind of bargaining among animals. There is a continuous threat, continuous rise of the likelihood of fighting, and occasional actual fighting. This is probably because of the limitation on what can be designed into the rather simple brains and communication systems with which animals are equipped. Human beings, having much larger computer capacity, can make conscious bargains in these cases. Note, however, that for the bargain to be rational for the large, more powerful human, the prospect of the weaker human losing his temper and attacking – even though he faces a present discounted negative value on the attack – is a necessity. The probability of losing one's temper and attacking against odds would have survival value, even though the attack itself will normally have negative payoff. This is particularly so if the larger and stronger human being hopes to continue to exploit the smaller human being over time, and hence would be most unwise to kill him. Thus the historically observed fact that slaveowners used positive incentives very commonly to get more work out of their slaves can be explained.

This problem is, of course, very similar to what we find in game theory. The mixed strategy which is the optimal solution of many matrices will normally provide for at least some probability of an individual player being called upon to play a strategy which, taken in and of itself, is the worst on the board. Nevertheless, adopting a mixed strategy in which he sometimes engages in this apparently foolish behavior is optimal. The human being would presumably *not* adopt the dangerous strategy every fifteenth time because when the fifteenth time came, he would rationally calculate it is weaker. A built-in, automatic biological mechanism – the loss of temper – can, however, give the same results.

So much, however, for this reason why we would anticipate the complete reliance upon coercion and physical strength would not be optimal. If we grant that it is not optimal, i.e. that sometimes there is a trading range, then the discipline of continuous dealings becomes important. Suppose, for example, that we first consider a situation in which there is a strong man and a weak man occupying the same area, but that the weak man physically is not capable of supporting both of them; hence, the strong man engages in some production himself and, in addition, preys upon the weak man to the maximum extent which he thinks is feasible. Granted the possibility of the weak man losing his temper, the strong man would be well advised to restrict his predation to some extent. Thus, the weak man will in fact occasionally have things which the strong man would want.

It is likely that the strong man will have things that the weak man would want also, and the prospect of trade would arise. In order for this trade to be possible, the weak man must feel confident that if he produces something above and beyond his normal payments to the strong man, the strong man will not simply seize it. Thus the strong man would, if he were sensible, have a fairly regular schedule of predation, but would be willing to make trades on things above and beyond that regular schedule. The reason is the discipline of continuous dealings. If the strong man regularly seizes three coconuts from the weak man, but on one occasion when the weak man happens to have a papaya and offers to trade it for some of the strong man's products, the strong man seizes it, then the strong man can feel confident that never again will the weak man, if he happens to have some additional papaya, offer to make the trade. The question is whether the present discounted value of the profit on a number of future trades is greater or less than the value of papaya which the weak man has at the moment. This should, of course, be added to the possibility of loss of temper on the part of the weak man when the papaya is grabbed.

Note that the credit has not entered into the computations so far. Neither the strong man nor the weak man is attempting to trade something in the present for something in the future. All the contracts are contracts for simultaneous performance. The only restraint on the discipline of the continuous dealings so far is a restraint upon seizing whatever the other party has brought for the trade, instead of trading for it. There is, of course, the willingness of the stronger to give up something in return for the papaya. It is interesting that these conditions do not apparently ever occur in the animal kingdom; hence, pure trades do not seem to be observed there.[2]

Trades of this sort clearly could improve the well-being of both parties. It might be possible for the stronger to acquire for himself the bulk of the improvement, but that would simply be a statement as to where they are on the new and improved Paretian frontier, rather than a denial that they would move outward. Note, however, that this particular variant of continuous dealings will continue to exist only so long as there are no significant accumulations of property. The stronger man does not take the weaker man's property because of the present discounted value of profits in future trades. If the weaker man's property becomes a large enough quantity, then this condition would cease to be true and seizure of the property would be rational.

So far we have discussed the problem entirely in terms of the use of force and violence, but fraud, stealth, and deception are also possible. They are harder to guard against and, in fact, guarding against them normally involves fairly large resource investments. Thus the existence of these possibilities will divert a good deal of energy from the society toward protective activity and away from production, with the result that the total product will be lower.

As a third problem, there has so far been no mention of credit. There will, however, be occasions in which a trade which is not simultaneous would pay; trade in which A must do something today and B reciprocate with some action or property tomorrow. The discipline of continuous dealings could permit such trades to go on, but only, again, so long as the repayment that B must make tomorrow is less in value than the present discounted value of future profits. This condition is found even today in illegal activity. Black market dealers and professional gamblers are very, very careful to keep a good reputation because it is their reputation for prompt payment which makes it possible for them to continue in business. They are, indeed, probably more careful about prompt performance than a businessman who can make a contract which will be enforced by the courts.

So far, we have seen a number of cases where trading can be organized, and the reason it can be organized is simply the discipline of continuous dealings. The individuals find the present discounted value of future dealings greater than the profit they can make from seizing property or refusing to make payment today. It is clear, however, that there are many situations in which we could not depend upon this very simple variant of the discipline of continuous dealings. The obvious case, of course, is simple accumulation of property until such time as the total amount accumulated is greater than the present discounted value of a set of transactions. Surely a fairly small amount of property would normally have that characteristic, granted the fact that it must counterbalance *not* the total value of future transactions but merely the profit on them.

A credit transaction raises the same problem. Transactions in which large payments will be made in the future would be impossible if we depended solely on the discipline of continuous dealings.

Introduction of enforcement apparatus, Mr Gunning's giant, would deal with this problem by making it possible to both accumulate and to enter into credit transactions. The enforcement apparatus could also be used to deal with the theft, stealth, and deception way of obtaining funds. In essence, the enforcement apparatus – instead of attempting to guard everything continuously – threatens the individuals with severe punishment *if* they violate some set of rules. The punishment is heavy enough so that the present discounted value of such rule violation is negative. This technique can be used to make it possible to accumulate capital, engage in extensive credit transactions, and make it unnecessary for the average citizen to put very much of his energy into guarding his property against stealthy removal. It can also be used to eliminate the advantage that the strong has over the weak, although here the arguments for doing so are not so obvious. Indeed, historically, there have been a great many societies in which the people who entered them as slaves have tended to remain slaves for long periods of time. We would anticipate that moving out of the simple Bush-type world would be highly beneficial even if the benefits were distributed in a manner which was highly unequal. Those that had might gain, and those that had not might make little or no improvement in their status. Egalitarians might find the prospect painful, but it would be admitted – even by them – that it was better than the jungle.

The introduction of some kind of enforcement apparatus, then, would be desirable to all members of the society, albeit it might be more desirable to some than to others. It would be possible to distribute the profits from the establishment of such an enforcement apparatus in exactly the same ratio as the wealth held by the various denizens of the jungle before the apparatus was established. It would also be possible to adjust this distribution in several ways. The bulk of the profit could accrue to some people and not to others. It would also, we should note, be possible that the state of nature would change. It might be that certain people with relatively little wealth or income in the state of nature as it was originally set up would gain greatly by the transfer to the new system, while some individuals who had done very well under the previous system would find their income going down very sharply. In essence, we are not getting away from the state of nature; we are simply changing the technological characteristics of individual power. If we set up an enforcement apparatus, those characteristics which lead to large income in a jungle may cease to lead to large income now. Diplomacy, salesmanship, and careful judgment of other people's opinions and values may make it possible for a person in the new society with an enforcement mechanism to apply force to an individual who physically is much stronger and who, in a single combat, would certainly win. This is not because we are no longer dependent upon force and violence, but because the technological conditions for using them have changed. Under the new scheme, an individual's ability to use force and violence is not so closely correlated with his personal strength and cunning.

Let us make the simplest assumption of transition conditions from the jungle to one where there is an enforcement apparatus. Assume, then, a jungle in which there are some bands – like the pride of lions – and that one of these bands succeeds in destroying or enslaving all of the others, and establishes firm control. This control would, firstly, lead to a considerable change in the income distribution in the jungle in that the members of the winning band would have much larger incomes, and the losers would have lower incomes. It would be rational for the stronger members of the winning band to permit sizable improvements in the income of the weaker members at the expense of non-members of the band, simply in order to retain the support of these weak members. The cohesion of the new government would depend on suitable rewards for all members.

This new controlling group would presumably establish a system under which it 'exploited' the remainder of the population to some degree which it thought was efficient. If, however, it wishes to maximize its drawings from the remainder of the population, it would be well advised to establish a set of rules under which this subject portion of the population devotes relatively little time to fighting with each other or guarding its own wealth against other members of the subject population, and/or attempting to get wealth of members of the subject population. By reducing the input of the subject population in these activities, it would make it possible for the subject population to produce a larger net revenue to the new ruling group.

Under these circumstances, the discipline of continuous dealings would have relatively little to do with the relationships among and between the subject population. They would be controlled by external sanctions imposed by the rulers. It would be possible for the subjects to accumulate capital – feeling confident that other *subjects* would not be able to take it away – to enter into large contracts for future performance under the impression that they would be enforced, and in other ways take advantage of economic opportunities which would not exist if the only enforcement mechanism was the discipline of continuous dealings. It would be to the advantage of the ruling group to provide the necessary enforcement.[3]

If the collection of people now incorporated under the rule of the 'upper class' is not the entire population of the world, then the possibility of clashes with external groups would exist and it would be in the best interests of the ruling group to protect its subjects against predation from the outside.[4]

There are, however, two other possible social relations which we have not so far discussed. One of these would be the relations between the ruling group and the subjects, and the other would be the relations within the ruling group itself. Since the ruling group itself is the police force which keeps the peace among the subjects, there is no police force to control its behavior, either with regard to the subjects or with regard to other members of the ruling group. This is a problem which must, under our present model, be dealt with once again by the discipline of continuous dealings.

Looked at from the standpoint of the ruling group, the optimal policy would be to select a set of payments which members of the subject group must make to the ruling group which maximizes the return. Presumably, there are two variables. Firstly, the fees, etc. charged to the ruled people should be arranged insofar as possible to provide them with incentives for hard work. For example, if the ruling group takes all of the coconuts any individual produces above the barest subsistence for his family, the individual would have little motive for producing coconuts. On the other hand, if the ruling groups take some large quantity of coconuts from each individual and then pay little attention to whether or not his family subsists, it would provide maximum incentives for hard work on the part of the subjects, provided of course that it would be possible for most families to continue to subsist on the amount remaining.

In addition to decisions as to the appropriate type of fees to impose upon the subject group and the laws which bind the behavior of the members of the subject group with respect to each other in an efficient way, the actual decision on the total amount of transfers to the rulers must be made with some care. In general, increasing the percentage of the product produced by the subject group transferred to the ruling group will reduce the total product. At some point, the increase which is obtained from increasing the percentage of production transferred will be counterbalanced by the fall in the total product. That is the point of maximum taxable capacity, and should be the area at which the ruling group aims. Note that if the ruling group is sensible, it will choose this rate at such a level that a good deal of inequality is possible among the subject people. This is in order to give the subject people incentives for hard work. If they can, indeed, improve their own status if they work hard and if they will starve to death if they do not, they are likely to be more productive than if they are all kept right on the brink of starvation.

Note that this last rule to some extent depends on both the possibility of loss of temper and the difficulties of information. If the ruling group were capable of exactly computing the potential productivity of each member of the subject people, it could set a tax upon such people at a rate which kept them just at the level of starvation at their maximum work-level. It is unlikely, however, that a ruling group will ever have that kind of knowledge. Further, the prospect of such behavior setting off fairly large scale loss of temper, with the losses that this would lead to on the part of both the ruled *and* ruling groups, is a consideration.

If the ruling group proposes to use an efficient system of drawing funds from the ruled group, then it must set up some way of administering these transfers and of controlling individual members of the ruling group who might wish to exceed the standard. Suppose, for example, that the ruling group consists of 100 people and the subjects number 2000 to 3000. Mr Smith, one member of the ruling group, is interested in seizing an additional coconut from Mr Jones, one of the ruled. If he is permitted to do so, this will mean that the security, and hence the incentive, of the ruled is reduced. The gain will go entirely to Mr Smith and not at all to the other members of the ruling group. The ruling group has, then, a motive for preventing this kind of thing from happening.

Note that the reason that the ruling group has motives for preventing this individual depredation, or depredation at a level or according to a structure which is not optimal, is the discipline of continuous dealings. They are compelled, in motivating behavior on the part of the subjects which will eventually produce a maximum income to the rulers, to give themselves a pattern of behavior on which the subjects can depend. Thus the discipline of continuous dealings – having been eliminated for intrasubject dealings – is returned for government–subject dealings. It is subject to exactly the same requirements that we had before. If the profit from a single act of depredation is greater than the losses from the elimination of future profits on regular transactions, then the government would be well advised to grab. The subjects, if they have an opportunity, will almost always be well advised to attempt to throw out the rulers. The rulers must see to it that the subjects never have such an opportunity. Note, however, that the discipline of continuous dealings, in dealing between the ruling group and the ruled, is essentially a public good from the standpoint of individual members of the ruling group. Since most of the cost of reducing the security of the subjects will fall on the other members of the ruling group, while the entire profit of the particular bit of depredation will accrue to the person who does it, the individual members of the ruling group would be motivated to violate the general rules which maximize income to the ruling group. The discipline of continuous dealings would indicate that the ruling group members would have motives to, if they could, discipline each other in order to maximize the long-term value of group membership.

So far we have discussed the relations between various members of the ruled, and between the rulers and the ruled. We have not discussed the relationships between members of the ruling group. They could be in a state of nature with respect to each other, i.e. the income derived from the exploitation of the ruled would be divided among the rulers in accordance with the Bush model. This would be like the lion pride in which the lower ranking members accept inferior status because it is still better than not being a member of the pride.

There are, however, profits available to the members of the ruling group from restricting their own internal relationships to a more orderly pattern. The ability to trade under conditions in which the discipline of continuous dealings will not afford guarantees, the accumulation of capital or other property beyond the level which would be protected by the discipline of continuous dealings,[5] and the possibility of making long-run contracts for large amounts would also be things which the ruling group would like to obtain for themselves. These are all areas where positive profits can be made by moving *out* of the Bush-type state of nature. Our subject society so far has moved the ruled out of this state of nature, but not the rulers.

A particularly important aspect of the long-term contract would be provision for the old age of members of the ruling group. The discipline of continuous dealings would never tell you not to seize the wealth of an old and feeble man, because he would never be in a position to retaliate. If you wish to assure a reasonably pleasant life in your old age, or if you are badly injured, or, for that matter, to members of your family if you die,[6] you would be interested in moving from the discipline of continuous dealings to some method of enforcing agreements, property rights, etc., which is superior to it.

The restrictions on the individual depredations of members of the ruling group upon the ruled, and upon the behavior of the rulers with respect to others, could be arranged by setting up some set of rules and arranging to have them 'enforced.' The problem is establishing an enforcement mechanism which will not, in and of itself, become another ruling group, thus putting the present ruling group – or the bulk of it – into the subject category, while reviving the basic problem for the new ruling group.

The simplest way of doing this would be to use the old-fashioned posse or vigilante method. Suppose, then, whenever any member of the ruling group either engages in unauthorized depredation upon the subjects or another member of the ruling group, or fails to carry out a contract, etc., all the rest of the members of the ruling group gather in a mass and inflict some punishment upon him. The members of the ruling group are, by adopting this institution, imposing some cost upon themselves in order to enforce the rules, i.e. they must occasionally take action as members of the posse. This is, of course, the reason why Becker, etc. calculate optimal degrees of enforcement for various laws. Let us assume, as seems reasonable, that the cost will be less than the benefit. Under these circumstances, the members of the ruling group are prevented from violating contracts, etc. by the threat of retaliation, just as are the members of the subject population. The organization is only a little different. The individual members of the ruling group are impelled to join the posse, however, by the discipline of continuous dealings. They know that if they do not join the posse at one particular time, then the posse may not turn out to help them in the future. Under the circumstances, it is very unlikely that the present discounted value of failing to turn out for the posse will be higher than the costs which would be imposed by not receiving its protection later. Thus the discipline of continuous dealings would lead to people turning out as members of the posse, and the posse would impose a 'rule of law' on the whole population, including its members when they acted as individuals.

Note that there is nothing in the model so far to prevent a group of members of the ruling class, or indeed a group of members of the ruled class, from forming a counter-group and attempting to defeat the posse. Presumably there would be potential coalitions capable of doing this available at any time. It is not clear, however, that such coalitions would pay. Once again, the discipline of continuous dealings is involved. But here the discipline should be imposed by making it 'illegal' to even begin the organization of such a group. If the detection apparatus is efficient, it could detect formations of such coalitions before they are far enough along so that they would have much chance of success.

The posse, of course, is a relatively inefficient mechanism. In general, we tend to turn toward specialization and division of labor. Setting up a special organization for the purpose of policing the rules would be an improvement in efficiency, if some method could be designed which will prevent this special group of policemen from becoming themselves a ruling group. There are two basic methods for this purpose. The first of these is simply to have the police weak enough so that the ruling group can readily defeat them. The long-standing tradition in England that there be no standing army is an example. The general weakness of the American government, the provision that individuals may carry arms, the weakness of the king in medieval Europe before the armed nobles, and many other examples of this method may be described.

It is unlikely, however, that this method in and of itself is optimally efficient for large groups. A more efficient method is to set up the enforcement apparatus in such a way that it is not capable of organizing itself for the purpose of overthrowing the existing regime. This requires that the enforcement apparatus be composed of quite a number of different people, and that their organization be such that they could not instantaneously convert themselves into a ruling group. A conspiracy within this large organization would be necessary and there would be an effort to detect such conspiracies early, with the result that they could be disposed of before they are large enough to be dangerous. It is not obvious that this is possible; indeed, the history of coups would seem to indicate that it is quite difficult, but it is surely not utterly impossible either. In any event, this is the mechanism upon which most societies have depended.

Note, then, that although we have come a long way from Hobbes' bush, we still depend on physical power to enforce the rules. We still depend, also, upon the discipline of continuous dealings, but the discipline of continuous dealings is now used only for a small part of society. It is only those members of the police force who are expected to report potential conspiracies among their fellow officers who find it necessary to make such discipline of continuous dealings calculations. They, if they feel that the present discounted value of the conspiracy is higher than the probable rewards of continuing in their present activity, would not report it. The rest of society, however, faces the much more efficient system of rules and enforcement of those rules by a body which is enough stronger than they are individually so that they are not well advised to resist it, and hence waste resources. As a consequence, society would be much more efficient. Indeed, the whole point of civilization may be said to be the pushing back of the jungle and the discipline of continuous dealings into a minor role. We cannot, however, completely eliminate them because they are the only motives available, in the last analysis, to motivate enforcement of the rules.

As a final *coda*, I should like to talk very briefly about cooperative states. The state I have described so far involves a ruling group and a much larger ruled group. Normally we would like to be in states which are somewhat more egalitarian than that, unless we are fairly confident we will be in the ruling group. We can imagine the society as a whole going through the same line of reasoning we have so far described for the ruling group only. They would not, of course, be interested in the relations within the 'ruled' group because this would not exist; but they would have the same motives for establishing controls within the new ruling group which is all of society, and could end up with approximately the same solution. One can imagine various other ways in which one could make the transition from the jungle to civilization, depending on the power structure at the time that the transition began.

It should be noted, however, that we are in a way still in the jungle. It is still true that our society in the last analysis depends on the combination of force and discipline of continuous dealings in order to retain its ability to enforce its rules. It may, of course, fail because the rules are bad or because it loses the desire to enforce them; but, even with good rules and a full willingness to enforce them, society will still be built on a Hobbesian foundation.

NOTES

1. Ardrey says that the principal cause of death among lions is fights with other lions. (See *African Genesis* [New York: Delta, 1963], pp. 41 and 103).
2. There are some cases where animals or plants engage in preprogrammed behavior which has some of the characteristics of trades, if looked at from the standpoint of the entire species. Individual trades, however, appear to be unknown.
3. Of course, the degree of enforcement is subject to appropriate calculations along the lines of Becker, etc., but it will not be discussed here.

4. Once again, the resources to be put into this protection are not something we will discuss here. They would not be infinite.
5. The ruling group might specialize in chateaux and other consumption goods.
6. It is not obvious that close relations among members of the family would be in accord with Bush's state of nature, but it is characteristic in economics to simply exempt family matters. Let us hope this custom will be terminated in the future, but it will require further research.

5. Social interaction without the state[*]

Christopher Coyne

Any society of force – whether ruled by criminal bands or by an organized State –
fundamentally means the rule of the jungle, or economic chaos.

Murray N. Rothbard, *Power and Market: Government and the Economy*

Social order is perhaps the most enduring issue in the social sciences. Thirty
years ago Gordon Tullock analyzed this problem in 'The edge of the jungle'
(1972), an essay in which he explores social interaction without the state as
well as the evolution of the state as a necessity for the facilitation of social
interaction.

Tullock begins by accepting Winston Bush's (1972) postulate that in
'genuine anarchy' two patterns of individual behavior may arise. One possibility is the Hobbesian jungle in which, without a central authority, individuals can either expend their energy on the production of goods or simply take
goods from others by force. The second possibility reflects the Proudhonian
notion that in the absence of social rules, individuals will develop their natural
talents and live in harmony. Besides accepting these notions of anarchy,
Tullock makes several modifications. He acknowledges the possibility of
'cooperative organizations' that may engage either in peaceful interaction or in
fighting with other groups or individuals. Moreover, he postulates that individuals or groups will not trade when the stronger can simply take from the
weaker.

In this article, I first clarify the meaning of anarchy. I then argue that
Tullock's concept of anarchy is flawed and that it leads to an inaccurate analysis of law without the state. Next, I reassess Tullock's analysis of the interaction of individuals and groups in a social setting with no central authority as

---

[*] This paper was first published as 'Order in the Jungle: Social Interaction without the State',
The Independent Review, **VII** (4), Spring 2003, ISSN 1086-1653, Copyright © 2003, pp.
557–66.

An earlier version of this article was presented at the Eighth Austrian Scholars Conference
at the Ludwig von Mises Institute, Auburn, Alabama, March 2002. For useful criticisms and
suggestions, I thank Peter Boettke, Bryan Caplan, Tyler Cowen, Peter Leeson, Eric McDaniel,
Edward Stringham, and an anonymous referee for *The Independent Review*. I acknowledge
also the H.B. Earhart Foundation and the Mercatus Center for financial support of the research
for this article.

well as his conclusion that the state is a necessary institution. Finally, I explore the facilitation of social order and interaction in anarchy. In passing through this discussion, we will come to realize that Tullock's entire critique of anarchy applies equally to any notion of the state.

ANARCHY DEFINED AND THE DEVELOPMENT OF LAW WITHOUT THE STATE

To begin, let us develop a clear understanding of the meaning of genuine anarchy and of the basic postulates of anarchist theory. Tullock presents the concept of anarchy as one of two extremes. We have either a Hobbesian jungle, in which individuals must rely on their natural talents to produce, take goods by force, and protect their own lives and property, or we have a Proudhonian utopia, in which individuals focus on developing their natural talents, conflict is absent, and all exist in harmony. Does Tullock's binary conception adequately express the concept of anarchy?

According to the Merriam–Webster dictionary, anarchy is defined as 'a political theory holding all forms of governmental authority to be unnecessary and undesirable.' Clearly, anarchists may believe in the importance of social norms, rules, laws, and controls. What anarchists oppose is the provision and enforcement of such social constraints by a central, compulsive, state monopoly. Anarchists argue that the government's ability to alter laws as it sees fit corrupts and violates the true rule of law (Osterfeld 1989).

Must a central authority create the laws? If not, who or what will develop them? Anarchists maintain that the laws need not be imposed by a central authority – that is, laid down as authoritative law – but can and do arise through customary arrangements and understandings that evolve over time. Customs serve as signposts that guide the actions of individuals in their interactions with others. As customs prove successful and gain acceptance, people gain the ability to anticipate others' actions and reactions (Hayek 1973).[1]

Authoritative law requires the use of extensive force for both implementation and enforcement, in contrast to customary law, which arises through social interaction. Juxtaposing customary and authoritative law, Bruce Benson has observed, 'if a minority coercively imposes law from above, then that law will require much more force to maintain social order than is required when law develops from the bottom through mutual recognition and acceptance' (1990b, 12). The coercive state evidently is not a prerequisite for the development of social norms, rules, and laws.[2]

Anarchists are not under the illusion that in the absence of a compulsive state no social conflict will occur. Rather, they presume that the market will provide the means to facilitate and maintain social order and interaction, including the development of rules and laws as well as their enforcement (Stringham 1999). The choice is not between having social rules enforced by a compulsive state and not having social rules at all. What is really at stake is the means by which the development and enforcement of such rules takes place; the root issue is state versus private provision. Tullock not only fails to consider customary law but also neglects the possibility of the private provision of enforcement. Anarchists argue that the state is not necessary to resolve disputes or to enforce laws. They claim that individuals will have strong incentives to form mutual support groups with others to deal with conflicts and legal problems (Benson 1990b).[3]

Having clarified the concept of anarchism and the development and enforcement of rules and laws in the absence of the state, we can understand better how various flaws in Tullock's analysis arise. The error lies not in semantics, but in a fundamental misconception of what the notion of anarchy entails. If we consider only two choices, both of which exclude the possibility of market provisions – total chaos where life is nasty, brutish, and short, or total harmony in the absence of conflict – we easily reach the conclusion that a compulsive state is needed as an effective enforcement mechanism. The former choice is dismissed on the grounds of continued violence and conflict, and the latter is rejected because a conflict-free society is impossible to imagine. Once the possibility of the market provision of rules, laws, and enforcement mechanisms is admitted, however, the conclusion that the state is the necessary and only source of order is exposed as a misconception.

TULLOCK'S ANALYSIS OF EXCHANGE, INTERACTION, AND ENFORCEMENT

Exchange is more beneficial than everyone's simply taking by force and violence. The market provides a framework that allows all – both the physically weak and the strong – to reap benefits by concentrating on the form of production in which each possesses a comparative advantage and then exchanging outputs with others. Tullock seems to agree when he acknowledges that 'we would anticipate the complete reliance upon coercion and physical strength would not be optimal . . . if we grant that . . . sometimes there is a trading range, then the discipline of continuous dealings becomes important' (1972, 67). Although Tullock recognizes the potential gains from trade, he anticipates potential problems in the absence of some protection mechanism.

Considering a situation in which two persons – one weak, one strong – inhabit the same area of land, and the weak person cannot produce enough to sustain both individuals, Tullock supposes that the stronger individual would produce but also would exploit the weaker individual up to the point that the victim will accept without retaliation. Of course, to maintain ongoing trade ('continuous dealings'), the weak person must expect to receive something in exchange; otherwise, he will stop producing. Although in this scenario continuous dealing serves as a check against complete exploitation of the weaker by the stronger, Tullock is concerned that it does not serve to eliminate predation completely. 'Thus the strong man would . . . have a fairly regular schedule of predation, but would be willing to make trades on things above and beyond that regular schedule' (68).

Furthermore, the concept of continuous dealings has other limitations. According to Tullock, continuous dealing will persist only as long as no considerable accumulations of property exist. 'The stronger man does not take the weaker man's property because of the present discounted value of the profits in future trades. If the weaker man's property becomes a large enough quantity . . . seizure of the property would be rational.' Nor is force the only potential problem in such a setting: 'fraud, stealth and deception are also possible' (68). Yet another problem arises with the introduction of credit or exchanges in which at least one party does not actually exchange a good or service at the time of trade. 'It is clear . . . that there are many situations in which we could not depend upon the very variant of the discipline of continuous dealings. . . . Transactions in which large payments will be made in the future would be impossible if we depended solely on the discipline of continuous dealings' (69).

Tullock's solution to these perceived problems is to introduce what Patrick Gunning (1972) calls the 'supergiant' (that is, government), which threatens individuals with punishment if they violate the rules (Tullock 1972, 69). Tullock recognizes that the result might be a ruling group that controls a much larger ruled group. In deciding what fees to extract from the ruled, Tullock claims, the rulers' goal would be to reach what he calls the point of maximum taxable capacity – namely, that point at which an increment of taxes would be offset by a fall in society's total product.

Remarkably, after pointing out the limitations of continuous dealings in the uninhibited market, Tullock grounds his entire theory of government on this very foundation: 'They [the rulers] are compelled, in motivating behavior on the part of the subjects which will eventually produce a maximum income to the rulers, to give themselves a pattern of behavior on which the subjects can depend' (72). If the subjects are unhappy with the level of taxation – that is, if they gain a lesser value than they surrender in taxes – they 'will almost always be well-advised to attempt to throw out the rulers. The rulers must see to it that the subjects never have such an opportunity' (72). Whether the rulers will prevent such an uprising by keeping taxes at the maximum taxable capacity or by threatening force, Tullock does not discuss. Finally, although he notes that nothing in his analyses prevents the formation of competing groups by members of the ruling group or of the ruled group, he quickly dismisses the idea: 'But here the discipline should be imposed by making it "illegal" to even begin the organization of such a group' (74).

Tullock unequivocally arrives at the need for a coercive government as a direct result of his failure to consider the market's potential to serve as the mechanism facilitating societal relations. Every potential difficulty that he finds in the absence of a coercive state, however, will exist also in the presence of the state.

A RECONSIDERATION OF SOCIAL INTERACTION AND EXCHANGE IN THE ABSENCE OF THE STATE

In Tullock's analysis of interaction between two individuals, one physically stronger than the other, he concludes that an incentive exists for the stronger to trade with the weaker but also for the stronger to take from the weaker so long as the weaker's cost of retaliating exceeds his cost of continued submission to the exploitation. If significant accumulations of property exist, the stronger takes from the weaker if the value of the taking exceeds the discounted expected profits from future trades. Although Tullock recognizes property rights, he does not discuss how they are assigned or enforced (1972, 68). We must ask, then, why the weaker would allow the stronger to take his property, especially if he has accumulated large amounts.

The advocate of pure laissez-faire might note that even in a Hobbesian situation individuals have some idea about how others will act. In any coordination scenario, certain focal strategies or courses of action are more obvious than others. To be sure, there is a wide range of possibilities. Nor will others always act as expected. Nevertheless, two or more persons in a situation in which they must choose how to interact will perceive certain focal points (fight, exchange, and so forth) that will be obvious to them, if not to everyone. Therefore, each individual will have a bundle of expectations of how others will act. For example, if Jones, a physically weaker individual, is considering a first-time interaction with Smith, a physically stronger individual, he may have some expectation of making a mutually beneficial exchange. Likewise, he may have some expectation of being attacked or exploited by Smith and may protect himself as this expectation warrants. As individuals continue to interact over time, they will become more confident about how their counterparts will act. In addition, we must recognize that predation is costly. Smith initially must consider the probability that Jones will not retaliate when attacked. He must consider also the probability that if Jones does retaliate, he himself potentially will bear part of the cost in terms of either bodily injuries or the loss of part (or all) of his preattack endowment of assets. Given each individual's expectations of how others will act, there are several possibilities, all arising on the market, that allow weaker individuals to protect themselves from predation by the strong.

The most obvious way for the weak to protect themselves is by increasing their personal protective measures, which may include simple tactics such as keeping doors locked or installing alarms as well as more costly options such as accumulating weapons to compensate for deficiencies in physical strength. Other alternatives also permit individuals, whether physically weak or strong, to protect their property more effectively. One potential solution is for the weak to join together to form support groups to assist members exploited by those who are physically stronger. In such a scenario, what the individual members lack in physical strength, they compensate for in numbers. Examples of such cooperative groups are community watches, neighborhood patrols of streets and buildings, and escort services to accompany and protect those desiring such assistance (Benson 1990a, 30–31; 1998, 80–86). Moreover, entrepreneurs may cater to the market demand by selling protection services to the weak.[4] Examples of such market services include the patrols formed or financed by businesses to protect their property. We see such activity in malls, office and apartment complexes, amusement parks, and resorts (Benson 1998, 92; Stringham 1999, 56). University police provide yet another example of the private production of security and policing in a private community (Stringham 1999).

Exploitation and predation obviously are not unique to the uninhibited market but also arise from the state. And just as laws, rules, norms, and the institutions of enforcement (private courts, support groups, and so forth) develop on the market, so too will institutions that serve to protect the individual and his property. Moreover, individuals will be able to satisfy their specific needs with regard to the amount, quality, and cost of the services they obtain.

Although Tullock recognizes that continuous dealings, at least for immediate transactions, will serve to facilitate societal relations, he clearly underestimates the importance of the role they play in the interactions between individuals on the uninhibited market. The key elements of continuous dealings are the participants' reputations, which are grounded in other people's subjective views and beliefs. On the free market, entrepreneurs, driven by the profit motive, attempt to maximize profits and minimize losses. In an effort to maintain current market share and gain new market share, entrepreneurs attempt to meet customer needs best in terms of product quality, service, and price – crucial variables in determining a seller's reputation. The entrepreneurial quest reveals itself in advertisements, which seek to establish a brand name and shape a product's image and therefore to establish the seller's reputation. In this connection, we also observe firms guaranteeing their products and services and offering continued maintenance services in order to strengthen their reputation. We see the value placed on reputation when an acquiring firm makes a goodwill payment – the price of the firm's reputation – to the seller. As George Stigler points out, 'Reputation is a word which denotes the persistence of quality, and reputation commands a price (or exacts a penalty) because it economizes on search' (1961, 224). One might question what is to be done in situations where the reputation of one of the traders is unknown. Such situations, however, provide a market opportunity for an entrepreneur to supply information regarding the reputation of the seller and his product (Klein 1997). These information sources also aid in overcoming the problems of fraud, stealth, and deception to which Tullock refers. Examples of such services include *Consumer Reports* magazine, which provides information, testing, and rankings for numerous consumer products; '1-800-Dentist,' which provides information on dentists to potential patients; and Moody's, Standard & Poor's, and Morningstar, which provide financial analysis, rankings, and information for various companies in many industries. Even with a coercive state, we see entrepreneurs providing services that record and make available comments and complaints about various sellers. Examples of services that provide information on sellers are credit card companies, credit rating agencies, and Ebay. Finally, we might note that Tullock fails to consider the possibility that government agents themselves will deceive and defraud the ruled. Because other potential, competitive government organizations are to be banned, and 'fees' are to be charged no matter what, the ruled have no effective recourse even if they recognize such fraud and deception.

What about the longer-term and credit transactions that Tullock views as so problematical for anarchy? Even for them, recent research (Stringham 2003) has shown that we need not abandon the concept of continuous dealing and that we can have confidence that the market will provide efficient mechanisms and institutions to facilitate transactions. Researching the role of reputation and continuous dealings in the development of financial markets in seventeenth-century Amsterdam, Stringham has found that traders developed reputations that allowed them to interact in financial transactions of varying maturity dates and complexities. Cheating or reneging rarely occurred because such transgressions would mar the miscreant's reputation permanently.

Yet another potential market solution to possible difficulties in longer-term dealings is for a third party with a well-known and highly regarded reputation to vouch for and ensure execution by the party with a lesser-known reputation in exchange for a fee. In this case, the third party that vouches for those involved in the transaction assumes responsibility in the case of default. Furthermore, as noted previously, customary law will develop over time to facilitate longer-term transactions through contracts and the enforcement of such transactions. One such example is the law that governs international commercial dealings, which is separate from any specific national law. Merchants trading across national borders must enter into agreements and settle disputes without the assistance of a coercive government. In many cases, international trade associations have developed their own procedures to resolve conflicts (Benson 1990b).

A RECONSIDERATION OF TULLOCK'S NOTION OF GOVERNMENT

Tullock seems to have blind faith that the ruling group, acting as a rational income maximizer, will rarely abuse its power. When abuse does in fact occur, he relies on other members of the ruling group to discipline those who have acted inappropriately. This discipline supposedly will occur at the hands of a 'posse,' voluntarily formed and composed of ruling members, which will inflict a punishment on the offender. However, Tullock fails to consider the possibility that the same type of law enforcement to deal with conflict might occur on the market. As noted earlier, many historical examples show the formation of support groups to assist members in settling disputes. Underlying Tullock's oversight is his characterization of the rulers as monetary income maximizers. It is critical to remember, however, that through action people attempt to maximize psychic income. This is not limited to monetary income but includes nonpecuniary forms of income as well. Rulers may gain (psychic) income by holding and wielding power even though they may not maximize monetary revenue by doing so. And, if they do so, their actions may conflict with the ruled group's interests far more than Tullock's analysis suggests.

Further, the government in the Tullock formulation fails to solve the problem of the social order. What prevents internal strife among the rulers from causing a return to the initial state of the Hobbesian jungle? If we accept that a ruling group can achieve a peaceful equilibrium, why can't a similar equilibrium be attained on the market without government?

If the ruled are dissatisfied with the rulers, Tullock concludes that the former should seek to throw the latter out. This possibility is a dubious one, inasmuch as Tullock believes that the ruling group should have the ability to grant itself a monopoly over governing – that is, the ability to outlaw all other competing organizations that might form. Under such conditions, why can't the same government officials prevent the ruled from ousting them from their positions of power by threat of force? Along the same lines, Tullock's government also can outlaw any private watch groups that pose a potential threat to the rulers' power. The fear of fraud, stealth, and deception should apply even more to a coercive state, given its ability to outlaw the mechanisms that arise in the uninhibited market to disseminate information about the parties involved in transactions.

Moreover, within Tullock's framework, the notion of continuous dealings is inapplicable – that is, in the case in which one of the parties is a coercive government. The concept of continuous dealings rests on the assumption that parties continue to interact over time because all involved expect to benefit. If one or more parties believe they will not benefit from the exchange, they can voluntarily cease to exchange with one party and instead begin to interact with other parties. When the coercive state is one of the parties involved, however, such continuous dealings cannot be a possibility because some parties are forced to continue the exchange. The very existence of a coercive state completely obviates the possibility of genuine continuous dealings. Once these factors are considered, Tullock's theory of government, grounded in continuous dealings and the discipline of the ruling group from within, is weakened significantly. The only remaining check on government is that the rulers will want to maximize their monetary income and therefore will provide incentives for the ruled to maximize output. Because Tullock has conceded to the government the ability to grant or exercise monopolies at will, however, what can stop the rulers from simply demanding that the ruled work under the threat of force?

CONCLUSION

In the foregoing discussion, I have reconsidered Gordon Tullock's analysis of social interaction in the absence of the state. In doing so, I have sought to clarify the meaning of anarchy and have considered the market provision of the various institutions – laws, courts, enforcement mechanisms, information services, and so forth – that might develop to further social interaction (and, indeed, already do to some extent). In considering the possibility of the market supply of these institutions, I have identified critical oversights in Tullock's analysis. His conclusions rest on the unsupported assumption that the perceived problems that arise in anarchy can be averted somehow by a coercive government. This assumption takes for granted that the strong will act differently, depending on the existence of a state.

In exploring 'genuine anarchy,' as Tullock set out to do, we must consider as a viable option the market provision of key institutions facilitating social interaction. Numerous social orders fall between the Hobbesian jungle and the Proudhonian utopia. By extending the idea that individuals act in a rational, self-interested manner to the analysis of social interaction without the state, we come to understand better the importance of social interaction and cooperation and the genuine possibility that individuals can promote such interaction and cooperation by means of market-supplied institutions.

NOTES

1. For examples of reciprocal exchange and its role in law throughout US history, see Benson (1991).
2. For a discussion of the development of customary law and a comparison of customary and authoritative law, see Benson (1990b). For a discussion of potential problems and solutions in customary law, see Hayek (1973) and Osterfeld (1989).
3. For a discussion of the operation of private courts, see Barnett (1986); Benson (1990a, 1990b and 1998); Friedman (1989); Osterfeld (1989); and Rothbard (1973).
4. For more on private security, see Benson (1990a, 1990b, 1998); Hoppe (1998). For an analysis of the private production of defense, see Hoppe (1999). For a discussion of private police and security services and the interaction of competing agencies and private prisons, see Osterfeld (1989) and Sneed (1977).

REFERENCES

Barnett, Randy E. 1986. 'Pursuing Justice in a Free Society: Part Two – Crime Prevention and the Legal Order'. *Criminal Justice Ethics* (Winter–Spring): 30–53.

Benson, Bruce L. 1990a. 'Customary Law with Private Means of Resolving Disputes and Dispensing Justice: A Description of a Modern System of Law and Order Without State Coercion'. *Journal of Libertarian Studies* 9: 25–42.

—— 1990b. *The Enterprise of Law: Justice Without the State.* San Francisco: Pacific Research Institute for Public Policy.

—— 1991. 'Reciprocal Exchange as the Basis for Recognition of Law: Examples from American History'. *Journal of Libertarian Studies* 10: 54–82.

—— 1998. *To Serve and Protect: Privatization and Community Criminal Justice.* New York: New York University Press for The Independent Institute.

Bush, Winston. 1972. 'Individual Welfare in Anarchy'. In *Explorations in the Theory of Anarchy*, edited by Gordon Tullock, 5–18. Blacksburg, Va.: Center for the Study of Public Choice.

Friedman, David. ,1989. *The Machinery of Freedom: Guide to a Radical Capitalism.* Chicago: Open Court.

Gunning, J. Patrick. 1972. 'Towards a Theory of the Evolution of Government'. In *Explorations in the Theory of Anarchy*, edited by Gordon Tullock, 19–26. Blacksburg, Va.: Center for the Study of Public Choice.

Hayek, Friedrich A. 1973. *Rules and Order. Vol. 1 of Law Legislation and Liberty.* Chicago: University of Chicago Press.

Hoppe, Hans-Hermann. 1998. 'Fallacies of the Public Goods Theory and the Production of Security'. *Journal of Libertarian Studies* 9: 27–46.

—— 1999. 'The Private Production of Defense'. *Journal of Libertarian Studies* 14: 27–52.

Klein, Daniel B., ed. 1997. *Reputation: Studies in the Voluntary Elicitation of Good Conduct.* Ann Arbor: University of Michigan Press.

Osterfeld, David. 1989. 'Anarchism and the Public Goods Issue: Law, Courts, and the Police'. *Journal of Libertarian Studies* 9: 47–68.

Rothbard, Murray N. 1973. *For a New Liberty: The Libertarian Manifesto.* San Francisco, Calif.: Fox and Wilkes.

Sneed, John D. 1977. 'Order Without Law: Where Will Anarchists Keep the Madman?' *Journal of Libertarian Studies* 1: 117–24.

Stigler, George J. 1961. 'The Economics of Information'. *Journal of Political Economy* 69: 213–25.

Stringham, Edward. 1999. 'Market Chosen Law'. *Journal of Libertarian Studies* 14: 53–77.

——— 2003. 'The Extralegal Development of Securities Trading in 17th-century Amsterdam'. *Quarterly Review of Economics and Finance* 43: 321–44.

Tullock, Gordon. 1972. 'The Edge of the Jungle'. In *Explorations in the Theory of Anarchy*, edited by Gordon Tullock, 65–75. Blacksburg, Va.: Center for the Study of Public Choice.

6. Towards a theory of the evolution of government*

J. Patrick Gunning

Professor Bush recently presented a model which depicted an equilibrium for a social situation which begins in the Hobbesian jungle. In his model, he demonstrated that gains from trade would always exist unless theft and violence were reduced to a zero level. Consequently, the equilibrium that Bush established was one in which continuous tradings would reduce the level of these mutually undesirable activities to zero. Bush's analysis leads one to believe that the Hobbesian jungle is a disequilibrium state in which the preferences and abilities are uncertain. The gradual reduction of the uncertainty through the learning experience will lead to the elimination of theft and extortion.

Although there is nothing wrong with Professor Bush's analytics, I believe that he omitted two very important aspects of the Hobbesian jungle. First, although it is true that for infinitely recurring contacts between two persons with given characteristics, certainty will emerge; it seems more realistic to assume that individuals will alter their characteristics as time passes. Secondly, and more to the point of this paper, contacts are not likely to be infinitely recurring. In both of these cases, the relevant problem concerns individuals' attempts to cope with the continuing uncertainty about the behavior of others in potential mutually beneficial trading situations.

The task of this paper is to explain the emergence of government by recognizing its role as a provider of the service of contract enforcement. Enforcements of contracts reduces the uncertainty of individuals in nonrecurring situations.

I. A MODEL OF INDIVIDUAL BEHAVIOR

To begin, let us define an individual in the following manner:

* This paper was first published in *Explorations in the Theory of Anarchy*, edited by Gordon Tullock, The Public Choice Society Book and Monograph Series, Center for the Study of Public Choice, Blacksburg, VA, USA, 1972, pp. 19–26.

$$U = f(X_1, X_2, \ldots, X_n, L); f'(X_1), f'(X_2) \ldots f'(X_n) > 0; \qquad (6.1)$$
$$f'(L) < 0.$$

$$X_1 = g_1(L); g_1'(L) > 0;$$
$$X_2 = g_2(L); g_2'(L) > 0;$$
$$\cdot$$
$$\cdot \qquad\qquad\qquad\qquad\qquad (6.2)$$
$$\cdot$$
$$X_n = g_n(L); g_n'(L) > 0.$$

The functions, g, refer to own production functions. They indicate the quantities of labor (or time, if you prefer) that are necessary to produce various events with one's own labor time. If a second individual exists, the first person can produce one of the events in a way that differs from his own production function. For the simplest case, suppose that the first individual recognizes that the ith event – and only the ith event – in his utility function will be produced by the second individual if that second person can be persuaded to do so. It will be assumed for simplicity that stealing is impossible. Such an assumption is more easily defended in a two-person model than in a larger model.

In the general case, an individual will observe two ways to persuade: by a threat and by a bribe. The threat consists of using a certain amount of resources to make the threat credible. The bribe function consists of using a certain amount of labor to produce an event desired by the second individual. Whether he chooses to bribe, threaten, or produce the event himself depends on the values of the respective functions. The bribe and threat functions, as the individual perceives them, can be represented algebraically:

$$X_i = b(1); b'(L) > 0; \qquad (6.3)$$

$$X_i = t(L); t'(L) > 0. \qquad (6.4)$$

II. BRIBES AND THREATS

It will be convenient to begin with a discussion of bribing. The simplest bribe function seems to consist of a trade of a change in one person's behavior for a change in another's. For example, a giant may offer to feed a pygmy some coconut milk if the pygmy will sing a song for him. Or, vice versa, the pygmy may offer to sing his song if the giant gives him some milk. One necessary condition for a bribe to occur is that a bargaining range must exist. If a bargaining range does not exist, no amount of bargaining will result in a bribe.

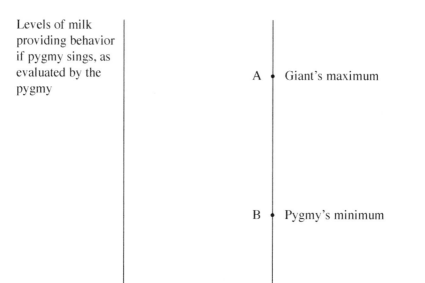

Levels of milk
providing behavior
if pygmy sings, as
evaluated by the
pygmy

A ● Giant's maximum

B ● Pygmy's minimum

1   Units of song-singing

Figure 6.1   Bribe function

In the simplest case, where the song-singing is a single discrete activity, the range can be expressed by a straight line. For example, in Figure 6.1, the bargaining range is represented by the line segment AB. If the maximum amount of coconut milk that the giant is willing to pay exceeds the minimum amount that the pygmy will accept (as shown in the figure), a bargaining range will exist and a trade may occur. It is said that a trade *may* occur because there are at least two obstacles. It is the attempt to eliminate these obstacles which might lead the traders to hire a third party to enforce a trading agreement.

The first of these is the obstacle of timing. Will the milk be provided before, during, or after the performance? If it is before, how can the giant be guaranteed that the performance will occur? If it is afterwards, how can the pygmy be assured that the giant will actually give it? If it is during, it may affect the quality of the performance. The importance of timing is inversely related to the number of times that the same trade (or other similar trades) is expected to recur. If a trade is expected to occur only once, it would always be beneficial for the one whose behavior occurs latest to refrain from that behavior. As the expected number of recurrences of trading situations approaches infinity, timing becomes unimportant. For example, in a recurring situation, the giant's failure to give milk after a song was sung (assuming that is the sequence of behavior) would jeopardize future trades.

Even if the trades are expected to be infinitely recurring, there may be no trade even though a bargaining range exists. Suppose that both the giant and the pygmy are equally certain that trades will continue forever. Suppose further, however, that they differ in their ability to predict changes in demand conditions. For example, coconut milk may be addictive, but only the giant may know the extent of its addictive powers. The pygmy may have an inkling that the milk is addictive, but he may be quite uncertain about the extent. In this circumstance, mutually beneficial trade may be impossible unless the pygmy can be insured against a rise in price at future negotiations.

The threat function is very similar to the bribe function. As a practical example, assume that the giant wishes to persuade the pygmy to sing his song through coercion. To do so, he announces to the pygmy that, if he does not sing, the giant will behave in such a way as to inflict pain on the pygmy (perhaps he says that he will beat the pygmy over the head). A necessary condition for song-singing to occur in the threat case, as in the bribe case, is that a bargaining range must exist. A picture similar to that of Figure 6.1 can be drawn. In Figure 6.2, the bargaining range is again represented by the line

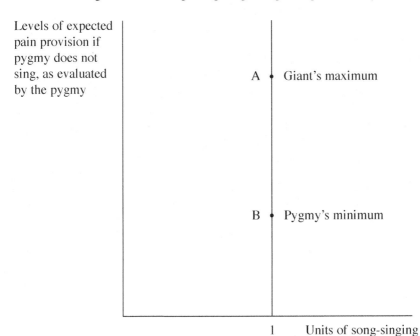

Figure 6.2   Threat function

segment AB. As in the bribe case, timing is also important. Should the threat-credibility behavior take place before, during, or after the song? If it is before, it will have no effect on the decision; if it is during, it may affect the quality of the performance; if it is afterwards, the giant cannot be certain that the song will be sung. Also like the bribe case, the quantity of threats may be lower if there is uncertainty about future changes in demand. The giant may be unwilling to threaten the pygmy if he believes that song-singing is addictive.

There is one important difference between bribes and threats that arises only under uncertainty. Suppose, in a two-person model, that the pygmy knows the utility function and constraints facing the giant and that the giant knows the utility function and all but one of the constraints of the pygmy. Assume that the constraint concerns the activity of song-singing, an activity which yields external benefits to the giant. Now the pygmy will generally attempt to conceal the constraint (his ability and willingness to sing songs) from the giant. The extent to which he carries out his attempts at concealment, however, depends on whether he expects to be bribed or threatened to perform that activity. If the pygmy expects to be threatened, he will attempt to convince the giant that song-singing is extremely difficult. If he expects to be bribed, he will do the same thing, but only to the extent that his concealment behavior begins to affect the giant's willingness to negotiate.

III.   AN ENFORCER OF CONTRACTS

Suppose now that there exists some third party, say a *super-giant*, who is able to impose the most severe penalties on both the giant and the pygmy. The super-giant could conceivably add considerable efficiency in the dealings between the giant and the pygmy. This is because he has the unique ability to enforce contracts between the two parties. It is clear that there are at least two services which could be provided. The first concerns the enforcement of promises to perform activities at a later time. For non-recurring exchanges in which the timing problem is present, two traders would be willing to pay an enforcer to insure by threats that the activities which are traded are carried out by both parties. Secondly, the traders would hire an enforcer to insure against differences in information about future changes in demand which might result from something like addiction.

It is important to note that the relationship between the enforcer and potential traders must be a recurring one for the traders to be willing to hire him. This is because the service of enforcement is one in which the enforcer's activity is expected to occur after the traders' activities. If the enforcer of contracts has not established a reasonably good reputation for carrying out his threats when an agreement is not kept, the traders would certainly be foolish to hire him.

IV. EXTENSIONS

The task of this paper has been to show that it is possible to explain the emergence of government on the basis of a government's specialized ability to enforce contracts. It was recognized that the entity(ies) with such specialized abilities will also be a relatively good extortionist. For the sake of brevity, some very important issues have been passed over.

The first of these is the nature of the competition of potential enforcers. One would expect such competition to differ substantially from the typical textbook representation of competition of suppliers. This is because competitors are engaged in attempts to extort as well as to sell services.

A second possible extension is the use of the model to explain the emergence of different kinds of governments. For example, the model could be used to explain the emergence of the United States government in something like the following manner. Initially, it consisted of a set of persons who were hired to monitor the provision of war services by the various colonies. Mechanisms were built into the initial system, by design or chance, which prevented unintended intimidation by any state or coalition. These mechanisms were also useful in providing the service of contract enforcement, since a primary requisite for such provision is the ability to withstand threatening behavior by individual traders. At the beginning, the traders consisted largely of the states of the union. As a result of the success of the mechanisms used to enforce contracts at the federal level, however, various factions which comprised the individual states began to install similar ones in their own states.[1]

Under this interpretation, the various governments of the United States are viewed as the culmination of attempts by coalitions to establish an entity which was able to enforce contracts. In addition, it is undoubtedly true that the establishment of governments was also a manifestation of extortionate behavior.[2] This is demonstrated by factual evidence which shows that the power to veto a government's formation or activity was not granted to all those who felt its effects. Indeed, it seems clear that many state governments were established and controlled by minorities of adult male landowners. Later in history, some governments were given the task of punishing runaway slaves who had no voice whatsoever in the making of laws.

Finally, the contracts which need enforcing may be much more complicated than the ones considered in this paper. The actual contract may contain elaborate liability provisions in order to cope with a multiplicity of sequential actions on the part of the traders. In addition, one provision of a contract may conflict with other provisions in the same or in a different contract. To the extent that the United States constitution can be considered a social contract, it is evident that the task of the Supreme Court is to continually identify and interpret the conflicting contractual provisions contained therein.

V. CONCLUSIONS

If anarchy is defined as social interaction under uncertainty, then it will disappear as individuals find methods of reducing that uncertainty. As a society begins to move away from anarchy, the entity called the enforcer will emerge. The only important condition for the enforcer's emergence is that individuals or groups differ substantially with respect to their ability to provide the service of contract enforcement.

Previous writings concerning the evolution of government activities have stressed the ability of a government to supply and demand payment for public goods. The enforcement of contracts was regarded as just one of many kinds of public goods. Although it was recognized that governments have the power to extort, an extortion theory of the emergence of government has not been proposed until just recently.[3] The theory of this paper is that practically all of the behavior which is normally attributed to governments can be explained on the basis of its contribution to both contract enforcement and to extortion.

At best, a theory of the emergence of government based on public goods supply is misleading. As a supplier of public goods, the government performs exactly the same service, albeit on a larger scale, that it performs in the enforcement of contracts. In the general case of exchange, individuals trade modes of behavior. It does not matter whether the behavior traded is the payment of taxes at a specified time, song-singing, or coconut milk provision. The analytics of the trade are identical, and the enforcer may be useful in both instances. The fact that provision of public goods may require agreement to pay taxes by more than two persons only serves to underscore the limitations of a two-person model and, consequently, the need for more elaborate models. The reason why a government emerges should not be that individuals recognize it as a more efficient provider of public goods. A government emerges because one individual or group believes that he can use it to coerce other individuals or groups, and it emerges because of the unmet demand for contract enforcement.

NOTES

1. The direction of causation may have been just the reverse in some instances, as the federal mechanisms may have been copied from those installed at the state and local level or from those installed abroad.
2. Professor Tullock has developed a theory of revolutions based primarily on the potential gains to those in power from extorting wealth from the populace. See Gordon Tullock, *The Social Dilemma* (unpublished manuscript), Ch. III, 'The Exploitative State.'
3. See note 2.

7. Do contracts require formal enforcement?*

Peter T. Leeson

INTRODUCTION

Patrick Gunning's 'Towards a Theory of the Evolution of Government' attempts to explain the emergence of government by 'its role as a provider of the service of contract enforcement' (Gunning 1972: 19). According to Gunning, anarchy is characterized by the Hobbesian state of nature. Specifically, he defines it as 'social interaction under uncertainty' (ibid.: 25).[1] 'It is true,' Gunning tells us, 'that for infinitely recurring contacts between two persons . . . certainty will emerge,' but he adds that, 'contacts are not likely to be infinitely recurring.' As a result, 'continuing uncertainty about the behavior of others in potential mutually beneficial trading situations' pervades anarchy (ibid.: 19).

In Gunning's essay, in order to alleviate uncertainty in trading, trading partners hire a third-party enforcer to ensure that contracts made are honored. The traders grant the enforcer the right to use coercive means 'to impose the most severe penalties on both' parties in the event that one or the other breaks the terms of the previously agreed-upon contract. In this way, Gunning states, out of an otherwise 'unmet demand for contract enforcement,' government is formed (ibid.: 26).[2]

This chapter uses the logic of individual interaction under anarchy, economic history and the insights of experimental economics to critically explore Gunning's claim that government is necessary for contract enforcement. Section 1 distinguishes coercive and non-coercive enforcement mechanisms. Section 2 explores the extent to which society requires third-party enforcement mechanisms to function properly. Section 3 considers contract performance in the context of non-coercive third-party enforcement, and Section 4 explores coercive third-party enforcement without government. Section 5 concludes.

* This paper is adapted from Leeson, Peter T. (2003), 'Contracts without Government', *Journal of Private Enterprise*, **18** (2): 35–54.

1.   COERCIVE AND NON-COERCIVE ENFORCEMENT MECHANISMS

We may classify contract enforcement mechanisms into two groups: coercive and non-coercive. Coercive enforcement mechanisms are those that entail direct punishment of the contract-violating party. Direct punishment includes punishments like jail time or fines. Non-coercive enforcement mechanisms also punish the violating party but use indirect means to do so. Ostracism, injured reputation, refusal of future interaction or general boycott, for example, would all be considered indirect means of 'punishment' under a non-coercive enforcement mechanism.[3]

Government is characterized by its monopoly on the use of coercion. Its contract enforcement mechanisms are consequently always coercive in nature. If one violates a contract with another party who then appeals to government, the state does not resort to ostracism or recommend to the aggrieved that he abstain from future dealings with the violator to punish him. Government uses coercive means – fine or imprisonment of the violator – to rectify the problem. In contrast, privately provided market contract enforcement mechanisms may come in *either* coercive or non-coercive forms. Here the violator may be ostracized, boycotted, or bad-mouthed, or, if a private contract enforcement agency exists, he may be levied a fine.

While coercive means may be employed under anarchy or government, it is important to recognize that only government's coercive means represent a monopoly power. Under anarchy, no private contract enforcement agency has a legal monopoly on the use of coercive punishment.

2.   DO WE NEED THIRD-PARTY ENFORCEMENT?

While Gunning maintains that *coercive* third-party enforcement of contracts is requisite for a functional society, it is not clear that he is correct. As noted above, it is not true that anarchy necessarily lacks coercive third-party enforcement as Gunning assumes, but this is an issue we will deal with later. For now, let us grant that Gunning is right – let us assume that anarchy is incapable of providing coercive third-party enforcement.

Does that mean government is necessary and that anarchy will not work?[4] The answer is evidently, no. The vast majority of our interactions in the marketplace do not hinge upon the existence of a coercive third-party enforcement institution to ensure that they are carried out smoothly.[5]

Consider the following example. An individual eating at a restaurant has a contract with the restaurant to provide him with food of the type and quality he selects from the menu for a certain price. If the food subsequently served to him falls short of the quality specified on the menu (or of the quality to be 'reasonably expected'), the restaurant has broken its contract with the diner.

Many diners have found themselves in this position at some point. How did they respond? Most diners expressed their dissatisfaction to the manager in some fashion, in hopes of securing remuneration. Chances are the restaurant owner agreed to their request because he feared losing their business and the problem was solved. But what if the restaurant owner rejected the diner's request and refused to repair the situation?

Many diners have found themselves in this situation before as well. How did they react then? They paid, and then, thoroughly dissatisfied, left, vowing never to patronize the establishment again. Note that it probably never crossed the diner's mind to appeal to the coercive third-party enforcing institutions available to him. He did not consider taking the restaurant owner to court for fraud or false advertising because the restaurateur failed to honor his side of the contract. The diner simply punished the restaurant owner himself by vowing never to return to his restaurant.

By doing this, the diner implicitly employed the so-called 'trigger strategy' from game theory – 'hit me once and I'll never play with you again'. Simple though it may sound, this is the first and most convenient method of contract enforcement that we have available to us under anarchy or any other system, for that matter. Indeed, it is probably the method of enforcement we use most often. Thus, for many purposes, this type of 'second-party' enforcement is just as effective as coercive third-party enforcement in mitigating contract repudiation.[6]

Experimental trials of 'trust games' corroborate our theory that third-party enforcement is largely unnecessary in order to get cooperation. In these games Player 1 has the option of either passing decision power and the possibility of mutually higher payoffs to his partner, or ending the game right there for a lower payoff. If Player 1 passes to his partner, his partner can either reward Player 1 by giving both Player 1 and himself some payoff larger than the payoff Player 1 could get by not passing decision power to Player 2, or he can take an even larger payoff yet leaving Player 1 with nothing. Thus, Player 1 must initially decide whether or not to trust Player 2 with the power to take advantage of the fact that he did not defect in round one, leaving both with the chance to earn more.

Not only is there no external enforcement here, but the interaction is of a one-shot nature. Despite this, these experiments consistently show considerable levels of cooperation, indicating that Player 1's trust is frequently rewarded (Smith, 1998). Indeed, 'the data strongly reject the game theoretic hypothesis that in a single interactive play of the game subjects will overwhelmingly play non-cooperatively, and that conditional on moving down, players 2 will overwhelmingly defect' (ibid.: 11). Some experiments show 75 percent of Player 1s passing off to Player 2s and out of those, 76 percent of

Player 2s choosing to cooperate (McCabe and Smith, 2000). In more elaborate versions of the trust game that involve the ability of Player 2 to punish Player 1 if he defects, cooperative play is even higher, suggesting that the ability of actors to punish those who cheat them in interaction considerably raises the likelihood that those they interact will choose not to cheat (Smith, 2003).

'Ultimatum games', where Player 1 is given a sum of money to divide as he sees fit between himself and Player 2 who may accept the offer yielding the offered payoff or reject the offer giving both players nothing, is also of a one-shot nature. Here Player 1 has incredible power to 'cheat' Player 2. But experimental trials demonstrate that this outcome is far less likely to occur than we would think. The modal offer by Player 1s is an even split, yielding an equal payoff for both players.

Even more striking than this result are experimental runs of so-called 'dictator games'. In this game Player 1 has *absolute power* over the payoffs himself and Player 2 will receive. In the ultimatum game it may be argued that Player 1 fears the rejection of his offer by Player 2 if he does not split the given sum of money equitably. But in dictator games, the split offered by Player 1 cannot be rejected. Player 2 must accept the division of money as dictated by Player 1. While some Player 1s offer nothing to Player 2s, many more offer Player 2s a higher sum (Smith, 1998: 14–15). Indeed, in some trials, over 60 percent of dictators gave 20 percent or more of the total sum of money allotted to them to their counterparts (Hoffman et al., 1996).

Experimental results conclude that cooperation does not require a positive probability of repeat interaction for actors to cooperate (McCabe and Smith, 2003). Even in non-repeated interaction (with complete anonymity), when game theory declares players' dominant strategy is to defect, cooperation is not uncommon. Experimental economists attribute much of this to the fact that 'subjects bring their ongoing repeated game experience and reputations from the world into the laboratory' (Hoffman et al., 1996: 655). 'Goodwill' plays a role in ensuring cooperation even where we least expect it (McCabe and Smith, 2001). Actors' experiences and reputations built from repeated interactions largely shape their behavior in non-repeated interaction. In other words, even when engaging in one-shot interactions where there appears to be a strong incentive to cheat, quite often actors will choose not to. In the context of contract enforcement, that means that even when contact is not repeated, third-party enforcement is often unnecessary.

3.   NON-COERCIVE THIRD-PARTY ENFORCEMENT

According to Gunning, as long as there is infinitely recurring contact between individuals, anarchy presents no particular problem and government is not required. Once we step outside the world of infinitely recurring contact, however, anarchy becomes problematic. Radical uncertainty emerges between traders, preventing potentially mutually beneficial trades from occurring. By offering potential traders security that their contracts with others will be fulfilled, government rectifies the problem. In terms of Gunning's argument, if we can show error in his assertion that contact under anarchy is 'not likely to be infinitely recurring', then anarchy as a viable and desirable system of social arrangement is revived. But what if we have a situation where there is, in fact, no repeated interaction? If a diner wishes to patronize a restaurant only once and the proprietor knows this, what then? For Gunning, this is precisely when we need government to act as the coercive third-party enforcer – when interaction will not be infinitely recurring. Is he correct? If we can show why it is reasonable to expect high levels of cooperation to prevail despite the absence of infinitely repeated interaction, we will have removed the need for government on Gunning's own grounds.

Before proceeding with this argument, it is worth noting that it is not clear that as many of our interactions are of a 'one-shot' nature as Gunning thinks. In fact, brief reflection on our daily activities reveals quite the opposite. Many of our interactions are repeated again and again with the same people and therefore ensure high levels of cooperation without coercive third-party enforcement.

More importantly, however, the logic of market interaction under anarchy provides a non-coercive third-party contract enforcement mechanism *that simulates infinitely recurring contact and its cooperative outcome even when contact is not actually infinitely recurring.*

Under anarchy, although a seller may know that he will never deal with any given customer again (that is, contact is not infinitely recurring), he also knows that if he breaks his contract with this customer, this customer will inform many others that he did so. Because *actual* buyers are able to impart information about a seller's practices to *potential* buyers, for the seller, the prospect of dealing with potential buyers is effectively the same as the prospect of dealing with actual buyers again.[7] In terms of knowledge about the seller, every potential buyer in the marketplace is equivalent to an actual buyer. In this way, without government, the marketplace simulates infinitely recurring contact and achieves the cooperative equilibrium achieved by *actual* infinitely recurring contact.[8] This same mechanism holds in the event that a buyer violates his contract with a seller. Indeed, it not only acts to punish those who violate their contracts with others but also acts to punish those who are cheated but who fail to punish the cheater. Via this reputational element of market interaction, Gunning's problem with anarchy and need for government disappear. Note that while this form of contract enforcement is indeed a third-party mechanism, unlike the government enforcement that Gunning says we need, this form is non-coercive.

Market participants operating in the context of this mechanism are essentially following Axelrod's 'tit-for-tat' strategy. If a buyer or seller violates a contract, the aggrieved party informs others and the buyer or seller who violated the contract is punished. There is a penalty for cheating and cooperation does not ensue again until the buyer or seller who violated the contract demonstrates that he will not do so again. Experimental trials designed to test different strategies show the 'tit-for-tat' strategy consistently yields the highest payoffs. This being the case, it should come as no surprise that market interaction follows this pattern (Axelrod, 1984).

In contrast to our 'tit-for-tat' approach, Gunning implicitly models interaction under anarchy like a one-shot prisoner's dilemma game. In non-repeated interaction both individuals involved in a potential trade will have an incentive to violate the contract, preventing the execution of mutually beneficial exchange. But for the most part the conditions of interaction under anarchy, just like conditions of interaction in the real world, are not set up like a prisoner's dilemma. In the real world, potential traders may choose whom they would like to trade with, communicate with one another, and switch partners if they become dissatisfied with their original selection. Under these circumstances extremely high levels of cooperation prevail (Tullock, 1999).

Historically, non-coercive reputation-based forms of contract enforcement have been prevalent. Eleventh-century Maghribi traders, for example, operating in a framework of extremely limited legal contract enforceability and 'much uncertainty', made wide use of this system. Under Gunning's definition, these traders existed for the most part in an anarchic Hobbesian state of nature (Greif, 1989: 860).

But the outcome of this anarchy contrasts starkly with Gunning's prediction. According to Greif, '[t]he evidence suggests that the observed "trust" [between traders] reflects a reputation mechanism among economic self-interested individuals. By establishing ex ante a linkage between past conduct and future utility stream, an agent could acquire a reputation as honest, that is, he could credibly commit himself ex ante to not breach a contract ex post' (ibid.: 858–9). As theoretically anticipated above, historically, this non-coercive form of contract enforcement worked extremely well. Although most businesses were 'conducted without relying upon the legal system' or 'were not based upon legal contracts . . . Nevertheless, only a handful of documents reflect allegations about misconduct' (ibid.: 864).

More recently, the transition economies of Eastern Europe have provided evidence of the effective operation of non-coercive third-party enforcement. With government-provided third-party enforcement in shambles, 'private rather than state mechanisms are used to solve disputes. These mechanisms range from social norms and pressures, to arbitration' (Hay and Shleifer, 1998:

399). To the extent that contract enforcement occurs in these transitioning nations, it is 'against a background of self-enforcing market mechanisms' that we see it happening (Rapaczynski, 1996: 102).

Research by Leeson and Stringham (2005), Ellickson (1991), Bernstein (1992), and Benson (1989, 1990) provides additional historical evidence of the functioning of this mechanism in other areas of the market as well.[9] Recent work by Stringham (2003) illustrates the workings of this mechanism in the financial trading markets of seventeenth-century Amsterdam. Financial trading markets are often considered among the most elaborate and complex in the marketplace, yet even here reputation functioned effectively to enforce contracts in non-infinitely repeated interactions. Leeson's (forthcoming) research demonstrates the robustness of self-enforcing arrangements even in the face of potential obstacles to such arrangements – for instance, when there is significant social distance between actors.

Thus far we have considered the cases of how anarchy would handle contract enforcement (a) in the absence of any third-party enforcement mechanism whatsoever, and (b) in the absence of coercive third-party enforcement. These two mechanisms alone cast considerable doubt on Gunning's claim that we need government for contract enforcement. But we still need to explore the issue of coercive third-party contract enforcement without government.

4.   COERCIVE THIRD-PARTY ENFORCEMENT

Even if Gunning's claim regarding the necessity of coercive third-party contract enforcement is valid, there is no reason to believe that we need government to fulfill this role. Indeed, Gunning's entire account of how government emerges could just as well be applied to how private agencies under anarchy would emerge to meet the growing demand for coercive third-party contract enforcement.

Gunning assumes that under anarchy there will remain an 'unmet demand for contract enforcement', but given his story of government's evolution that applies equally to the evolution of private agencies for this purpose, his assumption seems questionable (Gunning, 1972: 26). If the problems of non-infinitely repeated contact described by Gunning cannot be solved without resort to coercive third-party enforcement, as we suggested in Section 3, a profit opportunity for offering coercive enforcement will emerge and some business will undertake this enterprise. The market for this form of contract enforcement is not fundamentally different from the market for any other good or service that consumers demand. There is nothing inherent in the service of coercive third-party contract enforcement that would exclude the possibility of its private provision *a priori*. In fact, historically, private contract enforcement worked quite well and for this reason remains far more common today than Gunning's work would suggest.[10]

5.   CONCLUSION

Patrick Gunning's 'Towards a Theory of the Evolution of Government' offers little insight into the necessity of the state. While there may remain some legitimate concerns about the functioning of anarchy, contract enforcement is not one of them. Both theory and history support the thesis that contract enforcement can be privately provided for without problem. If anything, it is the dynamics of interaction under government where special interests vie for privileged positions and prey on the produce of society that resembles the war of all against all. Far from the Hobbesian jungle that Gunning portrays it as, the stateless society is capable of successfully providing the means for effective contract enforcement that underlies the smooth operation of the market economy. Without government, market mechanisms efficiently ensure high levels of cooperation among a wide range of complex human interactions.

NOTES

1. This definition is far too broad. As the Austrian economist Ludwig von Mises pointed out, uncertainty is a prerequisite of any action whatsoever (1949: 105–6). If we had absolute certainty about the future we would have no reason to act, as the future would already be unalterably predetermined. Some degree of uncertainty must therefore permeate all of our social interactions. If Gunning's definition were accurate, nothing short of a society of omniscient individuals would be non-anarchic.
2. Tellingly, Gunning refers to the coercive third-party enforcer that emerges out of the state of nature as the '*super-giant*' (italics original) (1972: 22). Presumably we are not only to believe that government is necessary for contract enforcement but furthermore that a gigantic government is necessary to adequately perform this task.
3. For more on non-coercive enforcement mechanisms see Caplan and Stringham (2003).
4. Like Gunning, Hobbes himself rejected this possibility: 'he that performeth first, has no assurance the other will perform after; because the bonds of words are too weak to bridle men's ambition, avarice, anger, and other Passions, without fear of some coercive Power; which in the condition of here Nature, where all men are equal, and judges of justness of their own fears cannot possibly be supposed' ([1651] 1955: 89–90).
5. The notion that third-party enforcement is not necessary to assure contract performance is not new. Indeed, the idea can be found in the writings of economists from Hayek (1948: 97) to Marshall (1949: vol. 4, xi).
6. For a discussion of cooperative behavior despite buyer–seller informational asymmetries see Barzell (1982).
7. 'Actual buyers' are those that have already interacted with the seller. 'Potential buyers' are those who have not yet interacted with the seller but who may do so in the future.
8. For a formal treatment of this type of mechanism and its robustness under varying degrees of observability, see Kandori (1992).
9. For an exploration of workings of the reputation mechanism in labor markets, see Bull (1987).
10. See, for instance, Benson (1990).

REFERENCES

Axelrod, Robert (1984), *The Evolution of Cooperation*, New York: Basic Books.

Barzell, Yoram (1982), 'Measurement Cost and the Organization of Markets', *Journal of Law and Economics*, **25**: 27–48.

Benson, Bruce (1989), 'The Spontaneous Evolution of Commercial Law', *Southern Economic Journal*, **55**: 644–61.

Benson, Bruce (1990), *The Enterprise of Law: Justice Without the State*, San Francisco: Pacific Research Institute for Public Policy.

Bernstein, Lisa (1992), 'Opting Out of the Legal System: Extralegal Contractual Relations in the Diamond Industry', *Journal of Legal Studies*, **21**: 115–57.

Bull, Clive (1987), 'The Existence of Self-Enforcing Implicit Contracts', *Quarterly Journal of Economics*, **102**: 147–60.

Caplan, Bryan and Edward Stringham (2003), 'Networks, Law, and the Paradox of Cooperation', *Review of Austrian Economics*, **16**: 309–26.

Ellickson, Robert (1991), *Order Without Law: How Neighbors Settle Disputes*, Boston: Harvard University Press.

Greif, Avner (1989), 'Reputation and Coalitions in Medieval Trade: Evidence on the Maghribi Traders', *Journal of Economic History*, **49**: 857–82.

Gunning, Patrick (1972), 'Towards a Theory of the Evolution of Government', in Gordon Tullock (ed.), *Explorations in the Theory of Anarchy*, Blacksburg, VA: Center for the Study of Public Choice, pp. 19–26.

Hay, Jonathan and Andrei Shleifer (1998), 'Private Enforcement of Public Laws: A Theory of Legal Reform', *American Economic Review*, **88**: 398–403.

Hayek, F.A. (1948), *Individualism and Economic Order*, Chicago: University of Chicago Press.

Hobbes, Thomas ([1651] 1955), *Leviathan*, Oxford: Blackwell.

Hoffman, Elizabeth, Kevin McCabe and Vernon Smith (1996), 'Social Distance and Other-Regarding Behavior in Dictator Games', *American Economic Review*, **86**: 653–60.

Kandori, Michihiro (1992), 'Social Norms and Community Enforcement', *Review of Economic Studies*, **59**: 63–80.

Leeson, Peter (forthcoming), 'Cooperation and Conflict: Evidence on Self-Enforcing Arrangements and Heterogeneous Groups', *American Journal of Economics and Sociology*.

Leeson, Peter T. and Edward P. Stringham (2005), 'Is Government Inevitable? Comment on Holcombe's Analysis', *The Independent Review*, **9** (4): 543–9.

Marshall, Alfred (1949), *Principles of Economics: An Introductory Volume*, 8th edn, New York: Macmillan.

McCabe, Kevin and Vernon Smith (2000), 'A Comparison of Naïve and Sophisticated Subject Behavior with Game Theoretic Predictions', *PNAS*, **97**: 3777–81.

McCabe, Kevin and Vernon Smith (2001), 'Goodwill Accounting and the Process of Exchange', in G. Gigerenzer and R. Selten (eds), *Bounded Rationality: The Adaptive Toolbox*, Cambridge, MA: MIT Press.

McCabe, Kevin and Vernon Smith (2003), 'Strategic Analysis by Players in Games: What Information Do They Use?', in Elinor Ostrom and James Walker (eds), *Trust, Reciprocity, and Gains from Association: Interdisciplinary Lessons from Experimental Research*, New York: Russell Sage Foundation.

Mises, Ludwig von (1949), *Human Action: A Treatise on Economics*, New Haven: Yale University Press.

Rapaczynski, Andrzej (1996), 'The Roles of State and the Market in Establishing Property Rights', *Journal of Economic Perspectives*, **10**: 87–103.

Smith, Vernon (1998), 'The Two Faces of Adam Smith', Distinguished Guest Lecture, *Southern Economic Journal*, **65**: 1–19.

Smith, Vernon (2003), 'Experimental Methods in (Neuro)Economics', in Lynn Nadel (ed.), *Encyclopedia of Cognitive Science*, London: Macmillan.

Stringham, Edward (2003), 'The Extralegal Development of Securities Trading in 17th Century Amsterdam', *Quarterly Review of Economics and Finance*, **43**: 321–44.

Tullock, Gordon (1999), 'Non-Prisoner's Dilemma', *Journal of Economic Behavior and Organization*, **39**: 455–8.

8. Before public choice*

James M. Buchanan

A contact theory of the State is relatively easy to derive, and careful use of this theory can yield major explanatory results. To an extent at least, a 'science' exists for the purpose of providing psychologically satisfying explanations of what men can commonly observe about them. Presumably, we 'feel better' when we possess some explanatory framework or model that allows us to classify and interpret disparate sense perceptions. This imposition of order on the universe is a 'good' in the strict economic sense of this term: men will invest money, time, and effort in acquiring it. The contract theory of the State, in all of its manifestations, can be defended on such grounds. It is important for sociopolitical order and tranquility that ordinary men explain to themselves the working of governmental process in models that conceptually take their bases in cooperative rather than in noncooperative behavior. Admittedly and unabashedly, the contract theory serves, in this sense, a rationalization purpose or objective. We need a 'logic of law,' a 'calculus of consent,' a 'logic of collective action,' to use the titles of three books that embody modern-day contract theory foundations.[1]

Can the contract theory of the State serve other objectives, whether these be normative or positive in character? Can institutions which find no conceivable logical derivation in contract among cooperating parties be condemned on other than strictly personal grounds? Can alleged improvements in social arrangements be evaluated on anything other than contractarian precepts, or, to lapse into economists' jargon, on anything other than Paretian criteria? But, even here, are these criteria any more legitimate than any other?

In earlier works, I have tended to go past these fundamental questions. I have been content to work out, at varying levels of sophistication, the contractarian bases for governmental action, either that which we can commonly observe or that which might be suggested as reforms. To me, this effort seemed relevant and significant. 'Political economy' or 'public choice' – these seemed to be labels assignable to honorable work that required little or no

* This paper was first published in *Explorations in the Theory of Anarchy*, edited by Gordon Tullock, The Public Choice Society Book and Monograph Series, Center for the Study of Public Choice, Blacksburg, VA, USA, 1972, pp. 27–37.

methodological justification. It was only when I tried to outline a summary treatment of my whole approach to sociopolitical structure that I was stopped short. I came to realize that the very basis of the contractarian position must be examined more thoroughly.

We know that, factually and historically, the 'social contract' is mythological, at least in many of its particulars. Individuals did not come together in some original position and mutually agree on the rules of social intercourse. And even had they done so at some time in history, their decisions could hardly be considered to be contractually binding on all of us who have come behind. We cannot start anew. We can either accept the political universe, or we can try to change it. The question reduces to one of determining the criteria for change.

When and if we fully recognize that the contract is a myth designed in part to rationalize existing institutional structures of society, can we simultaneously use the contractual derivations to develop criteria for evaluating changes or modifications in these structures? I have previously answered this question affirmatively, but without proper argument. The intellectual quality as well as the passionate conviction of those who answer the question negatively suggest that more careful consideration is required.

How can we derive a criterion for determining whether or not a change in law, or, if you will, a change in the assignment of rights, is or is not justified? To most social scientists, the only answer is solipsist. Change becomes desirable if 'I like it,' even though many prefer to dress this up in fanciful 'social welfare function' or 'public interest' semantics. To me, this seems to be pure escapism; it represents retreat into empty arguments about personal values which spells the end of rational discourse. Perhaps some of our colleagues do possess God-like qualities, or at least think that they do, but until and unless their godliness is accepted, we are left with no basis for discourse. My purpose is to see how far we can rationally discuss criteria for social change on the presumption that no man's values are better than any other man's.

Is *agreement* the only test? Is the Wicksellian–contractarian–Paretian answer the only legitimate one here? If so, are we willing to accept its corollaries? Its full implications? Are we willing to forestall all social change that does not command unanimous or quasi-unanimous consent?

Provisionally, let us say that we do so. We can move a step beyond, while at the same time rationalizing much of what we see, by resorting to 'constitutionalism,' the science of rules. We can say that particular proposals for social change need not command universal assent provided only that such assent holds for the legal structure within which particular proposals are enacted or chosen. This seems to advance the argument; we seem to be part of the way out of the dilemma. But note that this provides us with no means at all for evaluating particular proposals as 'good' or 'bad.' We can generate many outcomes or results under nonunanimity rules. This explains my initial response to the Arrow impossibility theorem, and to the subsequent discussion. My response was, and is, one of nonsurprise at the alleged inconsistency in a social decision process that embodies in itself no criteria for consistency. This also explains my unwillingness to be trapped, save on rare and regretted occasions, into positions of commitment on particular measures of policy on the familiar efficiency grounds. We can offer no policy advice on particular legislative proposals. As political economists, we examine public choices; we can make institutional predictions. We can analyze alternative political–social–economic structures.

But what about constitutional change itself? Can we say nothing, or must we say that, at this level, the contractarian (Wicksellian, Paretian) norm must apply? Once again, observation hardly supports us here. Changes are made, changes that would be acknowledged to be genuinely 'constitutional,' without anything remotely approaching unanimous consent. Must we reject all such changes out of hand, or can we begin to adduce criteria on some other basis?

Resort to the choice of rules for ordinary parlor games may seem to offer assistance. Influenced greatly by the emphasis on such choices by Rutledge Vining, I once considered this to be the key to genuinely innovative application of the contractarian criteria. If we could, somehow, think of individual participants in a setting of complete uncertainty about their own positions over subsequent rounds of play, we might think of their reaching genuine agreement on a set of rules. The idea of a 'fair game' does have real meaning, and this idea can be transferred to sociopolitical institutions. But how far can we go with this? We may, in this process, begin to rationalize certain institutions that cannot readily be brought within the standard Wicksellian framework. But can we do more? Can we, as John Rawls seems to want to do in his monumental *Theory of Justice*,[2] think ourselves into a position of original contract and then idealize our thought processes into norms that 'should' be imposed as criteria for institutional change? Note that this is, to me, quite different from saying that we derive a possible rationalization. To rationalize, to explain, is not to propose, and Rawls seems to miss this quite critical distinction. It is one thing to say that, conceptually, men in some genuinely constitutional stage of deliberation, operating behind the veil of ignorance, might have agreed to rules something akin to those that we actually observe, but it is quite another thing to say that men, in the here and now, should be forced to abide by specific rules that we imagine by transporting ourselves into some mental–moral equivalent of an original contract setting where men are genuine 'moral equals.'

Unless we do so, however, we must always accept whatever structure of rules that exists and seek constitutional changes only through agreement, through consensus. It is this inability to say anything about rule changes, this inability to play God, this inability to raise himself above the masses, that the social philosopher cannot abide. He has an ingrained prejudice against the status quo, however this may be defined, understandably so, since his very role, as he interprets it, is one that finds itself only in social reform. (Perhaps this role conception reflects the moral inversion that Michael Polanyi and Craig Roberts note: the shift of moral precepts away from personal behavior aimed at personal salvation and toward moral evaluation or social institutions.)

Just what are men saying when they propose nonagreed changes in the basic structure of rights? Are they saying anything more than 'this is what I want and since I think the State has the power to impose it, I support the State as the agency to enforce the change'? We may be able to get some handles on this very messy subject by going back to Hobbes. We need to examine the initial leap out of the Hobbesian jungle. How can agreement emerge? And what are the problems of enforcement?

We may represent the reaction equilibrium in the Hobbesian jungle at the origin in the diagrammatics of Figure 8.1. If we measure 'B's law-abiding behavior' on the ordinate, and 'A's law-abiding behavior' on the abscissa, it is evident that neither man secures advantage from 'lawful' behavior individually and independently of the other man's behavior. (Think of 'law-abiding' here as 'not-stealing.') Note that the situation here is quite different from the

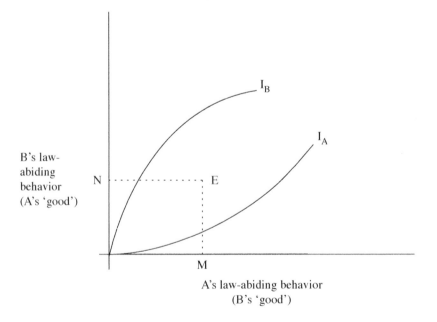

Figure 8.1 Law-abiding behavior and welfare

usual public-goods model in which at least some of the 'good' will tend to be produced by one or all of the common or joint consumers even under wholly independent adjustment. With law-abiding as the 'good,' however, the individual cannot, through his own behavior, produce so as to increase his own utility. He can do nothing other than provide a 'pure' external economy; all benefits accrue to the other parties. Hence the independent adjustment position involves a corner solution at the origin in our two-person diagram. But gains-from-trade clearly exist in this Hobbesian jungle, despite the absence of unilateral action.

It is easy enough to depict the Pareto region that bounds potential positions of mutual gains by drawing the appropriate indifference contours through the origin as is done in Figure 8.1. These contours indicate the internal or subjective rates of tradeoff as between *own* and *other* law-abiding. It seems plausible to suggest that the standard convexity properties would apply. The analysis remains largely empty, however, until we know something, or at least postulate something, about the descriptive characteristics of the initial position itself. And the important and relevant point in this respect is that individuals *are not equal*, or at least need not be equal, in such a setting, either in their relative abilities or in their final command over consumables.[3] To assume symmetry among persons here amounts to converting a desired normative state, that of equality among men, into a fallacious positive proposition. (This is, of course, a pervasive error, and one that is not only made by social philosophers. It has had significant and pernicious effects on judicial thinking in the twentieth century.) If we drop the equality or symmetry assumption, however, we can say something about the relative values or tradeoffs as between the relative 'haves' and 'have-nots' in the Hobbesian or natural adjustment equilibrium. For illustrative purposes here, think of the 'natural distribution' in our two-person model as characterized by A's enjoyment of 10 units of 'good,' and B's enjoyment of only 2 units. Both persons expend effort, a 'bad,' in generating and in maintaining this natural distribution. It is this effort that can be reduced or eliminated through trade, through agreement on laws or rules of respect for property. In this way, both parties can secure more 'goods.' The posttrade equilibrium must reflect improvement for both parties over the natural distribution or pretrade outcome. There are prospects for Pareto-efficient or Pareto-superior moves from the initial no-rights position to any one of many possible posttrade or positive-rights distributions.

Let us suppose that agreement is reached; each person agrees to an assignment of property rights and, furthermore, each person agrees to respect such rights as are assigned. Let us suppose, for illustration, that the net distribution of 'goods' under the assignment is 15 units for A and 7 units for B. Hence, there is a symmetrical sharing of the total gains-from-trade secured from the assignment of rights. Even under such symmetrical sharing, however, note that the relative position of B has improved more than the relative position of A. In our example, A's income increases by one-half; but B's income increases more than twofold. This suggests that the person who fares relatively worse in the natural distribution may well stand to gain relatively more from an initial assignment of rights than the person who fares relatively better in the pretrade state of the world.

Agreement is attained; both parties enjoy more utility than before. But again the prisoner's dilemma setting must be emphasized. Each of the two persons can anticipate gains by successful unilateral default on the agreement. In Figure 8.1, if E depicts the position of agreement, A can always gain by a shift to N if this can be accomplished; similarly, B can gain by a shift to M. There may, however, be an asymmetry present in prospective gains from unilateral default on the rights agreement. The prospective gains may well be higher for the person who remains relatively less favored in the natural distribution. In one sense, the 'vein of ore' that he can mine by departing from the rules through criminal activity is richer than the similar vein would be for the other party. The productivity of criminal effort is likely to be higher for the man who can steal from his rich neighbor than for the man who has only poor neighbors.

This may be illustrated in the matrix of Figure 8.2, where the initial pretrade or natural distribution is shown in Cell IV, and the posttrade or positive-rights distribution is shown in Cell I. Note that, as depicted, the man who is relatively 'poor' in the natural equilibrium, person B in the example, stands to gain relatively more by departing unilaterally from Cell I that person A. Person B could, by such a move, increase his quantity of 'goods' from 7 to 12, whereas person A could only increase his from 15 to 17. This example suggests that the relatively 'rich' person will necessarily be more interested in

| | | B | |
		Abides by 'law'	Observes no 'law'
A	Abides by 'law'	I 15, 7	II 6, 12
	Observes no 'law'	III 17, 3	IV 10, 2

Figure 8.2   Payoff matrix for choices to observe law

policing the activities of the 'poor' man, as such, than vice versa. This is, of course, widely accepted. But the construction and analysis here can be employed for a more complex and difficult issue that has not been treated adequately.

Assume that agreement has been attained; both parties abide by the law; both enjoy the benefits. Time passes. The 'rich' man becomes lazy and lethargic. The 'poor' man increases his strength. This modifies the natural distribution. Let us say that the natural distribution changes to 6:6. The 'rich' man now has an overwhelmingly more significant interest in the maintenance of the legal status quo than the 'poor' man, who is no longer 'poor' in natural ability terms. The initial symmetry in the sharing of gains as between the no-trade and the trade position no longer holds. With the new natural distribution, the 'rich' man secures almost all of the net gains.

The example must be made more specific. Assume that the situation is analogous to the one examined by Winston Bush. The initial problem is how is manna which drops from Heaven to be divided among the two persons. The initial natural distribution is in the ratio 10:2 as noted. Recognizing this, along with their own abilities, A and B agree that by assigning rights, they can attain a 15:7 ratio, as noted. Time passes, and B increases in relative strength, but the 'goods' are still shared in the 15:7 ratio. The initial set of property rights agreed to on the foundations of the initial natural distribution no longer reflects or mirrors the existing natural distribution. Under these changed conditions, a lapse back into the natural equilibrium will harm B relatively little whereas A will be severely damaged. The 'poor' man now has relatively little interest in adherence to law. If this trend continues, and the natural distribution changes further in the direction indicated, the 'poor' man may find himself able to secure even net advantages from a lapse back into the Hobbesian jungle.

The model may be described in something like the terms of modern game theory. If the initial natural distribution remains unaltered, the agreed-on assignment of rights possesses qualities like the core in an *n*-person game. It is to the advantage of no coalition to depart from this assignment or imputation if the remaining members of the group are willing to enforce or to block the imputation. No coalition can do better on its own, or in this model, in the natural distribution, than it does in the assignment. These core-like properties of the assigned distribution under law may, however, begin to lose dominance features as the potential natural distribution shifts around 'underneath' the existing structure of rights, so to speak. The foundations of the existing rights structure may be said to have shifted in the process.

This analysis opens up interesting new implications for net redistribution of wealth and for changes in property rights over time. Observed changes in claims to wealth take place without apparent consent. These may be interpreted simply as the use of the enforcement power of the State by certain coalitions of persons to break the contract. They are overtly shifting from a Cell I into a Cell II or Cell III outcome in the diagram of Figure 8.2. It is not, of course, difficult to explain why these coalitions arise. It will always be in the interest of a person, or a group of persons, to depart from the agreed-on assignment of claims or rights, provided that he or they can do so unilaterally and without offsetting reactive behavior on the part of the remaining members of the social group. The quasi-equilibrium in Cell I is inherently unstable. The equilibrium does qualify as a position in the core of the game, but we must keep in mind that the core analytics presumes the immediate formation of blocking coalitions. In order fully to explain observed departures from status quo we must also explain the behavior of the absence of the potential blocking coalitions. Why do the remaining members of the community fail to enforce the initial assignment of rights?

The analysis here suggests that if there has been a sufficiently large shift in the underlying natural distribution, the powers of enforcing adherence on the prospective violators of contract may not exist, or, if they exist, these powers may be demonstrably weakened. In our numerical example, B fares almost as well under the new natural distribution as he does in the continuing assignment of legal rights. Hence, A has lost almost all of his blocking power; he can scarcely influence B by threats to plunge the community into Hobbesian anarchy, even if A himself should be willing to do so. And it should also be recognized that 'willingness' to enforce the contract (the structure of legal rules, the existing set of claims to property) is as important as the objective ability to do so. Even if A should be physically able to force B to return to the status quo ante after some attempted departure, he may be unwilling to suffer the personal loss that might be required to make his threat of enforcement credible.[4] The law-abiding members of the community may find themselves in a genuine dilemma. They may simply be unable to block the unilateral violation of the social contract.

In this perspective, normative arguments based on 'justice' in distribution may signal acquiescence in modifications in the existing structure of claims. Just as the idea of contract, itself, has been used to rationalize existing structure, the idea of 'justice' may be used to rationalize coerced departures from contract. In the process those who advance such arguments and those who are convinced may 'feel better' while their claims are whittled away. This does, I think, explain much attitudinal behavior toward redistribution policy by specific social groups. Gordon Tullock has, in part, explained the prevailing attitudes of many academicians and intellectuals.[5] The explanation developed here applies more directly to the redistributionist attitudes of the scions of the rich, *e.g.*, the Rockefellers and Kennedys. Joseph Kennedy was less redistributive than his sons; John D. Rockefeller was less redistributive than his grandsons. We do not need to call on the psychologists since our model provides an explanation in the concept of a changing natural distribution. The scions of the wealthy are far less secure in their roles of custodians of wealth than were their forebears. They realize perhaps that their own natural talents simply do not match up, even remotely, to the share of national wealth that they now command. Their apparent passions for the poor may be nothing more than surface reflections of attempts to attain temporary security.

The analysis also suggests that there is a major behavioral difference fostered between the intergenerational transmission of nonhuman and human capital. Within limits, there is an important linkage between human capital and capacity to survive in a natural or Hobbesian environment. There seems to be no such linkage between nonhuman capital and survival in the jungle. From this it follows that the man who possesses human capital is likely to be far less concerned about the 'injustice' of his own position, less concerned about temporizing measures designed to shore up apparent leaks in the social system than his counterpart who possesses nonhuman capital. If we postulate that the actual income-asset distribution departs significantly from the proportionate distribution in the underlying and existing natural equilibrium, the system of claims must be acknowledged to be notoriously unstable. The idle rich, possessed of nonhuman capital, will tend to form coalitions with the poor that are designed primarily to ward off retreat toward the Hobbesian jungle. This coalition can take the form of the rich acquiescing in and providing defense for overt criminal activity on the part of the poor, or the more explicit form of political exploitation of the 'silent majority,' the Agnew constituency that possesses largely human rather than nonhuman capital.

This description has some empirical content in 1972. But what can the exploited groups do about it? Can the middle classes form a coalition with the rich, especially when the latter are themselves so insecure? Or can they form, instead, another coalition with the poor, accepting a promise of strict adherence to law in exchange for goodies provided by the explicit confiscation of the nonhuman capital of the rich? (Politically, this would take the form of confiscatory inheritance taxation.) The mythology of the American dream probably precludes this route from being taken. The self-made, the *nouveau riche*, seek to provide their children with fortunes that the latter will accept only with guilt.

All of this suggests that a law-abiding imputation becomes increasingly difficult to sustain as its structure departs from what participants conceive to be the natural or Bush–Hobbes imputation, defined in some proportionate sense. If the observed imputation, or set of bounded imputations that are possible under existing legal–constitutional rules, seems to bear no relationship at all to the natural imputation that men accept, breakdown in legal standards is predictable.

Where does this leave us in trying to discuss criteria for 'improvement' in rules, in assignments of rights, the initial question that was posed in this paper? I have argued that the contractarian or Paretian norm is relevant on the simple principle that 'we start from here.' But 'here,' the status quo, is the existing set of legal institutions and rules. Hence, how can we possibly distinguish genuine contractual changes in 'law' from those which take place under the motivations discussed above? Can we really say which changes are defensible 'exchanges' from an existing status quo position? This is what I am trying to answer, without full success, in my paper in response to Warren J. Samuels' discussion of the *Miller et al. v. Schoene* case.[6] There I tried to argue that, to the extent that property rights are specified in advance, genuine 'trades' can emerge, with mutual gains to all parties. However, to the extent that existing rights are held to be subject to continuous redefinition by the State, no one has an incentive to organize and to initiate trades or agreements. This amounts to saying that once the body politic begins to get overly concerned about the distribution of the pie under existing property-rights assignments and legal rules, once we begin to think either about the personal gains from law-breaking, privately or publicly, or about the disparities between existing imputations and those estimated to be forthcoming under some idealized anarchy, we are necessarily precluding and forestalling the achievement of potential structural changes that might increase the size of the pie for *all*. Too much concern for 'justice' acts to insure that 'growth' will not take place, and for reasons much more basic than the familiar economic incentives arguments.

In this respect, 1972 seems a century, not a mere decade, away from 1962, when, if you recall, the rage was all for growth and the newfound concern about distribution had not yet been invented. At issue here, of course, is the whole conception of the State, or of collective action. I am far less sanguine than I was concerning the possible acceptance of the existing constitutional–legal framework. The basic structure of property rights is now threatened more seriously than at any period in the two-century history of the United States. In the paper, 'The Samaritan's Dilemma,' noted above, I advanced the hypothesis that we have witnessed a general loss of strategic courage, brought on in part by economic affluence. As I think more about all this, however, I realize that there is more to it. We may be witnessing the disintegration of our effective constitutional rights, regardless of the prattle about 'the constitution' as seen by our judicial tyrants from their own visions of the entrails of their sacrificial beasts. I do not know what might be done about all this, even by those who recognize what is happening. We seem to be left with the question posed at the outset. How do rights re-emerge and come to command respect? How do 'laws' emerge that carry with them general respect for their 'legitimacy'?

NOTES

1. See Gordon Tullock, *The Logic of Law* (New York: Basic Books, 1970); James M. Buchanan and Gordon Tullock, *The Calculus of Consent* (Ann Arbor: University of Michigan Press, 1962); Mancur Olson, *The Logic of Collective Action* (Cambridge: Harvard University Press, 1965).
2. John Rawls, *Theory of Justice* (Cambridge: Harvard University Press, 1971).
3. The formal properties of the 'natural distribution' that will emerge under anarchy have been described by Winston Bush in his paper, 'Income Distribution in Anarchy'.
4. For a more extensive discussion of these points, see my paper, 'The Samaritan's Dilemma' (1971), to be published in *Economic Theory and Altruism*, edited by Edmund Phelps, Russell Sage Foundation (forthcoming).
5. See Gordon Tullock, 'The Charity of the Uncharitable,' *Western Economic Journal*, IX (December 1971), 379–91.
6. See Warren J. Samuels, 'Interrelations Between Legal and Economic Processes,' *Journal of Law and Economics*, XIV, 2 (October 1971), 435–50, and my 'Politics, Property and the Law,' *Journal of Law and Economics* (forthcoming).

9. Public choice and Leviathan

Benjamin Powell

In 'Before Public Choice' (1972), Buchanan began exploring interaction between individuals in anarchy. Buchanan further developed his ideas in *The Limits of Liberty* (1975). This chapter is a partial response to both of these works that focuses on whether his derivation of a 'protective state' from Hobbesian anarchy is justified. Buchanan's analysis concluded that a government must be formed for people to escape a 'nasty, brutish, and short' life in the Hobbesian jungle. This chapter presents a public choice analysis of a government comprising the same Hobbesian individuals Buchanan modeled in anarchy. The first section reviews Buchanan's framework and conclusions. The second section uses his assumptions about individual behavior in anarchy to analyze his proposed third-party enforcer – government. Once this public choice approach is taken I examine whether people would 'conceptually' agree to form a state for third-party enforcement.

THE BUCHANAN MODEL

Buchanan's analytical starting point is Hobbes's *Leviathan*.[1] Like Hobbes, Buchanan believes that conflicting claims over resources in anarchy will lead people to invest heavily in attacking others and defending against attacks. Society will plunge into a war of all against all, where the resulting lives will be nasty, brutish and short. Buchanan argues that individuals will achieve higher levels of utility if they leave anarchy and create an enforcement mechanism that forces them to respect each other's property.[2] He concludes that although anarchy, which allows for maximum personal liberty, is ideal, a government is necessary for people to achieve a higher level of utility. Unlike Hobbes, Buchanan believes the solution to anarchy is a limited government, not an all-powerful leviathan state.

Buchanan attempts to show why people would 'conceptually' agree to a social contract establishing a government. He never argues that historically an agreement actually took place.[3]

In Buchanan's model of anarchy, individuals' incentive to respect each other's property is examined. Buchanan looks solely at a person's economic

B
		Respect property	Don't respect property
A	Respect property	19, 7	3, 11
	Don't respect property	22, 1	9, 2

Figure 9.1   Payoff matrix for choices to respect property rights

incentives, acknowledging, but excluding, any moral reasons that might influence someone not to steal or commit an act of aggression. He frames the individuals' choices in a prisoner's dilemma game, as in Figure 9.1, where the numbers in the cells reflect A and B's utility.[4]

Although both people would be better off if they concentrated solely on producing, they are each individually better off engaging in some plunder, regardless of whether or not the other does. The bottom right corner is the Nash equilibrium, where both people are worse off than if they had respected each other's property. In this model the utility gains and losses are not symmetrical – reflecting differences in individuals' natural abilities.

Because both people are better off if they respect each other's property, they will enter into an agreement not to plunder. This agreement moves the equilibrium from the bottom right cell to the upper left cell. Buchanan wrote, 'Each person may respect the agreed-on assignment because he predicts that defection on his part will generate parallel behavior by the other party' (Buchanan, 1975: 85). In two-person interaction, if one person defects from the agreement, the other will immediately recognize it and also defect. Due to repeated plays, each person will abide by the contract knowing that if they do not, the other will also defect.

Buchanan claims that when there are many anonymous individuals in the contract it becomes optimal to defect. He wrote, 'As more parties are added to the initial contractual agreement, in which an assignment of rights is settled, the influence of any one person's behavior on that of others becomes less and less.' He continues, saying, 'In large-number groups, each individual rationally acts as if his own behavior does not influence the behavior of others. He treats others' behavior as part of his natural environment, and he adjusts his behavior accordingly.' His conclusion is, 'Each person has a rational incentive to default; hence, many persons can be predicted to default and the whole agreement becomes void unless the conditions of individual choice are somehow modified' (Buchanan, 1975: 85). Since it is individually optimal to defect, the society plunges back into the Hobbesian jungle where life is nasty, brutish and short.

Because of the individual incentive for defection, Buchanan concludes that a third-party enforcement mechanism is necessary.[5] Buchanan's conclusion is that the third-party enforcer has to be government. In the following section I explore the players' expected utility payoffs when government is analyzed with the same assumptions about individual behavior that Buchanan uses when modeling individuals in anarchy.

THIRD-PARTY ENFORCEMENT BY GOVERNMENT

The individual incentive for plunder in Hobbesian anarchy stems from the fact that there is no institution to punish people who defect from the social contract. The creation of an institution with the amount of power necessary to punish any defectors creates its own problems, though. Buchanan wrote, 'The design and location of this [enforcement] institution becomes all important, however; neither party will entrust enforcement to the other, and, indeed, the delegation of such authority to one party in contract violates the meaning of enforcement' (ibid.: 120–21). The ideal third-party enforcement mechanism would be some sort of machine that is entirely outside of the 'game'. This would be similar to a radar that could determine whether a pitch was a ball or strike in a baseball game. Absent the possibility of an impartial machine, an outside referee is optimal. This is the function of the umpire in a baseball game. If the catcher were calling the balls and strikes, the enforcement of rules would be incredibly biased. Buchanan wrote, 'In the game analogy that we have used several times before, the protective state is the umpire or referee, and, as such, its task is conceptually limited to enforcing agreed on rules' (ibid.: 206). Does the analogy of a baseball umpire apply to government as an interpreter and enforcer of rules?

The nature of the social contract, as described by Buchanan, is that everyone in a particular area unanimously agrees to the assignment of rights and then forms a government to enforce the assigned rights. The government, however, is not like the baseball umpire. The game being played is 'life' and the players, by the nature of the social contract, are all the people in a given location, including those who work for the government. The umpires are players. The government, as a third party, has the job of interpreting and enforcing the rules in discrepancies between players. It also has the job of interpreting what functions the social contract gave to itself.

Buchanan is widely known for introducing economic methodology to the analysis of government (Buchanan and Tullock, 1962). The public choice movement in economics challenged the romantic notions of how government works by insisting that the incentives facing bureaucrats and politicians must be analyzed. Public choice has been successful at showing that government failure is a likely outcome when interventions attempt to correct alleged 'market failures'. Ironically, in 'Before Public Choice', and in *The Limits of Liberty*, Buchanan does not analyze government with the same assumptions he makes about the people in anarchy. He leaves government 'conceptually external' and does not analyze the incentives facing individuals in that government. In the case of the models used in 'Before Public Choice' and *The Limits of Liberty*, the individuals modeled in anarchy lacked any moral or ideological constraints. These assumptions must be carried forth into our analysis of Buchanan's proposed solution – government.[6]

In the scenario of two citizens with government contract enforcement, citizens will now abide by their contracts with each other. However, Buchanan never models a second prisoner's dilemma of 'social' contract enforcement between the government and the citizens. The question becomes: will the government adhere to the initial social contract? If the government is the only interpreter and enforcer of the contract, then there is no third-party enforcement constraining it. There is a crucial difference between the incentives facing an official in the government and the people in the original prisoner's dilemma in Figure 9.1. If the government defects, the other players do not have the same option to defect because they still face an enforcer – the government. The game now can be modeled as in Figure 9.2.

		Citizen	
		Obey social contract	Don't obey social contract
Government	Obey social contract	19, 7	18, 1
	Don't obey social contract	25, 1	24, 0

Figure 9.2   Payoff matrix for choices to obey social contract

Following the assumptions from the model of anarchy, people, including government officials, only act according to their economic incentives. Even though the initial social contract or 'constitution' may have provided only for a limited government, the people in government will defect on that contract because there is no third party constraining them.[7] A representative citizen is modeled at the top in Figure 9.2. If the government abides by the agreed-on contract, the citizen will achieve a utility of 7. The government is now modeled on the side. It may depart from the contract (although it will interpret it to be within the contract) and confiscate a citizen's wealth. If the citizen attempts to defect after seeing that the government has, the government will use its enforcement monopoly and find him guilty of deviating from the contract (treason?) and will take away all his remaining utility. The reason the government does not take all the utility when it first departs from the contract is to leave the citizen some incentive to continue to abide by the contract.

The above example only shows one citizen's choice set against a government that departs from the social contract. The threat of many citizens simultaneously departing from the contract, in a rebellion, might provide some form of 'external enforcement' on the government. However, the individual calculus that each citizen faces when deciding to participate makes this a weak constraint because a public-goods problem has to be overcome (Tullock, 1971). In the real world morality and ideology help to overcome the public-goods problem in revolutions, but these things are assumed away in Buchanan's model, so only the narrow economic calculus can be looked at. The threat of rebellion will not force a government in Buchanan's framework to abide by the social contract.

In the simple prisoner's dilemma game above, government was modeled as a single individual; however, in reality governments comprise many individuals with a separation of duties and powers among them. Randy Barnett characterized the system by saying, 'The essence of this strategy [checks and balances] is to create an oligopoly or a "shared" monopoly of power. This scheme preserves a monopoly of power but purports to divide this power among a number of groups' (1998: 253). The above model can still accurately represent government with a separation of powers. Even with a separation of powers between different branches of government, or different levels of government through federalism, there are gains to be had from cooperation between the branches. Even though, in an individual round of play, the interests of different government branches may be opposing each other, over multiple plays they can all gain in utility from cooperating to expand the power of government. Barnett (ibid.: 254) wrote:

> Even in the beginning of such a regime, since each has the other by the throat, no one is willing to squeeze too hard. Eventually, entrepreneurs of power – master

politicians, judges, executives, or outsiders called 'special interest groups' – figure out ways to teach those who share the monopoly that each has an interest in cooperating with the others in using force against those who are outside the monopoly.

Rothbard (1973: 48) described the system of checks and balances by writing:

> As we have discovered in the past century, no constitution can interpret or enforce itself; it must be interpreted by men. And if the ultimate power to interpret a constitution is given to the government's own Supreme Court, then the inevitable tendency is for the Court to continue to place its imprimatur on ever-broader powers for its own government. Furthermore, the highly touted 'checks and balances' and 'separation of powers' in the American government are flimsy indeed, since in the final analysis all of these divisions are part of the same government and are governed by the same set of rulers.

Because of the assumption that individuals only act in their narrow economic interests, and feel no moral need to honor commitments, it must be questioned why a separation of powers would ever be obeyed. In the American system, the executive branch enforces, the judicial branch interprets, and the legislative branch writes laws. But with an executive branch that controls the enforcement agency of the army and police, why would the executive branch ever obey a court's interpretation, or the laws that Congress passes even if they did attempt to constrain the executive?[8] There is no reason for the branch of government that controls the coercive powers to obey any other branch, because the other branches simply do not have the coercive powers to force them to obey. Government collapses back into the initial prisoner's dilemma with the head of the coercive enforcement branch as the sole government decision maker because of the narrow assumptions of Buchanan's model.[9]

One slight modification might need to be made to the above utility payoffs between government and citizens. If the government continually steals all but subsistent living from its citizens, soon the people will stop producing much of a surplus for the government to seize. Depending on the type of government chosen and the leader's time preference rate, the government will find it in its own interest to seize less now in order to continue to seize more later.[10] Hoppe (2001: 18) describes the situation by saying, 'Assuming no more than self-interest, the ruler tries to maximize his total wealth, i.e., the present value of his estate *and* current income. He would *not* want to increase current income at the expense of a more than proportional drop in the present value of his assets.' Although this might change the magnitude of the payoffs, the result remains the same – government can defect because there is no third-party constraint on it. Unless citizens actually chose a social contract that maximized the rulers' income at the expense of the ruled, the government would defect. The Nash equilibrium remains the lower left box of the prisoner's dilemma game.

The essential feature of government is that it has a geographical monopoly over the use of coercive force. Because in Buchanan's model the only constraint on individuals' behavior in anarchy is economic incentives provided by the use of force from others, the only thing that can be expected to constrain government is also force. Since a government is defined as a geographic monopoly on the legal use of force, there is no social contract or piece of parchment that can constrain it. Hobbes's Leviathan will result from any attempt to establish a limited government to enforce contracts. Buchanan (1975: 87) seemed to recognize this when he wrote, 'There is no obvious and effective means through which the enforcing institution or agent can itself be constrained in its own behavior. Hence, as Hobbes so perceptively noted more than three centuries ago, individuals who contract for the services of enforcing institutions necessarily surrender their own independence.' Buchanan (ibid.: 88) later speaks of government as if it is external to the game, saying, 'The state emerges as the enforcing agency or institution, conceptually external to the contracting parties and charged with the single responsibility of enforcing agreed-on rights and claims along with contracts which involve voluntarily negotiated exchanges of such claims.' Leaving the state external to the game leads Buchanan to the erroneous conclusion that the state will necessarily enable people to achieve a higher level of utility.

Once it is consistently recognized that the state is not external to the game but is instead composed of players, a public choice analysis shows that individual utility levels could be even lower with a state than under the simple Hobbesian anarchy described in Buchanan's model. Which system will provide individuals with higher utility will depend on the time preference for wealth extraction of the leader of the government. The state will have the ability, because of its monopoly over the use of force, to seize more than anybody could under anarchy.[11] The state may refrain from maximum extraction in order to extract more in the long run by leaving the people more wealth to maintain their incentive to produce. The choice Buchanan leaves you with is between many roving bandits or one large stationary bandit, who is able to steal more than any roving bandit, but may limit his short-term theft in order to extract more in the long run.[12]

If people in anarchy face a choice between the natural distribution under anarchy or a Leviathan, it is not at all clear that conceptually they would ever unanimously agree to form a government. Buchanan is only able to find a justification for the existence of the state because he fails to analyze it with the assumptions he makes about individuals in anarchy. The use of force is the only available constraint with Buchanan's assumptions. Wagner (1993) has written that it is essential to align a system's guns in a way that it is in no one's incentive to fire. Buchanan gives all of the guns to one enforcer, so it is not constrained. Since Buchanan's original work, much has been written on polycentric legal and enforcement systems.[13] This literature describes situations where power is divided between different enforcement agencies so that they constrain each other. The task left for these systems is to see if they are theoretically robust enough to work with Buchanan's Hobbesian assumptions about behavior. Buchanan's monopoly enforcement by government still leaves him in the Hobbesian jungle where he started.[14] The only hope to get out of the jungle with these assumptions is a polycentric division of enforcement power.

NOTES

1. He was also influenced by Winston Bush's (1972) mathematical modeling of Hobbesian anarchy.
2. Buchanan (1975) separates his analysis into the 'productive state' which produces public goods and the 'protective state' which is the enforcement agency. This chapter deals exclusively with an analysis of the 'protective state'.
3. 'We know that, factually and historically, the "social contract" is mythological, at least in many of its particulars. Individuals did not come together in some original position and mutually agree on the rules of social intercourse. And even had they done so at some time in history, their decisions could hardly be considered to be contractually binding on all of us who have come behind' (Buchanan, 1972: 27). His work is thus untouched by Lysander Spooner's (1870) attack on the legitimacy of a constitution.
4. Figure 9.1 is from Buchanan (1975: 84). A similar figure appears in 'Before Public Choice' but due to a typographical error the payoffs do not result in the same equilibrium.
5. To some extent, continuous dealings, even among a large group of people, can serve as an enforcement mechanism (Stringham, 2003). In this chapter I will accept it as true that some type of third-party enforcement is necessary.
6. Nozick (1974: 5) recognizes this basic point and suggests that we might want to use the 'minimax' criteria in comparing anarchy to states, saying, 'the state would be compared with the most pessimistically described Hobbesian state of nature. But in using the minimax criterion, this Hobbesian situation should be compared with the most pessimistically described possible state, including *future* ones. [In] such a comparison, surely, the worst state of nature would win.'
7. Even if a 'veil of ignorance' (or uncertainty) is assumed the result does not change. The citizens could write an optimal social contract (constitution) not knowing what their positions will be. As soon as the contract is put into effect, some particular people must fill the roles of government to enforce contracts. They will now know who they are and will be able to defect on the contract that was initially written behind a veil of ignorance.
8. Landes and Posner (1975) have written that an independent judiciary enables Congress to extract more rents because it forces Congress to abide by a law that it passed giving a privilege to one group. Without a credible commitment that Congress will not reverse a privilege granted in the following period, special interest groups would not be willing to pay much to Congress for privileges because their expected rents would be small. This does not affect the analysis in this chapter though. The judiciary is only obeyed because it enables Congress to receive more rents from individuals through lobbying. The executive branch can still defect from its original contract with citizens to expropriate resources and the judiciary has no enforcement recourse. The judiciary is only obeyed in the areas where it helps Congress (or a similar argument for the executive branch) receive more money, not less.
9. This does not mean that ideology, tradition and morality play no role in helping to provide somewhat of a check on the expansion of a limited government into a Leviathan, but since these same things are assumed away in Buchanan's analysis of anarchy, they cannot then be reintroduced when analyzing government.

10. See Olson (2000) and Hoppe (2001) for analyses of how time horizons will impact rulers' incentives for theft.
11. Rothbard (1973 [1996]: 47) notes that 'Historically, by far the overwhelming portion of all enslavement and murder in the history of the world have come from the hands of government.' Providing evidence for this observation is Rummel (1994), who attempts to document the number of citizens killed by their own governments in the twentieth century.
12. This is the situation McGuire and Olson (1996) and Olson (2000) model. See Powell and Coyne (2003) for a critique showing that Olson's stationary bandit does not necessarily improve individual welfare compared to anarchy.
13. For detailed analysis of many of the workings of similar polycentric systems see: Rothbard (1973); Friedman (1989); Benson (1990; 1998); Barnett (1998: 238–97) and Stringham (1999). For recent debates about power relations, networks and collusion in a polycentric system see Cowen (1992), Friedman (1994), Sutter (1995), Cowen and Sutter (1999), and Caplan and Stringham (2003).
14. As Alfred Cuzan (1979) noted, we never get out of anarchy by forming a government. We only move from market anarchy to political anarchy.

REFERENCES

Barnett, Randy (1998) [2000], *The Structure of Liberty*, New York: Oxford University Press.

Benson, Bruce (1990), *The Enterprise of Law: Justice without the State*, San Francisco, CA: Pacific Research Institute for Public Policy.

Benson, Bruce (1998), *To Serve and Protect*, New York: New York University Press.

Buchanan, James (1972), 'Before Public Choice', in *Explorations in the Theory of Anarchy*, edited by Gordon Tullock, Blacksburg, VA: Center for the Study of Public Choice.

Buchanan, James (1975) [2000], *The Limits of Liberty*, Indianapolis, IN: Liberty Fund Inc.

Buchanan, James and Tullock, Gordon (1962) [2001], *The Calculus of Consent*, Ann Arbor, MI: The University of Michigan Press.

Bush, Winston (1972), 'Individual Welfare in Anarchy', in *Explorations in the Theory of Anarchy*, edited by Gordon Tullock, Blacksburg, VA: Center for the Study of Public Choice.

Caplan, Bryan and Stringham, Edward (2003), 'Networks, Law, and the Paradox of Cooperation', *Review of Austrian Economics*, **16**: 309–26.

Cowen, Tyler (1992), 'Law as a Public Good: The Economics of Anarchy', *Economics and Philosophy*, **8**: 249–67.

Cowen, Tyler and Sutter, Daniel (1999), 'The Costs of Cooperation', *The Review of Austrian Economics*, **12**: 161–73.

Cuzan, Alfred (1979), 'Do We Ever Really Get Out of Anarchy?', *Journal of Libertarian Studies*, **3**: 151–8.

Friedman, David (1989) [1995], *The Machinery of Freedom*, La Salle, IL: Open Court.

Friedman, David (1994), 'Law as a Private Good: A Response to Tyler Cowen on the Economics of Anarchy', *Economics and Philosophy*, **10**: 319–27.

Hobbes, Thomas (1651) [1994], *Leviathan*, Cambridge, MA: Cambridge University Press.

Hoppe, Hans-Hermann (2001), *Democracy – The God That Failed*, New Brunswick, NJ: Transaction Publishers.

Landes, David and Posner, Richard (1975), 'The Independent Judiciary in an Interest Group Perspective', *Journal of Law and Economics*, **18**: 875–901.

McGuire, Martin and Olson, Mancur (1996), 'The Economics of Autocracy and Majority Rule: The Invisible Hand and the Use of Force', *Journal of Economic Literature*, **34**: 72–96.

Nozick, Robert (1974), *Anarchy, State and Utopia*, New York: Basic Books.

Olson, Mancur (2000), *Power and Prosperity*, New York: Basic Books.

Powell, Benjamin, and Coyne, Christopher (2003), 'Do Pessimistic Assumptions Justify Government?', *Journal of Libertarian Studies*, **17**: 17–38.

Rothbard, Murray (1973) [1996], *For a New Liberty*, San Francisco, CA: Fox & Wilkes.

Rummel, R.J. (1994), *Death by Government*, New Brunswick, NJ: Transaction Publishers.

Spooner, Lysander (1870) [1992], 'No Treason No. IV: The Constitution of No Authority', in *The Lysander Spooner Reader*, San Francisco, CA: Fox & Wilkes.

Stringham, Edward (1999), 'Market Chosen Law', *Journal of Libertarian Studies*, **14**: 53–77.

Stringham, Edward (2003), 'The Extralegal Development of Securities Trading in Seventeenth-Century Amsterdam', *Quarterly Review of Economics and Finance*, **43**: 321–44.

Sutter, Daniel (1995), 'Asymmetric Power Relations and Cooperation in Anarchy', *Southern Economic Journal*, **61**: 602–13.

Tullock, Gordon (1971), 'The Paradox of Revolution', *Public Choice*, **11**: 89–100.

Wagner, Richard (1993), *Parchment, Guns and Constitutional Order*, Aldershot, UK and Brookfield, USA: Edward Elgar.

10. Cases in anarchy*

Thomas Hogarty

I. INTRODUCTION

Anarchy, customarily regarded as an exotic state of society possessing only 'academic' interest, has recently attracted widespread attention as a focal point for discussion of public institutions, social mores, the state of the economy and government itself. Most of the discussion has, not surprisingly, been concerned with the desirability or otherwise of (relatively) anarchic states; however, to be useful as even a mere focal point for discussion, the state of society we call anarchy must be subjected to positive analysis.

The most direct approach to this goal is theoretical analysis [2, 3, 13]; an alternative approach – and the one taken here – is an examination of isolated instances of anarchy. A typical model of anarchy would consider one or a few issues, such as an equilibrium distribution of income, the impact of time related factors (e.g., continuous dealing), etc. The objective of such a model would be definitive conclusions (predictions) about specific aspects of behavior.

In contrast, we hope to examine a wider range of behavioral issues, including those relating to the origin and termination of anarchy. At the same time, however, available evidence is sufficient neither to conclusively confirm nor refute our hypotheses or those of others. At best we can only hope to: (1) illustrate behavior patterns analyzed in more formal models; (2) suggest useful hypotheses (assumptions) for future models; and (3) provide points of reference as a general aid to future discussion.

In what follows, we first present a short conceptual framework (set of hypotheses) relating to behavior under anarchy. We then discuss, in general terms, the problem of experimental control as it relates to the issue of observing behavior in anarchy. Finally, we present a brief summary of three recorded 'case studies' of anarchy, followed immediately by some overall implications and conclusions.

* This paper was first published in *Explorations in the Theory of Anarchy*, edited by Gordon Tullock, The Public Choice Society Book and Monograph Series, Center for the Study of Public Choice, Blacksburg, VA, USA, 1972, pp. 51–64.

II. THE CONCEPTUAL FRAMEWORK

The propriety of a given definition depends primarily on the uses to which it is put. For present purposes, we can usefully define anarchy as a state of society characterized by the absence of law coupled with anonymity. The latter characteristic is introduced to eliminate the 'Andaman Islander Solution' [1, 6–7]. The Andaman Islanders, a primitive people, exist in a society without (formal) law, regulating behavior by means of 'public opinion' (i.e., ostracism).

The first issue concerns the origins of anarchy. Perhaps in ages past so-called 'cave men' lived under anarchic conditions. In any event, the interesting issue concerns how – starting from an initial position of civilization – anarchy might arise. A simple model which describes such a process is the following. Let:

L = legitimacy = probability of successful defense by a government against challenges to its authority;
A = probability of anarchy; and,
N = number of challengers.

The relation among these variables is:

(1) $N = f(L)$
(2) $A = g(N)$
(3) $A = h(L)$

with

$$\frac{dA}{dL} = \frac{dA}{dN} \cdot \frac{dN}{dL} < 0$$

because

$$\frac{dA}{dN} > 0 \text{ and } \frac{dN}{dL} < 0.$$

This simple syllogism indicates that the likelihood of anarchy depends on the legitimacy of the government existing in a particular society at some point in time. The word legitimacy is often, unfortunately, confused with distinct factors such as popularity. While popularity is perhaps a useful indicator of legitimacy, the latter is a distinct concept. For example, a medieval king might have been exceptionally unpopular; however, if his rule were thought to have divine origins, the number of pretenders to the throne would be insignificant. Thus, tradition and perceived competence may confer legitimacy on an extraordinarily unpopular government. In addition, popular election may not be sufficient.[1]

Thus, our first hypothesis is that anarchy is most likely to follow a government with low legitimacy. Tentatively, one might say that the type of government with the lowest level of legitimacy is a provisional government, one whose tenure is presumed temporary (but unspecified) and/or whose existence is buttressed by neither constitution nor tradition. Thus, our first hypothesis can be restated as the prediction that anarchy will be immediately preceded by a government usefully labelled as provisional.

Our second hypothesis is that in anarchy, dominance is likely. That is, the 'natural' distribution of income for some individuals will be less than that required for survival.[2] To be sure, this hypothesis is trivial so long as the aggregate income of a society implies *per capita* incomes significantly below the survival level (rate). However, we suggest the stronger form of the hypothesis will also hold. Even if *per capita* incomes are substantially above survival levels, some individuals will be killed or starved to death in a state of anarchy.

The third hypothesis concerns the formation of coalitions. We anticipate at least attempts to form coalitions; moreover, these attempts will be systematically related to relative abilities. Those individuals whose abilities in theft and violence are relatively large will tend to coalesce in bands of optimal size; those individuals whose abilities in productive activities are relatively large will also tend to coalesce, but with far greater difficulty.

Recall our first hypothesis that anarchy will follow the demise of (some) civilization. In the prior civilized society, we may suppose that certain individuals found illegal (criminal) activity more beneficial than normal productive activity. These individuals, upon the arrival of anarchy, will actually 'feel more at home' than they did in the society of rules. Such individuals will tend to coalesce in bands, the number and size of the bands depending on local circumstances.

In contrast, those individuals whose productive talent was well rewarded in civilization will desire a restoration of law and order; however, such individuals will encounter greater difficulty in coalescing because their goal (a system of law) is more complex than the simple raiding activities of the criminals. Establishment of rules usually presupposes consensus – even of a limited sort. On the other hand, the criminals will tend to establish a crude hierarchy, the chief being the one with greatest ability.

Thus, our third hypothesis is that the first coalition(s) will comprise those individuals who have both a comparative and relative advantage in activities such as violence and theft.[3]

III. THE ISSUE OF EXPERIMENTAL CONTROL

Suppose we desired an experiment to ascertain the impact on American society of eliminating government at all levels (federal, state, local). Presumably, some elite group could select as president some candidate whose approval rating in, say, the Gallup Poll was abysmally low. The elite group could then instruct their chosen president to ignore all advice and challenges to his authority until the resulting chaos plunged the country into complete anarchy. We might then be ready to observe the behavior of American citizens. Similar experiments might be designed for Argentina, Pakistan, Finland, etc.

Hopefully, all readers regard the above paragraph as absurd. Yet such ludicrous suggestions aptly illustrate the problem of (an) experiment(s) in anarchy. Human behavior under anarchic conditions would vary by time and place, by historical experience, etc., etc. Stability in behavioral patterns is something to be determined, not assumed; moreover, as noted in the earlier reference to the Andaman Islanders, phenomena such as familiarity, social conventions, and commonality of goals will strongly influence individual and group behavior under anarchy.

In short, if we are to evaluate the impact of no government, control over other factors is required. Unfortunately, no simple *dictum* to hold other things constant will suffice. The things to be held constant depend in part on the questions for which answers are sought. For example, if we desire to know the extent to which (conditions under which) private, informal agreements can be substituted for public, formal rules, then societies such as that of the Andaman Islanders merit detailed study. On the other hand, such societies are of marginal interest if the state, in lieu of withering away, is to be dismantled in a relatively short time period, say, one to ten years.[4] Our interest is primarily in the latter sort of experiment. That is, what would be the effects if anarchy were 'suddenly' to prevail in a modern, civilized society such as the US? Accordingly, we suggest that a reasonable experiment (case study) in anarchy would have four characteristics:

(1) the experiment would involve a time period of moderate length;
(2) the subjects participating in the experiment would have little or no chance of withdrawal (escape);
(3) the subjects participating would not be relatives, close friends, or comprise a group of 'like-minded' people gathered for a specific purpose; and,
(4) the subjects' behavior would be noted and recorded by a competent, preferably scientific, observer.

The importance of the first characteristic is readily illustrated. Consider the classic case of fire in a crowded theater. Typically, the theater-goers would rush for the exits, perhaps push and trample one another, etc. This sort of exper-iment permits almost no generalizations about behavior under anarchy. Similar problems would be encountered in a study based on the 'black plague' in Europe. Over a prolonged period, the behavioral patterns attributable to the fact of anarchy alone cannot be isolated. For example, the wanderings of people may lead to assault or murder merely because of differences in language, custom, etc. In brief, a long time period means that none of the 'other things' are constant.

The second characteristic is important simply because behavior will differ drastically if individuals can escape with relative ease. Thus, consider an isolated mining town whose mayor, judge, and sheriff die unexpectedly. If replacement of these individuals is not foreseeable in the near future, the best alternative for the local merchants and other inhabitants may be early departure for the nearest town. Depending on the time period involved, the remaining inhabitants will likely comprise a very unrepresentative cross section of society.[5]

The third characteristic hardly warrants discussion, but its importance can be illustrated by reference to recent attempts – in the US and elsewhere – to establish communal societies. The attempts, whether eminently successful or not, are inconclusive. The participants are volunteers, tend to share specific goals, and – after a fashion – resemble clubs or 'closed' societies such as the Amish people. Such communities may be ideal for improving our understand-ing of the possibilities for (limits of) human cooperation, etc. They tell us little about the impact of anarchy on an average society.

The fourth characteristic is cited merely to emphasize the fact that recorded instances of anarchy are extremely rare. This fact in itself is suggestive, but that is a matter we shall return to in the last section.

The three cases we present possess these four characteristics in varying degrees. In addition, while each of the cases has other, undesirable character-istics (e.g., the second case is pure fiction), these undesirable characteristics overlap to only a small extent (e.g., the first case is a carefully controlled experiment in animal behavior under anarchy while the other two concern human behavior). Hence, we feel that, taken together, these cases fulfill the objectives stated in the introduction.

IV.   THREE CASES OF ANARCHY

A.   The Brown Rat

The brown rat, one of man's major biological competitors, exhibits behavior which demonstrates something akin to learning. Knowledge about poisons is transmitted throughout a given rat pack by the behavior of the first rat to approach an unknown food. More importantly, knowledge of poisonous foods is apparently transmitted from generation to generation and 'the knowledge long outlives those individuals which first made the experience' [10, 161]. For these and other reasons, rats have been used in experiments involving questions of human behavior on an extensive scale.

Rats typically exist in extended families or packs, each clan comprising the various descendants and relatives of a given pair. Owing to proximity in the 'natural state,' the members of a given 'rat pack' apparently recognize each other by smell [10, 162].[6]

An experiment bearing directly on the subject at hand was performed some 20 years ago by a naturalist named Steiniger and recounted in a popular book by Lorenz [10, 158–9].

> Steiniger put brown rats from different localities into a large enclosure which provided them with completely natural living conditions. At first the individual animals seemed afraid of each other; they were not in an aggressive mood, but they bit each other if they met by chance, particularly if two were driven toward each other along one side of the enclosure, so that they collided at speed. However, they became really aggressive only when they began to settle and take possession of territories. At the same time, pair formation started between unacquainted rats from different localities. If several pairs were formed at the same time the ensuing fights might last a long time, but if one pair was formed before the others had started, the tyranny of the united forces of the two partners increased the pressure on the unfortunate co-tenants of the enclosure so much that any further pair formation was prevented. The unpaired rats sank noticeably in rank and were constantly pursued by the two mates. Even in the 102-square-yard enclosure, two or three weeks sufficed for such a pair to kill all the other residents, ten to fifteen strong adult rats.
>
> The male and female of the victorious pair were equally cruel to their subordinates, but it was plain that he preferred biting males and she females. The subjugated rats scarcely defended themselves, made desperate attempts to flee, and in their desperation took a direction which rarely brings safety to rats, namely upwards. Steiniger repeatedly saw weary, wounded rats sitting exposed and in broad daylight high up in bushes and trees, evidently outside occupied territory. The wounds were usually on the end of the back and the tail, where the pursuer had seized them. Death was seldom caused by sudden, deep wounds or loss of blood but more frequently by sepsis, particularly in the case of bites which penetrated the peritoneum. But usually the animals died of exhaustion and nervous overstimulation leading to disturbance of the adrenal glands.

B. Children on a Deserted Island

In Golding's *Lord of the Flies* [5] we have an imaginary instance of anarchy involving boys aged (approximately) 6–12. However, the book is no mere adventure story since it incorporates (some of) our meager knowledge of human nature into a 'test situation,' namely, one of anarchy.

The story begins with a gathering of boys stranded on an island by a plane crash. The boys, numbering a dozen or so, are gathered by the summons of a 'conch' (large seashell) usable as a horn. Some of the boys arrive individually; the remainder – consisting of choirboys led by Jack Merridew – arrive as a unified group.

Besides Jack, the oldest among the boys are Ralph, who originally discovered the conch, and 'Piggy,' the most intellectual of the boys. While Jack appears as the natural leader, Ralph is elected chief by the gathered assembly.

Initially, the situation is orderly. Ralph, as chief-elect, designates Jack and his choirboys as 'hunters'. The other boys are given the task of building a fire, to be used as a signal for passing ships. Nonetheless, while there's a provisional government, including chief, there is little organization. Attention to maintenance of the fire wanes as the boys pass time in swimming. What little organization exists is centered in Jack and his band of hunters.

Jack and another boy, Roger, evidence some tendency toward violence, but both are inhibited. Jack, in his initial attempt to kill a pig with his knife, develops 'cold feet' [5, 27]. Roger hurls stones in the vicinity of a smaller boy, Henry, but is inhibited – apparently by prior parental conditioning – against aiming directly at Henry [5, 57]. These inhibitions are subsequently overcome, when anonymity is attained. Initially, Jack and Roger 'paint' themselves for concealment, i.e., as an aid to their hunting. The masks, however, have the unintended effect of liberating the boys from shame and self-consciousness. In short, a *form of* anonymity is attained.

Over time, Jack becomes more ambitious, challenging the legitimacy of Ralph's rule. So what if elected? 'You can't hunt, you can't sing –' [5, 84]. Nonetheless, Jack's major bid to be elected chief is frustrated [5, 117–18]. Humiliated, Jack runs off, refusing to remain part of the original group. At first, Jack is joined only by (some of) his choirboys. However, this number suffices for an initial raid whose limited goal is fire.[7] While raiding, Jack attempts to induce members of the main group to join his band.

Eventually, all join Jack's group except Ralph, Piggy, Simon, and two small twins (Sam and Eric). Simon, a loner among the boys, is accidentally killed by Jack and his band, who mistake Simon – emerging from the brush at night – for a pig. Later, Jack and his band successfully raid the others' camp (now consisting of Ralph, Piggy, and two small twins) for Piggy's glasses. In a subsequent confrontation at Jack's hilltop camp, Piggy is killed by Roger,[8] and the twins are 'drafted' into Jack's band. Ralph departs, only to be hunted the following day. Fleeing from the band, Ralph is rescued by a British Naval Officer who has arrived – with a party of men – on the beach.

C. Andersonville

Prisons comprise miniature societies unto themselves and can be used as a fertile source of data for social science research. The classic study by Radford

[11] illustrated basic economic behavior under reasonably controlled conditions. The recent autobiography by H. Charierre [4] illustrated the interaction between prison administration and the economic activity of prisoners. Andersonville, the title of a book [9] and a POW camp during 1864–65, also illustrates behavior such as Gresham's Law (251).[9]

Nonetheless, Andersonville merits attention as a case study in anarchy because: (1) it is a fertile source of hypotheses; (2) it represents a level of experimental control not commonly achieved; and (3) it is closer to fact than fiction.[10]

The Andersonville camp (officially Camp Sumpter) was hurriedly constructed in 1864 so that the stream of union soldiers being captured might be accommodated. Originally designed as barely acceptable internment for a maximum of 10 000 men, the camp ultimately comprised a destination for about 40 000 prisoners (598). Command was divided into three separate departments: one man in charge of troops, another in charge of the prison, a third in command of the post. The prison officer, Henry Wirz, did not arrive until the prison population reached a level of about 7000.

New prisoners [termed 'fresh fish' (156) by the old prisoners] arrived continuously in carloads. Inasmuch as there was no facility for separating the new from the old prisoners, records of the prison population were never accurate and orderly, gradual settlement of the new prisoners among the old was impossible. If the new prisoners had the misfortune to arrive at night, they were not only unable to see but subject to predation by the raiders.

Escape, difficult at first, became virtually impossible with the establishment of a 'deadline' twenty feet inside the stockade.[11] The establishment of the deadline itself dispossessed many of the prisoners, who were understandably angered. The stockade was eventually enlarged to comprise a rectangular area with a perimeter of some 4800 feet. However, this enlargement occurred when the population swelled to 29 000 prisoners, so that density was *still* high (395, 397).

Long before this population density was attained, however, complete anarchy existed. Whereas initially new prisoners were attacked *en masse* only at night, now daylight raids on (*groups* of) old and new prisoners became commonplace (187–8):

What was the need of waiting for night? At first Willie Collins and those like him had a notion that guards might shoot. They recalled the death of Tomcat O'Connor, they saw no reason to die jumping as he had died. But one morning John Sarsfield himself, with his minions, was standing near the North Gate when a small detachment of Westerners (they included pickets gobbled up by a swift Confederate movement in northwest Georgia) found themselves staring at Andersonville for the first time. These people had not been robbed of their blankets. As did many folks from the West, they wore blanket rolls in Confederate fashion, they carried no knapsacks.

The blanket rolls seemed bulky to Sarsfield's practiced gaze. He shouldered forward and wrenched the roll away from the nearest prisoner. The man hallooed, Sarsfield knocked him flat, the balance of the fresh fish leaped toward Sarsfield, Sarsfield's Raiders swatted, stabbed, kicked. This fight was over in less than a minute. Six of the Westerners lay on the ground and the rest had fallen back into the watching throng – several others shy of their blanket rolls, as was the first man. All of the new-come prisoners were bleeding, two were unconscious. Sarsfield's Raiders were the richer by eleven blanket rolls filled with combs, socks, extra shoes, Bibles (these could be bartered), gilt melaineotypes, housewives, knives, eating utensils, and name-it-if-you-like. The guards on the parapet stations had not fired a shot; they watched idly or in downright amusement . . .

Willie Collins and Pat Delaney lifted a leaf from Sarsfield's book. Sarsfield was intelligent; it was said that he had read law, had served three years in the army, had been wounded, his wound had healed, he had been promoted First Sergeant and later commissioned; his commission had arrived but he had not mustered when he was captured. Hence he'd landed here with the enlisted men. Folks said that a bright fellow like Sarsfield had known all along that the guards would not fire. Or perhaps he had made a private agreement with the guards; and now guards might profit from each robbery occurring before their eyes and under the muzzles of their unfired muskets. No longer could the vice be relegated to darkness. It was here in daylight, stalking; it was an animal grown tall as the Methodist Church steeple back home, it was Force and Force only, it could and would maul you to a wet bloody rag if you lifted your fist in protest, or sometimes even if you lifted your voice.

In such chaotic conditions, the more primitive among the prisoners could reap a harvest. The raiders were happier in Andersonville than they had ever been before (191). In the outer world they had been insignificant, eternally existing in dread of discipline. Here the only discipline consisted of that which they administered. In fact, the raiders steadfastly refused to enlist in the Confederate Army: those soldiers were perhaps less well fed than they. Of what significance was a promise of female companionship when food and drink could be secured through robbery – and later – trade with the guards?[12]

The optimal size raiding band numbered *no more than* a dozen or so (186) with the result that several independent bands of raiders were operating (186–7).

Over a period of months the quality and quantity of the daily rations declined. The corn bread contained larger amounts of cobs (251) and it was claimed that *per capita* rations amounted to less than one-half the amount required for survival (233). Moreover the distribution of rations was *occasionally* on a 'first come, grab as you can' basis (234).

In sum, as time passed and the population of the camp grew, the odds of survival became lower for the ordinary prisoner. *If one could*, he became a raider. However, membership in that club *generally* required either a criminal background or contact with a raider leader prior to internment (179–97, 355). In some cases, one might become a peripheral member of a raider band by dint of special ability/service (e.g., superior eyesight to spot raiding opportunities, skill in cooking, etc.). One enterprising fellow told fortunes to a raider leader (232) and sold information to the camp commander (233).

A *very few* prisoners were able to engage in normal labor activity profitably. Seneca McBean, six feet four inches tall, successfully operated a laundry – accepting any and all currency – because he could defend himself against the raiders (211). Nathan Dreyfoos, newly arrived sergeant, possessed not only natural leadership ability, but shears and skill as an amateur boxer and (not so amateur) fencer. Wielding a homemade sword consisting of a pointed stick, he too could defend himself against the raiders (263).

McBean and Dreyfoos, the latter a self-proclaimed barber (214), eventually began operating a combination laundry and barbershop, attracting increasing numbers of prisoners to their area. The customers came not only to barter for their services, but also because they felt safe around McBean and Dreyfoos (263). In short, the volume of laundry and barbering services sold depended, *inter alia*, on the proprietor's ability to discourage the presence of raiders in their midst.

The members of the raiding bands seemed to coalesce naturally, if not effortlessly. Each band had a dominant chief, who welded the members into an effective attacking organization. Distribution of booty seemed to present little problem inasmuch as the typical band was small, organized along functional lines,[13] and essentially comprising a hierarchy. The raiders shared a common origin consisting of experience in unlawful behavior.

What of the ordinary prisoner? If they were to coalesce, barriers would have to be surmounted (265, McBean speaking):

> Ah . . . trouble is, we *ought* to rely on Westerners. I'm one, I understand them, they understand me. Most of your New Yorkers – saving the raiders – and Pennsylvanians – They stick by themselves. Even the New Jersey boys tend to cleave together, and dog bite the man on the outside. Did you ever see anything like the way Massachusetts folks hang tight? And so with most of New England. Now, Michiganders are something like them – but I'd say humanized. Westernized New Englanders? Is that what you'd call them? They talk much the same way. Say *I be* instead of *I am*. But they're more awake, more Western.

Eventually, *primarily through the efforts of McBean and Dreyfoos*, a coalition against the raiders began to form. Dubbing themselves 'Regulators,' they found it necessary to keep their plans secret and also elicit the aid of Wirz lest he regard the coming conflict as insurrection and order the guards to fire on the prisoners.

At a meeting with Wirz, Dreyfoos – accompanied by McBean and one other – obtains agreement: not only will the guards refrain from shooting, but the 'Regulators' will be supplied with clubs as well (325). The clubs were to have thongs lest they be readily seized by the raiders.

The battle, short but ferocious, was decided in favor of the Regulators (329–30). Several of the raiders were forced to run a gauntlet (327–9) while the chiefs were eventually hanged (377–80).[14]

With the elimination of the raiders, prison life remained harsh, but there was no further violence of a systematic, organized type. The level of violence dropped sharply and was essentially confined to individuals. The prisoners brewed beer from cornmeal and water (383) and new prisoners, even sailors arriving with seabags, were not molested by the old prisoners upon initial entry (415). Instead the newcomer was beset with offers to trade (417):

> One day there was excitement when a batch of freshies came in from some fort in the Carolinas, and one of them had smuggled a packet of candy: gaudy, viscous sticks striped with red and white. Promptly the candy was distributed to the four winds; the newcomer needed a blanket, a cooking can, things more imperative than candy.

And in general (422):

> There were times when sound of thirty thousand people assailed the senses more terribly than might have been imagined by one who was not there to hear them. Since the overthrow of the raiders the stockade was well-policed by Regulators, operating under command of the slow-spoken A. R. Hill of the One Hundredth Ohio Volunteer Infantry. Few civilian communities of comparable size could have boasted an equal passiveness and freedom from violent crime. But there were bound to ensue rivalry, fuss, abrasion. Men contended in a mere bickering or in a tussle to the death. Waldo took umbrage because Ned snored against the back of his head when they were pushed together at night, Amos claimed that Hez had stolen the bacon rind which Amos had bought on South Street the day before.

After the demise of the raiders, survival became an individual matter. The preferred physique for survival was that of the wiry, not the athletic man (502). Initial wealth (belongings brought to camp) was of course important, but not sufficient. Survival – other things equal – was best ensured by purposeful activity, preferably work. The man who could not – or would not – work did not obtain extra necessities such as rice, salt, beans, etc. (503).

V.   SUMMARY AND CONCLUSIONS

The three hypotheses enumerated at the beginning fared reasonably well, at least in the limited sense of not being disconfirmed.

Our first hypothesis – anarchy will follow provisional government – is supported by both the second and third cases. In Golding's novel [5], the boys established an interim government with Ralph as chief. This government was certainly temporary; moreover, it was not fully competent and was not traditional. Ralph could neither provide food nor effect a rescue; accustomed to the regimentation of parental rule, the boys' popular assembly lacked legitimacy. In Andersonville, the government headed by Wirz obviously had no constitutional origins and clearly could not be considered traditional. In addition, the government had very limited competence.[15] It could reduce escape to trivial levels, but was unable to provide adequate food, shelter, and medical attention.

The second hypothesis, namely, dominance of some individuals, also received general confirmation; however, evidence regarding the choice between slavery and death was mixed. In the deserted island case, Piggy was murdered, the twins Sam and Eric were enslaved, and Ralph was hunted. Ralph's fate, had he been captured, remains uncertain, but death seemed a likely outcome. In Andersonville, there were no slaves. Maintenance of slaves seemed impossible; however, the important fact is that those most useful as slaves (McBean and Dreyfoos) were able to defend themselves against slavery. Whether or not this correlation between defensive ability and talent in productive activity was fortuitous is difficult to determine.

All three cases demonstrate that: (1) one or more coalitions will be formed; and (2) the first coalition is likely to dominate, at least for a time. These cases also suggest some *tentative* conclusions about the (re)emergence of law and order. In the simplest case involving the brown rat, anarchy ends only when there is a single, dominant pair. This pair procreates and hence forms its own extended family. After several generations, we may suppose that new clans establish themselves, with resultant tribal rivalry.[16]

In the second case, Jack's band *may* have comprised a fragile coalition. Assuming Ralph had been killed, the band might have remained intact only so long as (1) resources were plentiful (numerous pigs to hunt, etc.) and (2) Jack could withstand any challenge to his leadership. Conceivably, Roger would have entertained ambitions to be chief. This might or might not result in establishment of a rival band.

In Andersonville, the initial coalition(s) of raiders was (were) overcome only with the aid of the 'pre-existing' provisional government. In the absence of such aid, the 'good' prisoners might have been unable to coalesce, much less defeat the raiders.

In any event, the Andersonville case also implies that property rights – as part of the law and order package – can emerge without externalities. Here, those skilled in productive activities had powerful incentives to establish rules.[17] Property rights would emerge when and if cooperative efforts in that regard became possible.

As regards the nature of coalitions, our hypothesis receives qualified support. There were no criminals on Golding's island. Yet Jack – and perhaps

Roger – seemed to have both a comparative and relative advantage in violent activities. Certainly both boys indicated such talent once they had painted themselves. In Andersonville, the biography of the raider Chief Willie Collins left no doubt about his prior criminal stature. Similar, but less dramatic, claims apply to other members of the raider bands. The only apparent case in which a member of a raider band had no criminal background was that of Myles Crickland [9, 355]. This Michigan lumberman had never stolen nor committed assault for personal gain. Yet Myles was a powerful man – potentially valuable as a raider – who, while being shipped to the POW camp, had fallen in with John Sarsfield, one of the raider chiefs.

The final, and perhaps most crucial, issue concerns the practical importance of anarchy as a viable alternative to those seeking a better society. We noted earlier the paucity of cases of anarchy. Instances of chaos abound, but anarchy – even in times of social upheaval and war – is rarely observed. Does this suggest that anarchy is merely a philosophical curiosity or, at most, an historically unimportant and necessarily temporary state of affairs?

A recent article by Milton Himmelfarb [7] implies the latter. Referring to comments by Julian Bond to the effect that vigilante methods be adopted by black communities to deal with the drug problem, Himmelfarb concludes that an inevitable result of failure in courtroom justice is an emergence of street justice. Not authoritarianism, but rather life in a society unable to control evildoers, is intolerable to the ordinary person.

'Suppose that in France, in 1968, the contest had been between the red-flag Communists and the black-flag anarchists. Does anyone doubt that every bourgeois *père de famille* would have voted red?' [7, 73].[18]

Evidently, some individuals are doubtful, at least to the extent that some regard anarchy as the (possibly unattainable) ideal state. In addition, 'some individuals' are no mere handful of zealots: the advocates of Marx's withered state far exceed in number the followers of Hobbes. Be that as it may, it must be admitted that even the most desirable of all anarchic states – The Garden of Eden – existed for only a brief period.

NOTES

1. Horne [8] notes that, following the German victory in 1870, the leader of the provisional French government (Thiers) faced the immediate task of a peace treaty. As it turned out, the Germans received: (a) Alsace-Lorraine; (b) an indemnity of $1000 million; and (c) a triumphal march through Paris. In return for the triumphal march, the Germans allowed France to retain the city of Belfort, which – in spite of a long seige – had never capitulated. Thiers had been chosen by an elected assembly comprised of 768 seats with 43 seats allocated to Paris [8, 255]. Parisians regarded the provinces (and the provincially dominated assembly) with contempt. Frenchmen (particularly Parisians) had become accustomed to centralized government – the center, of course, being Paris. In fact, the half century prior to

this witnessed four different types of regime (Bourbon, Orleanist, Republican, and Bonapartist); none had been elected, but each had been acknowledged abroad as the legal government of France [8, 300]. Within a matter of weeks, the Thiers government had departed to Versailles, to be replaced – at least temporarily – by the autonomous Parisian Commune.

2. For an alternative view, see Bush [3]. Assuming dominance of some individuals, the choice between enslavement and death is surprisingly complex [14]. Moreover, the choice need not be strictly dichotomous. Positive amounts of food and water, even at levels (rates) below that required for survival, *may* maximize the present value of the dominated enslaved person to his owner.

3. For example, assuming a normal distribution of talents in theft, some individuals will be far above average, and hence possess a relative advantage.

4. We assume that ten years is insufficient time for a society such as the US in 1972 to develop mores, institutions, etc., which would make formal government unnecessary.

5. Referring to the case of Paris in 1870–71 (see note 1), large numbers of Parisians had evacuated the city before the Thiers government assumed power. By the time the Commune was 'established' most of the middle class had fled Paris.

6. The smell referred to here comprises mostly the odors acquired in the area(s) comprising the pack's natural habitat.

7. Lacking matches, Piggy's glasses are used to start fires. Since Piggy remained with the original group, Jack and his band – as self-proclaimed outcasts – must snatch a burning branch.

8. A large rock with lever, devised as defense, is rolled down on Piggy, who is not crushed, but hurled some 40 feet down on the beach and smashed.

9. The number in parentheses refers to a page number in the hardcover edition cited in the reference section. This procedure will be followed throughout the discussion of Andersonville.

10. On this point, see Kantor's bibliography and attendant discussion. While actual conversations are of necessity fictional, the main characters existed in fact.

11. This was a line which, if crossed by a prisoner, made him liable to be shot by a guard.

12. Needless to say, data on trading volume were not maintained. However, it appeared that most trade was among the raiders and the guards. The ordinary prisoners, unless they were 'fresh fish,' had little worth trading.

13. For example, scout, able-bodied raider, cook, etc.

14. Willie Collins, perhaps the most feared of the raider chiefs, was so big that he broke the first (admittedly decayed) rope. Accordingly, he was literally hung twice – death by strangulation.

15. There can be little doubt that Wirz preferred order within the stockade. In almost constant pain from an old wound, Wirz was chagrined at his inability to accurately count the prison population. He regarded his subordinates as incompetent and, in general, was angered whenever situations within the stockade required his personal attention. The guards themselves were, at best, indifferent to the fate of the prisoners. There was no evidence to support a presumption of conscious collusion between the guards and the raiders. In contrast, the cooperation between Wirz and the Regulators encountered no 'sabotage' by the guards.

16. The reader who regards this simple case as naive is referred to Mario Puzo's best seller, *The Godfather*, or the classic case of the 'Hatfields and McCoys.'

17. One may wonder why McBean and Dreyfoos did not become raiders. At least three reasons can be offered: (1) McBean and Dreyfoos were unable to organize a band of minimum efficient size; (2) both men regarded the gains from shopkeeping as superior to those from raiding *for them*; i.e., their comparative and relative advantages in business activity dictated the choice; (3) both men forsaw an end to the war, with justice administered to the raiders, and both expected to survive until the war ended.

18. The Paris Commune of 1871, in large part a government of philosophical anarchists, was unable to survive. To be sure, this government was ousted by force, not a plebiscite; however, the government it succeeded *had been* popularly elected.

REFERENCES

1. Bohannan, Paul, ed. *Law and Warfare: Studies in the Anthropology of Conflict.* Garden City, NY: The Natural History Press, 1967.
2. Buchanan, James M. 'The Samaritan's Dilemma' (unpublished).
3. Bush, Winston. 'Income Distribution in Anarchy.'
4. Charriere, Henri. *Papillion.* William Morrow & Co., 1970.
5. Golding, William. *Lord of the Flies.* New York: Capricorn Books, 1959 (paperback).
6. Hicks, John. *A Theory of Economic History.* New York: Oxford University Press, 1969.
7. Himmelfarb, Milton. 'Sword of the Law,' *Commentary*, Vol. 53, No. 5, May, 1972, 71–3.
8. Horne, Alistair. *The Fall of Paris.* New York: St Martin's Press, 1965.
9. Kantor, MacKinlay. *Andersonville.* New York: World Publishing Co., 1955.
10. Lorenz, Konrad. *On Aggression.* New York: Harcourt, Brace & World, 1963 (translated 1966).
11. Radford, R.A. 'The Economic Organization of a POW Camp,' *Economica*, 12, 1945.
12. Tullock, Gordon. 'The Coal Tit as a Careful Shopper,' letter to editor of *American Naturalist*, 105, 1971, 77–80.
13. —— *The Edge of the Jungle.*
14. —— *The Social Dilemma* (unpublished).

11. Defining anarchy as rock 'n' roll: rethinking Hogarty's three cases

Virgil Storr

INTRODUCTION

> 'When I use a word,' Humpty Dumpty said, in rather a scornful tone, 'it means just what I choose it to mean – neither more nor less.'
>
> 'The question is,' said Alice, 'whether you *can* make words mean so many different things.'
>
> 'The question is,' said Humpty Dumpty, 'which is to be master – that's all.'
>
> Lewis Carroll, *Through the Looking-Glass*

Anarchy, simply put, means a society without government. Unfortunately, when most people use the word, they typically make it mean something like chaos, or social mayhem, or civil unrest; they equate anarchy with Hobbes's jungle where life is 'poore, nasty, brutish and short'. Anarchy, for them, is the penchant for society's destruction maintained by disaffected suburban youth who have an affinity with rock 'n' roll, drugs and black fingernail polish. It is children at play without adult supervision; it is streets without stop lights; it is the Wild Wild West with no sheriff or marshal. Few take anarchy seriously as an alternative socio-economic system to the one that we presently enjoy. And even fewer find it a viable or even desirable alternative to what we call 'democratic capitalism'. Professor Hogarty is no exception (neither, by the way, are any of the other authors in *Explorations in the Theory of Anarchy*).

In 'Cases in Anarchy', his contribution to the Center for the Study of Public Choice's interesting volume, Professor Hogarty tries to give us some insight into what an anarchic society would look like. More specifically, he attempts to present us with a 'positive analysis' of 'the state of society we call anarchy' by examining 'isolated instances of anarchy' (Hogarty, 1972: 51). Although Professor Hogarty's approach succeeds in many respects (it is both interesting and thought-provoking), it nonetheless fails to deliver on its central promise. We are treated to three interesting stories but none is recognizable as a case of anarchy, at least as envisioned by the anarcho-capitalist. Sadly, Professor Hogarty, like the other authors in *Explorations*, seems enthralled by the view of 'anarchy as rock 'n' roll'.[1] As a result, he is simply unable to conceive of either rules without legislation or order without government. This conceptual myopia, which plagues Professor Hogarty repeatedly during his presentation, prevents him from articulating a convincing case that a society without government will degenerate into Hobbes's jungle. That any other outcome is possible is not even considered. Those who have found something of value in visions of a libertarian (anarchic) society expressed by Rothbard, the Tannehills and others should, however, take a different approach to Professor Hogarty's work. Whether anarchy would come to resemble Hobbes's jungle is an important (if often answered; see, for instance, Tannehill and Tannehill, 1970) question. Let us, therefore, examine Professor Hogarty's analysis more closely.

THE CONCEPTUAL FRAMEWORK

Professor Hogarty begins by defining anarchy as 'a state of society characterized by the absence of law coupled with anonymity'. Proponents of anarchy would have no real cause to quarrel with this definition, except they may wish to distinguish *the law as government-enforced prohibitions* from *the law as social order* (that is, the opposite of a *lawless* society). Professor Hogarty does not make such a distinction. Although anarchists would swiftly agree with Professor Hogarty that anarchy requires the absence of government, they would not be so quick to agree with his assumptions that absent government there would be disorder.

Along the same lines, Professor Hogarty introduces an anonymity condition to his definition, in order to, as he says, 'eliminate the Andaman Islander Solution' (Hogarty, 1972: 51). By employing this condition he hopes to rule out from the very beginning the possibility that public opinion or moral suasion could be sufficient to regulate human behavior, as it was on the Andaman Islands. He believes that if all dealings are anonymous, then law, meaning here the presence and promise of government coercion, becomes the only way to regulate behavior. That repeated dealings are often enough to make individuals honor contracts in the absence of external enforcement and that much of our interaction as 'anonymous types' is regulated by social customs and not government directives is not acknowledged. He does not seem aware, for instance, that we shake hands, say good morning and are generally nice to each other not because we are coerced to do so but because, among other reasons, we were raised to.

Socially proscribed rules of behavior 'govern', for lack of a better word, even the most chaotic of circumstances. You may remember, for instance, that during the Los Angeles riots that followed the acquittal of the police officers that beat Rodney King a sign saying 'black-owned' was often sufficient to protect a store from being looted. Although much of the rioting took place in black neighborhoods, their anger was not directed towards other blacks; there was a socially enforced sanction in that circumstance against stealing from black-owned enterprises. Similarly, the *mosh pits* at the front of rock concerts where teenage boys throw themselves 'violently' into one another are themselves regulated by a set of complex rules that are not enforced by government or concert security. As one mosher explained, 'When participants lose their footing, moshers clear a space and give them a hand up; when someone dives from the stage, everyone focuses on catching him or her' (Reding, 1996: para. 4).

From his definition of anarchy as disorder, or what I call anarchy as rock 'n' roll, however, Professor Hogarty then constructs a simple model of how society might suddenly find itself in 'anarchy' and what is likely to happen in an anarchic community. He offers three disastrous hypotheses for us to consider. The first is that 'anarchy will follow the demise of (some) civilization' (Hogarty, 1972: 53). Government and civilization for Professor Hogarty are inextricably linked and, as such, anarchy, for him, is the social upheaval that accompanies something like a civil war or a palace *coup*. It is not the gradual withering away of the state predicted by Marx and the anarcho-socialists (Bakunin et al.), nor is it the quiet revolution envisioned by the anarcho-capitalists (Rothbard et al.). It is the aftermath of a collapse of civilization.

The second of Professor Hogarty's frightening predictions is that 'in anarchy, dominance is likely' (Hogarty, 1972: 53). According to Professor Hogarty, 'the "natural" distribution of income for some individuals [in anarchy] will be less than that required for survival'. Anarchy, then, will be a world of masters and slaves, a world of victimizers and victims, a world of haves and have-nots. A world where, in his words, 'some individuals will be killed or starved to death'. In short, one might argue that a state of anarchy will be a great deal like our current world – with one critical difference. Dominance is not only likely if government exists, but is one of its defining characteristics. Even those who celebrate the virtues of government define it as an organ with a monopoly on coercive force. As hard as it is for some to conceive of an ordered society without government, it would be even harder to conceive of government without dominance. Government ceases to be government when its coercive elements, its abilities to dominate its citizenry, are stripped from it.

The third of Professor Hogarty's dire predictions is that in anarchy individuals will attempt to form coalitions, and it is those individuals with a comparative advantage in theft and violence that will be the first to organize. As such, it is the worst and not the best in a society that will come to dominate because, according to Professor Hogarty, those individuals with a comparative advantage in productive activities will find it more difficult to coalesce than individuals with a comparative advantage in theft (ibid.). Although he does concede that whether his claim is true or not remains an open empirical question, he nonetheless maintains that his predicted outcome is likely because individuals who were criminals in a civilized world will be even more at home in an anarchic society. Bands of thieves, according to Professor Hogarty, will thus move quickly to establish a crude hierarchy based on merit, 'the chief being the one with the greatest ability' (ibid.). On the other hand, Professor Hogarty maintains, those members of society who desire law and order will find that the task before them is a complex one, as rules require consensus, and so they will be slow in enacting even the simplest provisions.

Professor Hogarty is indeed right to force us to consider what would prevent the worst from coming to dominate in anarchy. Professors Rothbard and Hoppe, for instance, as well as others in the anarcho-capitalist camp, have not shied away from that task and have argued quite convincingly about how individuals might protect themselves from being dominated (see, for instance, Hoppe, 1999). Professor Hogarty, however, should be equally prepared to answer a similar challenge aimed at democratic capitalism: what prevents the worst rulers from coming to control government? Democratic politics are by no means dominated by only benevolent rulers. And, in addition, governments have proven that they can be quite violent as well. The Holocaust, the atomic bombing of Hiroshima, the partitioning, conquest and colonialization of Africa and, more recently, the killing of Amadou Diallo and the sodomizing of Abner Louima were all performed by government agents.

Professor Hogarty's conceptual framework, as we have seen, then, is flawed on multiple levels. Let us, however, leave aside the problems inherent in Hogarty's conceptual framework for the time being and, instead, examine the three cases of anarchy that he suggests lend credibility to his predictions. Admittedly, if these cases did bear out Hogarty's fantastic predictions then we would perhaps be willing to overlook some of the problems with his model. Ours might be a quest for alternate explanations for (what turned out to be) sound predications rather than a quest for more satisfactory predictions.

THREE CASES OF ANARCHY

A.   The Brown Rat

The first of Hogarty's three cases of anarchy involves brown rats (not humans). It turns out that brown rats, 'who typically exist in extended families or packs' (Hogarty, 1972: 56), will exhibit the sorts of behavior consistent with Professor Hogarty's predictions about anarchy if they are stripped away from their familial packs and placed in an enclosed environment with rats from 'different localities'.

The naturalist Steiniger, Professor Hogarty recounts, 'put brown rats from different localities into a large enclosure which provided them with completely natural living conditions' (ibid.: 56).[2] Understandably, their first reaction was fear, followed quickly by aggression as 'they began to settle and take possession of territories' (ibid.). Pair formation, Professor Hogarty notes, took place at the same time as this territorial partitioning. And it was observed that if several couples formed at the same time, then their scraps for dominance tended to be protracted ones. If one pair formed before the rest, however, that couple, purportedly bearing out Professor Hogarty's predictions concerning dominance, cruelly squashed all their rivals with the intention of establishing their own pack.

Although Professor Hogarty would have us believe that Steiniger's experiment can be regarded as an example of anarchy, there are in fact several problems with using this experiment in that way, not the least of which is that there are important differences between men and rats (that prove relevant here). As Professor Hogarty rightfully points out, brown rats do exhibit something like learning, are able to transmit knowledge to each other and they are frequently used in experiments concerning human behavior. Even so, it should not be necessary to point out, they do not possess the cognitive capacity of humans, nor are their 'languages' able to express the same range of experiences and emotions as human languages. As such, one would expect human beings to deal with novel situations more 'competently' than rats and to find meetings with strangers (particularly if they are recognized as a like kind) less problematic (if such comparisons do not make too obvious the absurdity of using rats as proxies for humans). Indeed, assuming that language will not evaporate with government, men and women will have a pretty powerful alternative to violence; we can stop short of biting each other to register our disapproval or to resolve disputes.

Even if we were to accept Professor Hogarty on his terms and allow rats to stand in for humans, however, another problem with using Steiniger's experiment as a case of anarchy materializes. The anarchic situation it presents us with is entirely manufactured. We have already complained about Professor Hogarty's seeming assumption that anarchy can only be brought about by the chaotic collapse of weak governments. Our complaint hinted at the fact that it is not surprising that the sudden and dramatic collapse of a weak government might lead, indeed would lead, to a chaotic situation. But anarchy, even if initiated as Professor Hogarty imagines, is nothing like the violent dislocation that the rats endured in Steiniger's experiment. To be sure, it is not surprising at all that cornered and petrified rats behaved like cornered and petrified rats.

Additionally, it is unclear why the situation that the rats lived in prior to the experiment is not the one we should associate with anarchy. Before the experiments, the rats lived in extended family units called 'rat packs', their behavior unrestricted by any external force. These packs, it can be assumed, had or evolved some mechanism for regulating the behavior of its members as none of the violence that troubled the rat community in Steiniger's experiment (none of the 'desperate attempts [by rats] to flee' persecution (ibid.: 56)) seems to have plagued these pre-experiment communities (the violent behavior was out of the ordinary). Under anarchy, we might expect churches, clubs and other social organizations and families to evolve mechanisms (if they do not have them already) for regulating the behavior of their members.

B.   Children on a Deserted Island

Professor Hogarty's second case of anarchy suffers from many of the same flaws as his first one. For his second case, Hogarty employs Golding's *Lord of the Flies*.[3] In Golding's famous novel, according to Hogarty, 'we have an imaginary instance of anarchy involving boys aged (approximately) 6–12' (ibid.). The book, Professor Hogarty explains, 'incorporates (some of) our meager knowledge of human nature into a "test situation", namely, one of anarchy'. You might remember that Golding's tale tells the story of a group of boys who are marooned on an island without any adult supervision. Although their initial attempts at organizing themselves mimic the ordered society where they were from (they, for instance, elect a leader), within short order their society degenerates into chaos. By the end of the novel, one group of boys (the choir) had evolved into the dominant group and they controlled the island through brute force. Their island community was marred by violence, mayhem and even murder.

Perhaps we can forgive Professor Hogarty for confusing human beings with rats. After all, mainstream economics has for a long time now made a habit of modeling people as if they were rats. As Granovetter (1985) and others have argued, mainstream economists often model actors as automata, responding to changes in prices and circumstances like rats in a Skinner box respond to changes in the color of lights. But, although we can perhaps forgive Professor Hogarty for believing that human beings are like rats, we cannot so generously excuse him for confusing fictional children with adult human beings living in the real world. No one who has watched unsupervised kids in a playground would be surprised by Golding's saddening plot. Kids without adult supervision do not always play nicely with each other. It would be surprising, however, if adults even outside the watchful eye of police officers or some other agent of authority behaved in a similar way. Pickup basketball games without referees, tennis matches without umpires and conversations without mediators happen every day around the globe. Adults have simply learnt that it is more advantageous to play nicely with each other. It is unclear why individuals would forget these lessons in an anarchic situation. As stated earlier, several authors have demonstrated that the potential for repeated dealings is enough to keep us out of Hobbes's jungle.

It may also be argued that Golding's *Lord of the Flies* is not accurately read as a commentary on anarchy. It could just as easily be interpreted as a case of (the inevitability of) government tyranny. Remember, the first move that the boys made was to form a quasi-government; Ralph was elected their chief. This seat of leadership very quickly became a coveted position that was hotly contested. The *coup*, by the choirboys who served a quasi-military function (they were hunters), and their subsequent violent tenure is a familiar tale in North Vietnam, Nigeria, Cambodia, the Congo (Zaire) and elsewhere.

C. Andersonville

Andersonville, an overcrowded Confederate prisoner-of-war camp that operated during the Civil War, is Professor Hogarty's third and final case of anarchy.[4] Andersonville, at its peak, housed some 40 000 prisoners, who arrived in a continuous wave while the camp was operated. Rather than separating new from old inmates, the camp officials attempted to settle the new arrivals among prisoners who had been there longer (and so were already entrenched). As might be expected, it was quite common for new prisoners to be 'attacked *en masse*' by groups of raiders that had formed among the prisoners. These raiders would subject the new inmates to various kinds of abuse and would rob them of whatever possessions they had with them when they were admitted. This 'anarchy' persisted, Professor Hogarty points out, until a group of prisoners, called the Regulators, formed and overthrew the raiders (Hogarty, 1972: 61). According to Charierre (the Civil War historian cited by Professor Hogarty), 'Since the overthrow of the raiders the stockade was well-policed by Regulators ... Few civilian communities of comparable size could have boasted an equal passiveness and freedom from violent crime' (ibid.).

It is difficult to imagine that any serious proponent of anarchy as a form of social organization would accept that a prison, where government touches virtually every aspect of any individual's life, mimics an anarchic situation in any way. Indeed, there are important differences between what goes on in a prison and anarchy. The men with guns watching every move that the inmates make is one such difference that should be obvious to everyone. As Professor Hogarty himself points out, if the guards did not at least implicitly sanction the raids on new prisoners, they could not have taken place in broad daylight, as they did quite frequently.

Another important difference between a prison and an anarchic community is the incentive systems and opportunity set facing the people who live in either situation. In prison the opportunities for productive enterprise are severely limited; there's no agriculture, no manufacturing, no opportunities to amass wealth through any activity except smuggling, theft and other similarly piratical practices. The incentives facing prisoners thus differ significantly from the incentives facing free persons who have a far greater opportunity for positive sum transactions. In the absence of government, there is reason to believe that these opportunities would not evaporate but would rather increase. Remember, it is when government expands rather than contracts that opportunities for trade and production decrease.

Additionally, as with the *Lord of the Flies* example, it is also possible to offer an alternative interpretation of the case that Professor Hogarty presents. Why wouldn't you, for instance, associate the raiders with government and the Regulators with the private security agencies that would most certainly evolve under anarchy? Although the Regulators are not exactly what the proponents of anarchy had in mind when they talked about private security forces (they would for instance be worried about the quasi-monopoly on coercion that the Regulators established, though there were the guards), they have much more in common with private security forces than they do with governments (Hoppe, 1999). For one thing, they were voluntary; and second, they did not tax the people they protected.

CONCLUSIONS

Taken individually or as a group, these three cases of anarchy do little to convince us that anarchy is unworkable or undesirable. Indeed, only the word anarchy connects Professor Hogarty's conception of 'anarchy as rock 'n' roll' with the anarchic visions of Rothbard, the Tannehills and others. That anarchy is *ipso facto* chaotic, that in the absence of government our informal institutions all evaporate and that rats, fictional children and prisoners are adequate proxies for free adult human beings operating in an anarchic situation are all points on which Hogarty rests his argument. As we have seen, however, they have all proven to be problematic (even when we accept Hogarty on his own terms).

Even if Hogarty were to convince us that the cases he highlighted were in fact cases of anarchy, we would still have cause to discount the conclusions that he wishes to draw from them. As Hogarty himself concedes,

> Human behavior under anarchic conditions would vary by time and place, by historical experience, etc., etc. Stability in behavioral patterns is something to be determined, not assumed; moreover ... phenomena such as familiarity, social conventions, and commonality of goals will strongly influence individual and group behavior under anarchy. (Hogarty, 1972: 54)

Unfortunately, Hogarty seems unaware of how great a concession this is. It suggests that any case of anarchy degenerating into chaos should be taken with a grain of salt. Such cases, while proving that attempts at anarchy sometimes fail, that in the absence of government society might degenerate into chaos, necessarily stop well short of proving that anarchy is impossible. On the other hand, the cases of markets and regions operating outside the sphere of government control (often documented; see, for instance, Benson, 1990; Ellickson, 1991; Stringham, 2003) do speak to the possibility of an ordered society without government.

Read as an attack on anarchy, Hogarty's paper thus completely misses its mark. However, Hogarty does an excellent job of convincing us of the undesirability of lawlessness, not meaning here the absence of government enforced law but instead chaotic situations. Those anarchists who would wish for the violent overthrow of government to spur their anarchic visions may very well find several reasons in Hogarty's article to rethink those hopes. The straw man he seeks to tear down, however, is simply mislabeled. His target is not anarchy but something else.

NOTES

1. Like rock and roll, anarchy is often feared by those who do not understand it. It should be remembered, however, that what was noise only a half century ago has become the mainstream, the dominant form of music in this era.
2. With the obvious but unnoted exception that the brown rats were unnaturally separated from their packs.
3. One might immediately object that *Lord of the Flies* is a fictional tale and so its particular plot should not be given any weight over any of the millions of other plots that could be imagined. Indeed, Professor Hogarty would most likely offend the majority of cultural studies scholars who frequently use literature to make points about real-world circumstances by his using *Lord of the Flies* in the way that he does. That Golding's tale was such a wildly popular one cannot suggest that anarchy will lead to social destruction as Professor Hogarty might have us believe but only that people find tales of society degenerating into Hobbes's jungle interesting (if we are to be conservative in our claims) or believable (if we are to present the boldest claim possible). That people believe that civilization is fraily balanced on a foundation of government, however, neither affirms nor negates that claim. But let us ignore this objection for the time being.
4. Again, one objection can be voiced immediately. Indeed, it may be asserted that freedom to exit is an essential feature of anarcho-capitalism. As Hogarty points out about the Andersonville camp, however, 'escape, difficult at first, became virtually impossible with the establishment of a "deadline" twenty feet inside the stockade' (Hogarty, 1972: 58).

REFERENCES

Benson, Bruce (1990), *The Enterprise of Law*, San Francisco, CA: Pacific Research Institute for Public Policy.

Ellickson, Robert (1991), *Order without Law: How Neighbors Settle Disputes*, Boston, MA: Harvard University Press.

Granovetter, Mark (1985), 'Economic Action and Social Structure: The Problem of Embeddedness', *American Journal of Sociology*, **91**: 481–510.

Hogarty, Thomas F. (1972), 'Cases in Anarchy', in *Explorations in the Theory of Anarchy* ed. G. Tullock, Blacksburg, VA: Center for the Study of Public Choice.

Hoppe, Hans-Hermann (1999), 'The Private Production of Defense', *Journal of Libertarian Studies*, **14** (1): 27–52.

Reding, Andrew (1996), 'How the Mosh Pit Changed my View of Generation X', *Tucson Weekly*, 29 August, available at http://www.tucsonweekly.com/tw/08–29–96/mus.htm.

Stringham, Edward (2003), 'The Extralegal Development of Securities Trading in 17th-century Amsterdam', *Quarterly Review of Economics and Finance*, **43**: 321–44.

Tannehill, Linda and Morris Tannehill (1970), *The Market for Liberty*, San Francisco, CA: Fox & Wilkes.

12. Private property anarchism: an American variant*

Laurence Moss

Perhaps the most novel ingredient of the student protest movement both in this country and in Europe was the large number of 'New Left' radicals who adopted a more critical stance toward Marx and Lenin and embraced in their stead various anarchist heroes such as Proudhon, Kropotkin, and Bakunin. During the Paris uprisings of May 1968, C.L. Sulzberger of the *New York Times* reported that throughout Europe 'the real banner of unrest . . . is the black flag of anarchy and not the red flag of communism.'[1] That same year the noted authority on linguistics and unabashed critic of United States policies, Noam Chomsky, described the revival of anarchist theory and practice, among members of the New Left, as the 'most promising development of the past years' and expressed hope that this development would help choke off the impending 'American and world catastrophe.'[2] The rebirth of interest in anarchist thought furnished a steady market for soft-cover publishers who eagerly provided a long list of reprints of great nineteenth-century anarchist tracts. Whoever thought that Kropotkin's *Revolutionary Pamphlets* or Bakunin's *God and the State* would become something of campus best sellers;[3] yet in 1971 one prominent New York college was offering no less than three courses on anarchism and each was fairly well attended. Perhaps the most outstanding evidence of the new wave of interest in anarchist theory was the decision of the Southern Economic Association to devote an entire session to 'anarchism' at their November, 1972 meeting. I believe that I am correct in stating that this is the first time a major association of American economists has devoted an entire session to the 'economics of anarchy' and certainly this may be taken as evidence of the extent to which the anarchist revival has affected some of our own research interests.[4]

*   This paper was first published in *Further Explorations in the Theory of Anarchy*, edited by Gordon Tullock, The Public Choice Society Book and Monograph Series, University Publications, Blacksburg, VA, USA, 1974, pp. 1–31. It is an extended version of a paper read before the Southern Economic Association in Washington, DC, 11 November 1972. My thanks to Professor William Breit and Murray N. Rothbard for their comments and helpful criticisms. I, of course, accept full responsibility for the paper that follows.

When treating the development of anarchist thought in the West it is necessary to distinguish between two distinct strands of anti-state thought. The first, and by far the most popular among American and European intellectuals, involves a thorough-going attack on the institution of private property and the so-called ruthless market economy in which competition throws men against one another so as to sever the cords of an otherwise harmonious social order. Certainly the most outstanding, if not the earliest, proponent of this doctrine was Prince Kropotkin, who attempted to demonstrate how at all levels of nature and throughout the animal kingdom the force maintaining order in society and guaranteeing specie survival was 'mutual aid' and not competition. As a result of this analysis, Kropotkin opted for a stateless society organized around the abolition of private property and the institution of communistic methods of production.[5] This particular variant of anarchist thought was brought to America during the last quarter of the nineteenth century by figures like John Most, Emma Goldman, and Alexander Berkman and remains today the dominant strand of anarchist thinking among practitioners of the New Left.[6]

My principal concern in this paper is with the other and lesser known variant of anarchist thought which, because of its insistence on strengthening the institution of justly acquired property and allowing free rein to the alleged benevolent workings of a competitive market order, I shall call 'property anarchism.' The interesting thing about property anarchism is that it had its roots in America and flourished almost exclusively on this soil. The property anarchists are usually afforded no more than a footnote in histories of the subject and yet their 'school' was certainly one of the most interesting of all.[7] In the first section of my study I present an interpretative sketch of the economic doctrines of early property anarchist thought. Perhaps the most interesting aspect of their contribution was their attempt to reconcile individualism, private ownership of the means of production, competition, and the labor theory of value. In the second section I document the modern revival of property anarchism in the writings of Professor Murray N. Rothbard. While his reconciliation of property anarchism with the utility theory of value is not completely without precedent among his anarchist forebears, Rothbard's attempt to defend anarchist institutions within the context of modern welfare economics constitutes a thoroughly original addition to the development of property anarchist thought. After a summary review of Rothbard's contribution I shall critically examine his alleged proof that only anarchism can maximize social welfare. In the final section I offer some conjectural remarks about the probable impact of the property anarchist revival on the general development of economic science.

I

The beginning of an articulate private-property-anarchist tradition in the United States is marked by the appearance, in 1847, of Josiah Warren's *Equitable Commerce.*[8] Warren's treatise represents the first systematic attempt to provide an extended discussion of the principal institutions about which a stateless society must be organized if it is to produce an order consistent with 'equity' or social justice. Throughout the second half of the nineteenth century, the subsequent line of property anarchists hark back to Warren's treatise for both inspiration and doctrinal support.[9]

The work begins with a statement of what the author wishes to accomplish. Economic reform heads the list and Warren explains that the principal goal of an anarchist community must be that of securing the laborer his just reward.[10] In addition, the community must provide incentives for 'economy' in the production and use of wealth as well as the elimination of wasteful depressions resulting from fundamental imbalances in demand and supply. With economic reform will come the elimination of discord, war, and general insecurity that under present conditions results from uncertainty about life and property. All this without the sacrifice of the 'greatest amount of personal freedom'.[11] Such as list of lofty goals places *Equitable Commerce* squarely within the reformist literature of the ante-bellum period,[12] but unlike the general run of proposals for more state intervention in the economy Warren's proposals run in the opposite direction.

Warren's proposals, though few in number, were distilled and perfected out of almost twenty-five years of active participation in social reform experiments that were carried out on American soil. It will be instructive to review Warren's main principles of social organization in light of his own personal experience with social reform. First and foremost, Warren believed it necessary that the social community preserve individual sovereignty and not try to submerge the individual within a communistic structure. All transactions between individuals must be either completed at the moment they are performed or else the terms of future repayment must be specified at the time the transaction takes place. Warren continually harked back to his earliest experiences at New Harmony, Indiana, when as a young man of twenty-seven he joined Robert Owen's experimental community.[13] There Warren witnessed Owenite communism in practice which (according to his description) amounted to nothing more than a trying preoccupation with the pretty details of organization and a continual feud over the proper delineation of responsibility. Jones might perform a service for Smith and Smith would thank him promising to return the favor someday. This open-ended transaction, where the terms and time of future repayment were left unspecified, was destined to end in feud and strife. Warren linked all of the major difficulties of the Owenite

community to its common property scheme which obstructed the proper delegation of responsibility and obligation among its individual members.[14] Out of
these experiences Warren learned the importance of private ownership and the
delineation of individual responsibility as the basis for social organization.

Warren's second organizational principle concerned the reformation of the
basic act of economic exchange. The problem of securing for an individual the
full product of his labor could be accomplished if and only if commodities and
services were exchanged equally on a labor for labor basis. Each member of
the community was entitled to the full value of his labor and no more, for to
receive in excess of that amount meant that someone else in the community
was necessarily receiving less. Inasmuch as the source of all property was
labor, an individual could claim absolute sovereignty over only that portion of
social output that could be imputed directly to his own labor.

According to Warren, under contemporary conditions producers try to
extract from the consumer his maximum price regardless of what the
commodity originally cost to produce in terms of labor. This was the source of
the various non-labor incomes such as interest and profit. Cost only furnishes
the lower limit of market price but not its upper limit and herein lies the basic
source of economic injustice and impoverishment in modern society. If the
very act of economic exchange could be reformed so that cost and not utility
is the basis of price, Warren maintained then the most serious source of social
discord would be purged from society once and for all. Warren's goal was to
seek an institutional method by which labor cost would become both the upper
and lower limit of price and hence the determinant of price. This would guarantee an 'exchange of equivalents' between market participants and at the
same time insure the proper distribution of property among its rightful owners.
Thus, 'cost the basis of price' became Warren's second great organizational
principle.[15]

No sooner had Warren quit the Owenite community than he moved to
Cincinnati and inaugurated one of the most interesting social experiments ever
begun by a single individual. With only $300 of capital and in the midst of this
major Midwestern metropolis, Warren began a 'Time Store' to prove that his
cost principle was a viable tool of social reform. Warren purchased a variety
of urgently needed goods to fill the store and posted their invoices in the
window for all to see. To these wholesale prices he added 7 percent to cover
the 'contingent expenses' of shipping and overhead but no profits were added
to this basic price. A customer paid this price for the commodities purchased
entirely in cash but then paid Warren for his time according to an entirely
different principle. When a customer entered Warren's store, Warren would
begin clocking the time it took the customer to complete his business.
Regardless of the size of the order, Warren would demand for his own
compensation only an equivalent amount of time in the buyer's own labor. The

customer would sign over an IOU promising to pay Warren, on demand, an equivalent amount of time in his own labor. Thus, if the customer was a house painter and the transaction took ten minutes of Warren's time to complete, the customer would promise to supply ten minutes of his time as a painter. Warren collected these various labor notes (much as the modern customer collects 'green stamps') and redeemed them periodically for the labor services of his customers. The Cincinnati Time Store stayed in business from 1827 to 1830, when Warren, pleased with having demonstrated the viability of the cost principle, liquidated the operation.[16]

It was out of his experiences with the Cincinnati store that Warren developed the last of his great organizational principles: currency reform. In order to bring about 'equity' in trade it was necessary that the social community adopt an 'equitable money' in the form of labor certificates.[17] Such a money would have two radically new dimensions: first, it would make labor the new unit of account rather than gold or silver; and second, it would do away with the need for banks and bankers who by printing bank notes acquire an unjust claim on the labor of others while they themselves labor little, if at all. Every worker would be free to issue his own currency backed 100 percent by his own labor. Any scramble to liquidate labor notes would only lead to an increase in employment and greater social output. The problem of how to get individuals to accept each other's notes was academic at the very least.[18] Within the small anarchist community based on individualist principles, such as Warren was subsequently to develop, a signature on the bottom would be enough to guarantee the authenticity of the bargain. Unlike the communistic schemes where most transactions were left open-ended, the issuance of the labor note would serve to complete the transaction in the sense that the terms of future payment were agreed upon at the moment the transaction took place.

Throughout Warren's career, his labor note scheme underwent modification so as to better achieve his equitist ideals.[19] There can be no doubt that when Warren spoke of an equal exchange of labor he meant by this an equal exchange of the real pain cost expended in the production of the commodities traded. As early as the first edition of *Equitable Commerce*, Warren called for greater payment to those occupations beset with the greatest psychological repugnance.[20] The fact that the labor requiring the greatest intensity of effort was, in fact, most poorly paid struck Warren as a serious injustice of the present economic order. However, Warren also contended that when calculating the intensity of labor it was perfectly proper to make an allowance for previous training.[21] How then was one to establish an equation between an hour of a doctor's labor and an hour of a maid's labor if 'intensities of effort' and 'training cost' differ so radically? Certainly not by comparing relative wages in the outside labor market, because these prices reflect the perversion of making utility the limit of price rather than cost. Warren's solution was simply to allow each member of the community to decide the value of his own labor note: eventually, he argued, common consent would establish a set of viable norms.[22] To aid the participants in their calculations, Warren urged that a sort of bimetallic or, what is more exact, bi-commodity standard be developed. That is, each issuer of a labor note would promise to redeem his note with either his own labor or in so many bushels of Indian Corn. His reason for selecting Indian Corn was that its labor content was reasonably stable and the intensity of effort needed to produce it was known to all.[23] Thus each individual need merely set up an equation between his labor time and so many bushels of corn. If there were n types of labor in the economy then, under ideal circumstances, only $n - 1$ labor exchange ratios were needed for the maintenance of trade. The Indian Corn option also gave each issuer of labor notes an additional payment option should the issuer of the note be unwilling or unable to work for the bearer of the note 'on demand'. Warren insisted that within the context of an established anarchist community, public opinion would come to regulate the absolute accuracy of the labor hour for each type of labor.

Those who are skeptical about the possibility of such an economic system surviving its first week of operation need only be informed that Warren's labor note scheme actually operated to good effect at several experimental communities that he helped organize in the ante-bellum period. At an ex-Fourite community in Ohio, which Warren reformed along individualist lines,[24] corn was accepted as the medium of exchange and labor the unit of account. Despite the fact that the population of the community totaled in the thousands, the price of wheat oscillated around 6 hours to the bushel, the price of milk 10 minutes to the quart, and the price of boots averaged 18 hours to the pair. Furthermore, the range of variation was never more than 33 percent from these par values. Warren attributed the stability of the system to 'community sprit' which no doubt did contribute to the survival of both the Ohio community and a later Long Island anarchist community that Warren began in 1851.[25] But other mechanisms were at work besides 'Community Spirit,' as can be discerned from a careful reading of Warren's texts.

Clearly individuals competed for occupations much as they did in the outside world. If two shoemakers each opted for the consumer's patronage, the one offering shoes at the smallest labor cost would get all the business while the other would have to find another profession. Apparently these communities were small enough to only require the service of a few shoemakers, otherwise the possibility of the higher-cost producers setting the price while the lower-cost producers reap differential rent would no doubt have presented difficulties for his cost–price philosophy. As far as entering professions was concerned, producers competed in such a way that the one who was willing and able to sell at the lowest labor cost got the job. It is not clear that the services that required the greatest intensity of effort received the greatest or even moderately great rewards. Certainly there was no central authority to prevent a chimney-sweep from 'undervaluing' his services to gain employment. However, Warren did believe that by refusing to enforce the state-created apprentice laws in his communities, the mobility of labor between professions would be heightened.[26] Thus the possibility of a monopoly gain entering into labor's return would be lessened and with an increase in competition between labor groups, Warren believed that a structure of relative wage rates would emerge proportional to the relative pain costs involved in performing the labor.

In Warren's view the transition from statism to anarchism required withdrawing to small private communities and reforming the entire institution of economic exchange. As a precondition for joining, each member had to agree to the cost principle and adopt the labor note conception of equitable money. For Warren the stability of anarchist institutions depended on a fundamental change in methods of economic calculation from gold to labor units as well as a personal commitment to equitist ideals.[27] In the last of his writings, *Practical Applications*, Warren explained that two of his organizational principles – individual sovereignty and cost the limit of price – have their foundations in natural law, but the great organizational principle of 'equitable money' is purely a human contrivance developed so as to allow the natural law to operate unimpeded.[28] Thus, what is required for the construction and maintenance of property anarchism is a conscious effort on the part of its members to adopt Warren's philosophy and conform to its teachings.

The subsequent stream of private property anarchist literature was to remain true to Warren's ideals for over half a century. Individual sovereignty and the labor theory of value were to remain basic to its teachings. However, on the means to be employed a rather dramatic shift in emphasis took place. Where in Warren's philosophy the realization of anarchism was not automatic but rather depended on the community adopting the labor-cost–money mechanism, the subsequent stream of anarchist writers tended to argue that the transition to the equitist ideals could be achieved by way of the self-regulating mechanisms of the market. What had prevented the ideal from being realized was the state itself which by virtue of its coercive methods had managed to interfere with these automatic market mechanisms. The particular form of intervention consisted of monopolies which had violently managed to extract massive portions of the laborer's product leaving him in a state of virtual misery. Thus the solution to the social problem of securing the laborer his just reward involved not running away into small enclaves of anarchism but, rather, an active effort to repeal monopoly privilege and restore the natural conditions under which men could prosper.

Like Warren, this younger generation of property anarchists believed that man's right to ownership derived from his having combined his labor with nature in some fundamental way. Their essential contribution was to give this doctrine a radical bent, thereby avoiding the temptation of becoming apologists for the existing distribution of property titles. Unlike Locke, who had accepted the labor theory of property in his state of nature analysis but was unprepared to engage in a fundamental critique of then existing property relations on the basis of that theory, the property anarchists departed from Lockean conservatism in their attack on the legitimacy of state-created land titles.

Joshua King Ingalls is responsible for formulating the anarchist position on state-granted land titles. In his pamphlet, *Land and Labor*,[29] Ingalls argued that the productive powers of the soil were indestructible and did not owe to any man's individual efforts. Therefore, no man had a legitimate right to establish his perpetual dominion over what in actuality belonged to men in common. The only claim an individual had to fencing off a portion of land for his own was that he occupied the land and made use of it in the satisfaction of his individual needs. Upon his death or departure the individual's tenure ends and the next occupant, who employs the land productively while living on it, acquires a similar but temporary right to exclude others from the land. At all times the right of exclusion is temporary and not absolute. According to Ingalls, the present system of absolute land titles has permitted absentee landlords to acquire the land and speculate wildly about how much rent they can extract from the landless small farmers. In Ingalls' view, this was a violation of the labor theory of property. Thus the levying of rents above any legitimate charge for labor expended on improvements was not founded in natural law but resulted from the monopoly land system artificially imposed on the market by the state itself.[30] As a result of Ingalls' pamphleteering the chant of 'occupancy and use' became the rally cry of land reformers of anarchist persuasion in the post-Civil War period.[31]

With the landed monopoly destroyed and rental income driven to zero, there was only one thing left to prevent the working class from receiving the entire national income in the form of wages. That was the inclusion of profit and interest in the cost of producing commodities. Ezra Heywood stands out as one of the most prolific if not the earliest of the property anarchists to present the theoretical argument against the necessity of interest in a competitive market economy. In his pamphlet, *Yours or Mine* (1875), Heywood cites a host of economic writers to document the tendency for property (and capital) to deteriorate over time.[32] Hence, if a borrower of a shovel returns it to the owner in its original form, the lender should compensate the borrower rather than the other way around. In short, Heywood argued that in a competitive economy (or under natural conditions) the rate of interest would be negative or even zero but never positive.[33]

What then explained the fact that the market rate of interest was significantly greater than zero, enabling the owners of money to extract part of the workers' product? Simply the fact that by declaring certain types of money 'legal tender' and by limiting the number of banks of issue, the state had made money and credit artificially scarce and hence able to command a price in the market. Thus the source of a positive rate of interest was simply the absence of competition in banking. Heywood scolded the economics profession for expecting the benevolent effects of free competition to prevail under present conditions. He described this as absurd as 'expect[ing] free labor inside the old slave system.'[34]

The property anarchists were indebted to William Batchelder Greene for the actual details of their currency reform program. Greene first published his currency reform scheme in a series of newspaper articles in 1849. They were reprinted several times during his lifetime under the title *Mutual Banking*, and this small pamphlet ranked second to Warren's *Equitable Commerce* on the property anarchist's list of recommended readings.[35]

According to Greene, the natural function of banks in a market economy was simply that of financial intermediary between deficit and surplus spending units (usually households). This most fundamental of all banking transactions was mutually advantageous to both parties and hence the mutuality of the banking process. In addition, banks could also serve individuals by converting their real assets into more liquid forms. They could do this by issuing their own bank notes against secure physical assets (i.e., property or inventories).[36]

These natural banking functions have been perverted by the state which, by designating only certain types of notes to be 'legal tender' and refusing to permit its courts to settle debts in other types of money, has created an artificial scarcity of money and credit in the market. The workers must pay exorbitant amounts for credit, prohibiting their entry into business and forcing them to sell their labor at a disadvantage. Those who receive part of the worker's wages in the form of profit and interest are the beneficiaries of these state-created banking monopolies. They are the present holders of gold and silver who are able to secure charters allowing them to print greater nominal amounts of paper than the market value of the specie they hold. Thus, the enthronement of gold has operated to prevent the interest rate from falling to zero. Greene went on to declare the money monopoly the cause of business depression, declaring that there was no such thing as overproduction – only a shortage of money demand.[37]

Greene's scheme of currency reform involved the widespread adoption of 'mutual banks' where anyone could get notes by mortgaging real property. Banks would be allowed to issue notes whose nominal value did not exceed one-half the market value of the property secured. Only members of the bank would be entitled to loans and the condition of membership was that they accept the notes of the bank at par when engaging in trade with other individuals. In this way the supply of money and credit would expand to meet the needs of trade. It would be adequate to allow property owners to raise the capital with which they could start their own businesses and no longer have to sell their labor at a discount in the market.[38] Unlike Warren's scheme for currency reform, mutual money did not require the adoption of a new unit of account. Economic calculation could still be in 'gold dollars' but it would be the paper notes of mutual banks that would circulate. Apparently, the Civil War experience with Greenback money convinced the property anarchists of the viability of their scheme.[39]

Throughout the property anarchist literature there was wide acceptance of Greene's scheme. At face value it is another instance of the 'real bills' doctrine – the view that it is possible to have a 'self-liquidating' form of paper money that is not itself completely backed by the commodity-money it represents. The general criticism of all these schemes is that while the physical property backing the paper is fixed in amount its market value is not, and hence the system is never absolutely secure from a banking panic. Greene no doubt foresaw this possibility in that he required the banks to issue paper only up to one-half of the market value of the property pledged.[40]

The most serious omission of their analysis was their failure to realize that the demand for credit (i.e., loanable funds) is never completely inelastic but generally expands with a decline in the rate of interest. Should the supply of equitable money increase relative to that of gold and other commodities, market prices would begin to rise and mutual money would become 'depreciated.' As people began accepting mutual money at a discount, thereby breaking their promise with the mutual banks to accept the notes at par, it is not clear what recourse the banks would have. Should they 'punish' the discounters by calling in their loans, then a general liquidity panic would result. If however the individual citizens kept their promise to accept the notes at par, then (unless cash balances are significantly reduced) vast shortages of commodities would mount in various markets requiring non-price methods of rationing. The general weakness of their scheme stemmed from the fact that they were seeking to define mutual money in terms of at least two commodities: the physical property backing it and gold specie. This amounts to trying to regulate the market price between gold and other types of property and hence the mutual banking scheme is open to all the difficulties of a general price control policy.[41]

In order to propagate their scheme for currency reform among the workers, Heywood and Greene joined the New England Labor Reform League in 1869. Quickly they steered the association away from trade union activity which they considered to be largely ineffectual in permanently ameliorating the condition of the working class. Instead, Heywood and Greene wrote a declaration of the League's purposes and called for 'free contracts, free money, free markets, free transit, [and] free land'. For the next twenty-five years, the League remained under the sway of property anarchist doctrine.[42]

In 1872 a young radical and former MIT student, eighteen years of age, met the illustrious Josiah Warren and William B. Greene at the New England Labor Reform League's headquarters in Massachusetts. In three years' time, Benjamin R. Tucker was launched on his anarchist career. If Warren was the 'Thomas Paine' of anarchism, as he was called by one anarchist writer,[43] then Tucker was anarchism's Thomas Jefferson. Taking over Warren's theory of equitable exchange (exchange in accordance with labor cost), Ingalls' 'occupancy and use' theory of land titles, Heywood's attack on interest and the productivity of capital, and Greene's mutual banking scheme, Tucker fused these doctrines into one of the most formidable theoretical systems of the nineteenth century. Space does not permit a complete discussion of his contribution but several facets of his career deserve special comment.

By way of his erudite journal of anarchist thought, *Liberty*, Tucker provided a sophisticated forum for debate in which radicals of all persuasions were invited to take part.[44] Readers would send in letters and challenge Tucker's doctrines. Tucker would print their letters alongside his reply.[45] Despite numerous attempts, few could weaken his faith in the ability of competitive markets, operating within the context of mutual banking and limited land tenure, to achieve the equitist ideal of 'labor for labor' exchange. Tucker constantly prided himself and his followers on being the only unterrified free traders – unterrified to go beyond the half-way house of the Manchester liberals and advocate the elimination of all monopoly including the entire state apparatus. Whereas Warren sought to achieve the equitist ideal by forming little communities and developing new habits of trade, all the time ignoring the nation state and hoping it would go away, Tucker advocated *national* reform consisting of the elimination of all monopoly privilege and thereby unleashing the benevolent forces of market competition.

From the inauguration of *Liberty*, Tucker tried to form a coalition among the anarchists of both the communist and private property varieties in their common struggle against state socialism.[46] Tucker correctly declared Marx their mutual enemy, though he admitted that both Marx and the anarchists have their intellectual roots in the 'surplus value' doctrines of the classical economists. Whereas Marx would retain the state and subordinate the individual, Tucker would retain the individual and subordinate the state. Unfortunately, the promised coalition between the communist and property anarchists was never realized. John Most debated several of the issues, separating the two breeds of anarchists, and insisted that the abolition of private property was the only true road to reform, but whatever dialogue did take place was soon ended during the turbulent last decades of the nineteenth century. With Haymarket and the wave of anarchist-inspired assassinations of heads of state, Tucker found himself condemning the actions of the communist anarchists while at the same time condemning the brutal treatment of these anarchist-suspects in the hands of the police. Tucker's efforts to distinguish the tactics of his group from the violent efforts of the others were in vain and the word 'anarchy' took on the sinister meaning of 'disorder' or 'chaos' – the very opposite of what it has always meant to its devoted proponents. This, and the emergence of the large corporation as the dominant form of American economic life, no doubt contributed to Tucker's pessimism about the possibility of establishing a viable anarchist system. In 1908 he disbanded his journal and thereafter emigrated to France where he lived out his last years a sad recluse.[47]

With the onset of World War I, the Warren–Tucker school of property anarchism had passed out of existence.[48] It was not until the middle of the 20th century that something of a revival of interest in property anarchism began to take place. I shall discuss the intellectual foundations of this development in the next section below.

II

No discussion of property anarchism is complete unless it includes some mention of the most colorful of all the nineteenth-century anarchists, Lysander Spooner.[49] Born in Massachusetts and trained as a lawyer, Spooner discovered that state law required a two-year apprenticeship before he could practice law. He fought that law in the courts and won its repeal.[50] Thus began his illustrious career in social reform.

During the 1830s, Spooner joined up with the free-thought movement against religious orthodoxy and authored one of the more famous pamphlets of that campaign, *The Deist's Reply to the Alleged Supernatural Evidences of Christianity*.[51] His attack against illegitimate authority did not stop with the Church; next in line was the United States Constitution. Employing the very philosophy that inspired the Declaration of Independence and the American Revolution itself, Spooner in later years proved that the Constitution was an invalid contract and one in which a minority of special interests had managed to wrest power from the hands of the great majority. The pamphlet in which these views are expressed, *No Treason*,[52] remains one of the great polemics of the nineteenth-century radical movement.

The 1840s found Spooner in direct confrontation with the Federal government. Apparently Spooner had opened the American Letter Mail Company and was defiantly delivering mail between Boston and New York and later between Philadelphia and Baltimore in less time and at a cheaper price than the Federal Post Office.[53] Spooner argued that while the Constitution permits the Federal government to run a Post Office, it does not prohibit anyone from competing. After several months of court battle, Spooner ran out of personal funds and lost his fight. To his delight he had demonstrated the wastefulness of state action and became convinced that the market could accomplish any activity presently monopolized by the state more effectively and without coercion. The state, according to Spooner in a memorable passage, is far more evil than a highwayman who steals your money, beats you up, and runs away abandoning you on the road. The state beats you up, steals your property, and follows you down the road of life robbing you at every turn.[54]

Spooner's life and thought parallel that of the later group of property anarchists. Several years before Greene put forth his mutual banking scheme, Spooner had offered a similar analysis of poverty in America.[55] He affirmed man's natural right to monetize real property and advocated 'free banking.' The state, by enthroning gold and silver and prohibiting the issuance of other types of money against other types of durable property, had altered the distribution of income in society away from the workers and into the hands of a few large banking monopolists. By preventing the rest of society from obtaining credit, except at high rates of interest, the state was the source of instability in the market. Spooner went on to derive a 'law of prices' which demonstrated how, as trade becomes more diversified and as population grows, ever-increasing quantities of money are needed to finance trade. Unless banking is open to all, depression and despair will be the inevitable result.[56]

Where Spooner departs from the general line of thinking of the Warren–Tucker school is on the question of what constitutes an 'equitable exchange.' Towards the end of his life, Spooner came to reject the labor theory of value and the view that an exchange of equivalents was one in which equal quantities of 'pain cost' are transferred between buyer and seller. In a pamphlet published in 1879 entitled *Universal Wealth Shown to be Easily Attainable*,[57] Spooner attempted to reconcile the labor theory of property with the 'utility' or demand theory of market value. According to Spooner, each man had a natural right to the products of his labor but the amount of someone else's labor that his labor could command in exchange was in no way dependent on the intensity of one's own labor.[58] The value of the individual's labor depends on the value of what that labor produces. And the value of a laborer's product is decided in the market by the 'power and disposition of men to buy it, and give ... something *equally* desirable in exchange for it.'[59] Thus what was equilibrated in exchange was the utility gain of each trader.

Having embraced both the utility theory of value and the productivity theory of wages, Spooner explained that the source of all wealth could not be imputed to labor or brute effort alone. The source of the entire national product was labor *working with inventions*. Because of the importance of invention in ameliorating the condition of the populace, brain labor must be rewarded no less than hand labor. Spooner called for universal recognition of the right of all inventors to perpetual ownership in their inventions, and 'free money' so that inventors would have the means by which to put their inventions into practice.[60]

Spooner's attempt to combine the labor theory of property and the utility theory of value within the definition of 'equitable exchange' makes his writings something of a half-way house between the labor–cost anarchism of Warren and his successors and the present-day utility school of property anarchism headed by Professor Murray N. Rothbard. It is for this reason that I have included Spooner in this section rather than among his contemporaries. The existence of Spooner's *Universal Wealth* allows us to treat Rothbard's contribution as a direct continuation of the property anarchist tradition in the United States.

III

Any attempt to evaluate Rothbard's entire contribution to radical thought would require a thorough study many times the size of this present paper.[61] There is hardly an area of modern thought to which Rothbard has not contributed at least one scholarly paper and in certain areas, like economics and history, his contributions fill several volumes.[62] What is perhaps the most interesting aspect of Rothbard's work is how all of his various writings, written over a period of more than twenty years, fit together like prefabricated blocks upholding his lifelong belief in both the feasibility and ethical desirability of a stateless society.

Like his nineteenth-century forebears, Rothbard insists that there exists a body of law that takes precedence over state-created law and that each man is capable of acquiring absolute knowledge about what types of social action are 'good' and what types of social action are 'bad.' Each man has an absolute right to do his life and the extension of his life in the form of property. Social actions are of two types: (1) those that initiate violence against others, called 'coercive acts,' and (2) those that do not violate the natural rights of others called 'voluntary acts.'[63] The object of the common law is to decide in cases of interpersonal conflict whether the social action taken has or has not violated someone's natural rights and in the case where violations have taken place, the common law must decide which individuals are responsible for the action and what type of punishment is required. A society that employs the common law for this purpose we shall define as a society acting in accordance with 'the fundamental Libertarian Code.'[64]

In order for the anarchist community to function it is necessary that the bulk of its members adopt the fundamental Libertarian Code. There is a definite parallel here between Warrenite and Rothbardian anarchism in that both see the transition to an 'equitable society' as being dependent on a commitment by its members to abandon their old ways of thinking and adopt new ways. For Warren this involved adopting the labor note as the basic medium of exchange and a decision to carry out economic calculation in terms of labor units. For Rothbard the commitment involves the adoption of the fundamental Libertarian Code forbidding men from initiating force or coercion in their ordinary dealings with other men.[65]

Like his anarchist forebears, Rothbard employs the labor theory when deciding the primary distribution of income in an anarchist community. According to Rothbard, all legitimate titles of ownership descend from some individual having first mixed his labor with unowned resources. Subsequent property owners acquire their absolute right to property from the first owner by way of either exchange or inheritance (i.e., gift).[66]

Following Ingalls and the subsequent group of Tuckerite anarchists, Rothbard does not use the Lockean doctrine of 'labor-mixing' as a quick method for justifying the present state-effected distribution of property titles in modern society. Rothbard is quite willing to admit the need for radical real-locations of property titles in cases where surviving relatives of original owners can prove that the present 'owners' acquired their titles either directly or indirectly from illegitimate owners or by illegitimate means. In the case of land ownership, Rothbard is quite sympathetic to the call for radical redistrib-ution in favor of such groups as Ireland's Catholic farmers, Israel's homeless Arabs, Latin America's peasant tenant-farmers, etc.[67] Thus the labor principle of property titles will play an important part in the assignment of property titles in the anarchist community. Once property titles are 'justly' distributed, owners are free to charge rents, or sell them to others. Thus, unlike Ingalls and the Tuckerite group, Rothbard considers landlord–tenant contracts to be in line with the fundamental Libertarian Code.

Rothbard also parts company with the Warren–Tucker school of property anarchism on the question of what constitutes an 'equitable' or 'just' exchange. Like Spooner, Rothbard rejects the labor theory of value both as an explanation of relative prices and as a basis for defining what constitutes a 'just exchange.' However, whereas Spooner continued to search for a defini-tion of 'equivalency in exchange' and believed that he had found it in the util-ity gained by the two trading partners, Rothbard declares that all voluntary exchange has its basis in the exchange of unequals.[68] Herein lies the inherent power of the market to allow two or more individuals to gain without harming someone else. In the market individuals trade whenever they expect to gain something worth more to them than what they give up.

The possibility that two trading parties may both gain while causing some third party to suffer a utility loss makes it difficult for the majority of welfare economists to say that social welfare is always (or even most of the time) increased as a result of voluntary exchange. However, Rothbard clarifies the problem somewhat by insisting that when two individuals of 'good will' engage in an act of trade and inadvertently injure a third party either by, say, polluting his lungs or soiling his clothes, then the act of exchange is not voluntary and must be brought before the Libertarian Code.[69] The case of the third party who suffers no physical injury to his person or property yet develops a bad case of 'envy' upon seeing the two trading parties gain while he ends up further down the saggy part of the Lorenz Curve does present some difficulty to Rothbard's analysis. After all, can it still be said that voluntary exchange has enhanced *social* welfare? The exchange is clearly 'voluntary' and the third party can bribe, plead, and beg the other two to stop but he cannot legitimately invoke the Libertarian common law to make them stop because their actions are entirely non-coercive. Despite the distress of the 'envious' man, Rothbard still insists that voluntary exchange enhances social welfare.[70] A society in which all social action is voluntary is, according to Rothbard, what is meant by the 'free market.'[71] A market economy operating under the fundamental Libertarian Code will approximate this ideal better than any other social arrangement designed by man.

Like Tucker and his associates, Rothbard finds much about the market economy to commend on strictly moral grounds. However, not only is the market a 'moral' social arrangement; it is also an 'economically efficient' social arrangement. For the Tuckerites the unhampered market would harness the 'profit motive' and ride it toward the achievement of several important social goals. It would smash the state-created monopoly banking and lead to an increase in the quantity of money, driving the interest rate down and securing the laborer the full value of his product. Rothbard's analysis of the workings of the 'free market' is contained in his two-volume treatise *Man, Economy, and State* and, like the Tuckerites, Rothbard describes how it operates to the betterment of its members. Building on the theoretical foundations of Eugen von Bohm-Bawerk, Ludwig von Mises, Frank A. Fetter and other theorists of the marginal utility persuasion, Rothbard describes how 'entrepreneurs' operate in the market to continuously reallocate resources in order to secure the largest profits. This introduces a tendency for property to be valued according to its effectiveness in satisfying the most urgent wants to the consumers.[72] More specifically, the value of property in the market will tend toward the discounted sum of its future rentals. The discount rate is the one set by the market and reflects the opportunity cost of trading a unit of present income for one in the future. This opportunity cost is subjectively determined by the 'time preferences' of the individuals making up the market.[73] Thus, unlike the group of nineteenth-century property anarchists, Rothbard does not consider the interest rate the result of an artificial restriction of credit brought about by a banking monopoly. The interest rate plays an extremely important role in deciding the proper allocation of resources between present and future production.

Whereas Heywood and the Tuckerite school considered any interest rate greater than zero 'excessive,' Rothbard finds the interest rate often too low. This is the cause of great instability in the market economy as businessmen invest too heavily in the production of future goods while consumers do not provide the requisite amount of real savings. This 'excessive' investment is often financed out of bank credit, one result of fractional reserve banking, and is the cause of depression in the free market. Here Rothbard develops the Austrian theory of business cycle along the lines originally suggested by Mises.[74] But while Mises recommended more stringent controls over banking so as to move toward 100 percent reserve banking, Rothbard takes up the traditional anarchist cause of 'free banking.'[75]

According to Rothbard, any group may open a commercial bank in the market so long as they do not renege on their contract with their customers to redeem their deposit and currency liabilities 'on demand.' Should one bank decide to supplement its income from service fees by holding only fractional reserves and making loans with its 'excess reserves,' other banks would inform the public about the insolvency of the first bank. Should a banking panic develop where customers run to convert their notes and checking accounts back into the form of commodity money and the bank be found insolvent, the bank officials would be charged with 'fraud' and punished according to the fundamental Libertarian Code. Thus, according to Rothbard, 'free banking' tends toward 100 percent reserve banking thereby permitting the major source of economic instability to be eliminated once and for all from the market economy.[76]

The basic money of the anarchist community would be decided in the market as it has been for thousands of years. Chances are gold would be most popular as a medium of exchange and private firms would produce and mint it rather than the state. In equilibrium, gold dollars would be produced and sold up to the point where the marginal cost of producing a gold dollar is 'one dollar.' A deflation would be short-lived as the producers of money find their profit margins widening, thereby being signaled by the market to increase the supply of money. Inflations would engender a slowing down in the rate of growth of the money supply as profit margins in gold mining fall. In this way, severe departures from domestic equilibrium would be unlikely. The resource cost of the whole operation is high (depending on the elasticity of supply in the money industry), but not as high as the welfare cost of state mismanagement of the money supply. The comparison, Rothbard explains, is not between commodity standards and paper standards but rather between disciplined commodity standards and mismanaged state standards – a comparison which makes Rothbard's suggestion credible if not outright appealing.[77]

Thus, like Warren, Tucker, Spooner, and the other property anarchists, Rothbard attaches a great deal of importance to currency reform. However, while Warren wanted to change the 'unit of account' and return to labor units, and Tucker and Spooner wanted to expand the liquidity base of the economy so as to bring down interest rates, Rothbard is the hardest of 'hard money,' men as evidenced by his advocacy of 100 percent reserve banking and a strict commodity standard.

The most basic insight of social science itself is that there are unintended consequences of human action that are both important and amenable to scientific investigation. Rothbard insists that in a free market the unintended consequences of human action ultimately tend to the betterment of the individual members of society. Rothbard denies that in the absence of minimum wage laws, state-created union shops, licensing, apprentice laws, etc., there is any tendency for large scale unemployment to occur as an unintended consequence of human action. Also, the unintended consequences of voluntary action do not lead to too large a discounting of future investment opportunities,[78] or necessarily give rise to mass conglomerations of corporate power,[79] or lead to 'persistent' balance of payments worries,[80] or a large concentration of property in the hands of a few.[81] He does not deny that these calamities do plague the modern world today, but the source of all the difficulty is government intervention in violation of the fundamental Libertarian Code. Of course individuals in the market often make mistakes and the unintended consequences of their actions do not turn out as planned; but the market is also the most efficient distributor of 'erasers' yet known to man and it operates without the obnoxious loss of minority rights that emerges from the intervention of the state. In the final pages of his economic investigation into the workings of the economy, Rothbard concludes that the free market 'creates a delicate and even awe-inspiring mechanism of harmony, adjustment, and precision in allocating productive resources, deciding upon prices, and gently but swiftly guiding the economic system toward the greatest possible satisfaction of the desires of all the consumers. In short, not only does the free market *directly* benefit all parties and leave them free and uncoerced; it also creates a mighty and efficient instrument of social order.'[82]

Throughout my brief survey of Rothbard's thought I have referred to the importance of social action in accordance with the 'fundamental Libertarian Code.' But who is to enforce this Code in a 'free market' economy? Who is to protect the peaceful against the intentional or unintentional encroachments of others?

According to Rothbard, the market is quite able to minimize coercion by providing its own courts and police protection services, much as it provides the services of doctors and lawyers today.[83] The consumers must first demand the enforcement of the Libertarian Code – that is, they must demand anarchism. The profit motive will then see to it that the most efficient providers of high quality arbitration rise to the top and that inefficient and graft-oriented police lose their jobs. In short, the market is capable of providing justice at the cheapest price. According to Rothbard, to claim that these services are 'public goods' and cannot be sold to individuals in varying amounts is to make a claim which actually has little basis in fact. Suppose the state was responsible for the provision of movies and had developed the practice of projecting them in the sky at night. To argue that the market could not provide movies profitably is to mistake the existing technology of movie showing for the *only* technology of movie showing. Public goods advocates would be on sounder grounds if they advocated one-world government provision of so-called public good services, but they do not. If the entire world is not the optimum movie area, not the optimum court service area, not the optimum defense area, then what is? Rothbard does not know, but he does place his faith in the ability of profit-seeking entrepreneurs to find out and implement the most efficient methods and techniques for the provision of these services.[84] What makes Rothbard's whole discussion far more prophetic today than it sounded in the 1950s and early 1960s is the recent and unmistaken tendency for self-administered housing communities to spring up alongside cities and provide their residents with many 'public goods' privately and more efficiently than they are presently provided by the state.[85] Much of the recent Rothbardian-inspired literature of the current anarchist movement is concerned with citing the evidence for decentralized provision of so-called government services.[86] This type of analysis is geared toward Libertarians of the Hayekian variety who favor the state only because it, in some sense, can minimize coercion over a given territorial area.[87] Obviously, if it can be shown by example that anarchist institutions could minimize coercion more efficiently than state arrangements, then many conservative-Libertarians should take up the cause of property anarchism. And to date, most of Rothbard's student following have been recruited from the ranks of the student Libertarian movement in the United States.[88]

But the majority of professional economists are not Classical Liberals or Libertarians, and hence would be much more sympathetic to property anarchism if anarchist institutions could be shown to maximize social welfare. Rothbard understands this well and has attempted to give property anarchism a new twist by attempting to prove that only a stateless society can maximize social welfare.[89] I believe that Rothbard has gone only part of the way toward 'proving' his case and furthermore I do not believe that Rothbard can ever complete his argument while operating within the confines of his natural law philosophy. If I am correct, then the property anarchist tradition is either destined to remain an offshoot of the general Libertarian movement or else we can expect a reformulation of the basic doctrine outside the confines of natural law ethics. Let me develop these remarks by first formulating what I understand to be the 'Rothbardian case' for property anarchism.

To begin with, I must emphasize that Rothbard rejects the possibility of constructing a social welfare function consistent with the preferences of the individual members of society. He calls attention to the difficulties inherent in aggregating individual utilities and the impossibility of finding a 'unit of welfare' in a world where interpersonal comparisons of utility are impossible. For this reason Rothbard opts for a definition of social welfare carried out in terms of the 'principle of unanimity.'[90] However unlike the Paretean school which succeeds in defining the conditions under which economists may objectively say that a social action has *increased* social welfare, Rothbard demonstrates more of a concern with the conditions under which a social action may be said to have *decreased* social welfare. I believe that without much qualification most Rothbardians would consent to the following proposition:

(1)   If a social action leaves at least one person 'worse off' then, regardless of its effects on others, social economic welfare has been decreased.[91]

To this we add a second proposition which literally follows from the meaning of the word 'coercion'; this proposition is:

(2)   All coercive actions leave at least one person worse off.

It follows strictly as a matter of deduction that:

(3)   All coercive acts decrease social economic welfare.[92]

Now the bulk of Rothbard's writings on political economy are designed to show the coercive effects of all state intervention in the market economy. In his most recent economic writing, *Power and Market*, Rothbard provides a definitional schema into which all conceivable forms of state intervention may be classified.[93] Virtually every form of known intervention is analyzed, from corporate profits taxes to price control, and in every case resources are shown to be diverted from their free market allocation, relative price relationships upset, and individuals forced to use their property in ways less satisfactory to their interests. Rothbard's overall conclusion is that all state action involves 'coercion' at one level or another.[94] Suppose we grant Rothbard his principal conclusion, namely:

(4)   All state action involves coercive acts.

Then from propositions (3) and (4) it follows that

(5)   All state action decreases social economic welfare.

Having arrived at this rather sensational conclusion, does it follow that anarchism will maximize social economic welfare? The Rothbardians evidently feel that it need only be demonstrated that anarchist institutions will be able to minimize coercion by voluntary court and police institutions in order to seal their case for anarchism.[95] However, if we grant them their argument – that the quantity and quality of coercive acts will be lower under anarchism – does it now follow that anarchism maximizes social economic welfare?

Again the answer is no. The reason for my criticism at this stage is that from proposition (3), i.e., all coercive acts decrease social economic welfare, it does not follow that *only* coercive acts decrease social economic welfare. It may be the case that the class of social–economic-welfare-lowering actions is not exhausted by the class of coercive acts. Perhaps there exists an additional number of welfare-lower acts that would begin to flourish under anarchist institutions that in no way result in injuries (or threats of injury) to life and property. I do not know what these 'other' acts might be but certainly Rothbard cannot be certain that they do not exist.

Pushing the argument one step further. It may happen that someday, after a reconsideration of man's nature, another natural law theorist like Rothbard will conclude that social actions which create 'envy' in other men are morally evil. Inasmuch as Rothbard does not claim to be omniscient, he must admit that in principle this is possible. In this case it may happen that rational individuals actually prefer to have a state to prohibit (or limit) these other social–economic-welfare-lowering acts if these other acts rank lower on their preference orderings than the types of coercive acts that inevitably result from having a state.[96] Under these conditions the state emerges as the maximizer of social–economic welfare in the important sense that social–economic welfare would be decreased even further in the absence of the state.

Thus, at best, Rothbardian anarchism can prove that state action always decreases social welfare but it fails to support the argument that anarchism necessarily maximizes social–economic welfare even when the fundamental Libertarian Code is diligently enforced. At best property anarchism in its present revitalized form will appeal to Libertarians who tend to identify the entire class of welfare-lowering actions with coercive actions. This in itself is quite an achievement and something to Rothbard's credit. But some radical overhaul of the natural law basis of property anarchism will be needed if it is to appeal to the wider audience of non-Libertarian intellectuals. I predict that the future development of property anarchism will proceed with a reformulation of its ethical basis but it is beyond the scope of this essay to suggest the direction in which this inquiry might proceed.

IV

Rothbard's defense of anarchist institutions within the context of modern economic thought has succeeded in revitalizing the property anarchist tradition in this country after a half century of virtual neglect. Rothbard takes on all of the great concerns of his nineteenth-century forebears: the defense of individual liberty justice in exchange, the pricing and allocation of resources, currency reform, property title reform, tariffs, patents, etc., and offers a fresh look at these problems through the lenses of his own curious blend of natural law theory and Austro-American economics. In an age when emotional response and intellectual scholarship are assumed to be antagonistic literary qualities, it is not surprising that Rothbard's powerful writings appeal to the youth not yet fully acculturated with professional ritualization. It is not unusual to see some of our top students at schools like Columbia and Chicago carrying copies of Milton Friedman's provisional price theory text under one arm, a copy of Rothbard's latest apodictic indictment of the state under the other, and wearing a sweatshirt with Lysander Spooner's bearded portrait painted on the front. The implications of this phenomenon are clear.

With the aid of the tools of modern analysis we may expect to find a return among the younger generation of economists to the once great questions of political philosophy. For example, the important philosophical problem of reconciling individual autonomy with the doctrine of political obligation may turn out to be an economic problem in disguise. We may also expect a fresh look at the problem of 'optimum currency areas'; it may turn out that in the absence of state-imposed uniform currencies and fixed exchange rates, sticky wages and prices may not be as serious an obstacle to full employment as they are now. The whole question of 'collective goods' and the 'free-rider' problem may be shown to be readily handled on the market by the 'lumping' of services and their sale in well-defined units (certainly, the economic conditions under which services will be sold in bundles has not yet been adequately explored). I could go on, but my point is simply to illustrate what types of problems will appeal to the anarchist mind when studying economics. I sincerely believe that the property anarchist revival can only prove of lasting worth to the development of economic science.

I have tried in the course of this study to trace the roots of property anarchism in the United States. It has a long and interesting history harking back to the ideals of the Declaration of Independence and the Jeffersonian passion for creating the institutional framework within which individual personalities may flourish. We must neither be upset nor surprised by the growing popularity of this peculiar variant of radical thought today – (to paraphrase the words of one American radical) property anarchism is as American as apple pie!

NOTES

1. C.L. Sulzberger, 'Foreign Affairs: the Red and the Black,' *New York Times* (15 May 1968), p. 46. See also articles appearing on front page of *N.Y. Times* mentioning the anarchists among the Sorbonne rioters, 4 May 1968 and 7 May 1968.
2. Noam Chomsky, *American Power and the New Mandarins* (New York: Vintage Books, 1968), p. 19.
3. There is hardly a major example of nineteenth-century anarchist writing that is not currently available in reprinted form. My references throughout this paper are to the latest available editions of the works cited. The citations on the two works mentioned in the text are: Peter Kropotkin, *Kropotkin's Revolutionary Pamphlets*, ed. Roger N. Baldwin (New York: Dover Press, 1970). [Originally pub. 1927] and Michael Bakunin, *God and the State*, intro. by Paul Avrich (New York: Dover Press, 1970). [Originally pub. 1916].
4. To the best of my knowledge the only professional economists to take note of anarchism as an independent intellectual tradition were Richard T. Ely and his protégé John R. Commons. As early as the 1880s the property anarchists were disturbed about Ely's failure to distinguish between communist and property anarchism. Apparently Ely considered all anarchists 'communists': see for example, Ely, *Outlines of Economics*, written in collaboration with Ralph H. Hess (New York: Macmillan, 1937), pp. 995–6. The anarchist reaction to Ely's confusion is discussed in James Martin, *Men Against the State: the Expositors of Individualist Anarchism in America, 1827–1908* (Colorado: Ralph Myles, 1970), p. 284. See also Sidney Fine, ed., 'The Ely-Labadie Letters,' *Michigan History*, vol. 36 (March 1952), pp. 1–32.
5. See Peter Kropotkin, *Mutual Aid: A Factor of Evolution* (New York: McClure Phillips and Co., 1902).
6. Eunice Minette Schuster, *Native American Anarchism: A Study of Left-Wing American Individualism* (New York: DeCapo Press, 1970), pp. 159–87. First published 1932 as vol. 27, no. 1–4, in *Smith College Studies in History*. For an example of recent 'New Left' anarchist thought, see Daniel Guerin, *Anarchism*, intro. by Noam Chomsky (New York: Monthly Review Press, 1970).
7. The pioneering study of nineteenth-century anarchist thought in America is Schuster, *Native American . . .* (see especially, pp. 40–159 for his discussion of property anarchism). The most comprehensive study of property anarchism in the nineteenth century is still James J. Martin, *Men Against the State*; this work was first published in 1953 and has recently been reissued in soft cover. A comprehensive bibliography with commentary on the anarchist literature can be found in Martin, *Men Against the State*, pp. iii–xiii, 279–88, and 294–309. Most of the standard histories of economic doctrine have little to say about anarchism and certainly less to say about the property anarchists, with the exception of Joseph Dorfman, *The Economic Mind in American Civilization*, in four volumes (New York: Augustus M. Kelley, 1966); see especially vol. 2, pp. 671–8, and vol. 3, pp. 36–41.
8. Josiah Warren, *Equitable Commerce: A New Development of Principles, for the Harmonious Adjustment and Regulation of the Pecuniary, Intellectual, and Moral Intercourse of Mankind, Proposed as Elements of New Society* (Indiana, New Harmony, 1846). Reprinted in 1852 by Fowler and Wells of New York and this 1852 edition has just been reprinted and made available by Burt Franklin of New York. This work was preceded by a small pamphlet *Manifesto*, pub. in 1841, reprinted by Oriole Press, New Jersey, 1952. Warren's later writings are *True Civilization an Immediate Necessity and the Last Ground of Hope for Mankind. Being the Results and Conclusions of Thirty-nine Year's Laborings Study and Experiments in Civilization and as it is, and in Different Enterprises for Reconstruction* (Boston, J. Warren, 1863), reprinted by Burt Franklin of New York, 1967, and *Practical Applications of the Elementary Principles of 'True Civilization' to the Minute Details of Everyday Life* (Princeton, Warren, 1873). The best survey of Warren's life and principles is Martin, *Men Against the State*, pp. 1–102.
9. See for example Clarence Lee Swartz, 'Josiah Warren, the First American Anarchist,' *Liberty* (book review) 1906. Benjamin R. Tucker called his journal of anarchist thought 'the

foremost organ of Josiah Warren's doctrines,' Martin, *Men Against the State*, p. 203. Warren
acquired only one intellectual disciple in the strict sense of the meaning of the word 'disciple' and that was Stephen Pearl Andrews. After Warren's death, in 1874, Stephen Pearl
Andrews published two monographs restating the philosophy of his mentor under the title
The Science of Society (Boston, S. Holmes, 1888). Andrew's work has recently been republished by M&S Press, Weston, Mass.
10. Warren, *Equitable Commerce*, p. 45.
11. Ibid.
12. See Dorfman, *The Economic Mind*, vol. 2, ch. xxiv.
13. See Martin, *Men Against the State*, pp. 1–25.
14. Warren, *Manifesto*, pp. 3–4 and *Equitable Commerce*, p. 90.
15. The search for 'equality' in exchange by making price equal to (labor) cost becomes via
     Warren's influence the dominant concern of the nineteenth-century property anarchists.
     Warren claimed that under the present system, where utility sets price, the result is wide fluc-
     tuations in price and periodic depressions; see for example, *Equitable Commerce*, p. 65. The
     search for a definition of justice in terms of 'equivalency in exchange' dates to Aristotle's
     Ethics and without a doubt the property anarchists (due to Warren's influence) must be
     considered part of the Aristotelian tradition in ethical theory. However, there is no evidence
     to indicate that Warren ever read Aristotle's writings. Inasmuch as the 'equivalency' is
     defined in terms of labor inputs, it seems more likely that Warren's thinking about this prob-
     lem was influenced by Owen himself. See the latter's 'Report to Lanark,' in *A New View of
     Society and Other Writings*, intro. by G.D.H. Cole (London: Everyman, 1949), pp. 262–3.
     Unlike the subsequent generation of property anarchists, Warren's writings offer no evidence
     that he was familiar with the thought of any of the classical economists other than Owen
     himself.
16. On the details of the Cincinnati Time Store, see Martin, *Men Against the State*, pp. 11–25.
     Warren's idea of a labor note currency might owe to Owen's discussion of a similar scheme;
     see the latter's 'Report to Lanark,' pp. 262–3.
17. In *Equitable Commerce* Warren explains, 'We want a circulating medium that is a *definite
     representative* of a definite quality of property and nothing but a representative,' p. 67. On
     Warren's subsequent Time Stores and the use of labor notes, see Martin, *Men Against the
     State*, ch. 2.
18. In *Equitable Commerce*, Warren explains that the labor note would be non-transferable. In
     subsequent writings he dropped this restriction, see *Equitable Commerce*, p. 6.
19. See Martin, *Men Against the State*, pp. 26–87.
20. See for example, *True Civilization*, p. 74.
21. Ibid., p. 77.
22. Warren did argue the need for the issuer to number his notes so that the receiver could
     protect himself against 'over issue', *True Civilization*, p. 97. During the operation of the
     second Time Store, Warren found himself the victim of some customers overvaluing their
     labor in terms of his and over-issuing notes against their limited supply of labor time. Warren
     played down these problems in his writings but we do have a first-hand account of these
     difficulties as reported by someone who was familiar with Warren and what had happened;
     see Martin, *Men Against the State*, p. 43n.
23. Warren proposed the idea of using corn as an alternative form of payment as early as 1847;
     see *Equitable Commerce*, p. 116. This might owe to Adam Smith's own suggestion to use
     'corn' as an invariable measure but there is no evidence to indicate that Warren was famil-
     iar with Smith's discussion.
24. In 1846 a Fourite Phalanx closed in Ohio and as a consequence of its joint-stock arrange-
     ment, the land fell back to the principal stock holders. Warren appeared on the scene and
     helped them begin reorganizing along property anarchist lines. By 1851, thousands were
     participating in what became a prosperous and moral community conducting exchange by
     way of labor notes.
25. This community was started on a stretch of land suddenly made accessible to New York City
     by the opening of the Long Island Railroad. The community of Modern Times (now called
     Brentwood, Long Island) was the crowning achievement of Warren's experimentation.

Begun in 1851, it survived the Panic of 1857 because its labor note was not tied to gold. Later the community also fared well through the yellow journalism of Horace Greely and others who accused the Modern Timers of using anarchism as a front for sexual perversions. The Civil War finally contributed to the break-down of Warrenite anarchism on Long Island. See Martin, *Men Against the State*, pp. 64–87.

26. While operating his first Time Store, Warren posted a bill board on which people could list the type of things they desired and the type of things they were willing to offer in exchange. Warren called this his 'report of demand' and hoped in this way to eliminate speculation about people's needs by providing a central information board. Apparently, the whole enterprise was a failure as Warren noted a preponderance of unwanted occupations. Furthermore, the labor returns of women and children were priced far below those of adult men. Warren was puzzled about why demand and supply when expressed in labor units failed so often to mesh. The answer had to do with the current apprentice system in America which kept the best men out of the ripest professions. No sooner did he liquidate his first Time Store than he was out setting up a training school in Spring Hill, Ohio, where he taught young children apprentice-type professions in but two weeks. Clearly, apprentice laws served no purpose but to keep labor out of certain privileged occupations; cf. ibid., pp. 35–8.

27. Warren, *True Civilization*, p. 18.

28. Warren, *Practical Applications*, p. 23.

29. Joshua King Ingalls, *Land and Labor* (Princeton, 1872 approx.). Ingalls authored at least eight pamphlets that were published during his lifetime, three of which are *Economic Equities: A Compend of the Natural Laws of Industrial Production and Exchange* (New York: Social Science Publ., 1887); *Henry George Examined. Should Land be Nationalized or Individualized* (Princeton, 1888); and *Social Wealth: the Sole Factors and Exact Ratios in its Acquirement and Apportionment* (New York: Social Science, 1885).

30. Ingalls writes, 'Possession means *possession*, and can never become property, in the sense of absolute dominion, except by positive statute. Labor can only claim occupancy . . .,' *Social Wealth*, p. 125.

31. Following Ingalls, the property anarchists attacked Henry George's *Progress and Poverty* from the moment it appeared in 1880. Ingalls pointed out that the rise in land value is not due to the progress of society, as George maintained, but, rather, to the state-created scarcity of land. Furthermore, George would create one huge landlord (the state) and this would mean absolute monopoly, making all farmers tenants of the state. Cf. *Henry George Examined*. See also Benjamin R. Tucker's criticisms in *Instead of a Book, by a Man Too Busy to Write One*: first pub. 1897 (New York: Haskell House, 1969), pp. 299–357.

32. Heywood cites J.S. Mill, Bentham, F. Bastiat, and Amasa Walker as having themselves admitted that capital and property tend naturally to depreciate. This allegedly proves that capital and property are not productive and hence that the productivity explanation of interest was in error. See Heywood, *Yours or Mine: An Essay to Show the True Basis of Property, and the Causes of its Inequitable Distribution* (Princeton: Mass. Cooperative, 1875), p. 9. Heywood's many published writings also include: *Free Trade: Showing that Medieval Barbarism, Cunningly Termed 'Protection to Home Industry,' Tariff Delusion, Invades Enterprise, Defrauds Labor, Plunders Trade and Postpones Industrial Emancipation* (Princeton: Mass. Cooperative, 1883): and *The Great Strike: its Relations to Labor, Property and Government. An Essay Defining the Relative Claims of Work and Wealth Involved in the Irresponsible Conflict Between Capital and Labor* (Boston: B.R. Trucker, 1888). Heywood achieved a great deal of notoriety for the active role he played in propagandizing the free-love movement; see Martin, *Men Against the State*, pp. 105–25.

33. Heywood also dismisses Senior's theory of abstinence in *Yours or Mine*, p. 7.

34. Ibid., pp. 19–20.

35. William Batchelder Greene was the financial authority of the property anarchist movement. Influenced by Edward Kellogg's scheme (1843) for expanding the money supply but reluctant to concede additional money-issuing powers to the state, Greene adopted a mutual banking plan much influenced by the schemes of his Continental friend Pierre Joseph Proudhon. Greene's banking scheme was first published in the *Worcester Palladium* (1849) under a

pseudonym, then later reprinted under the title *Equality* and finally under its present title *Mutual Banking*. The pamphlet is reprinted in *Proudhon's Solution of the Social Problem, including Commentary and Exposition by Charles A. Dana and William B. Greene*, edited by Henry Cohen (New York: Vanguard Press, 1927), pp. 173–225. A useful summary of his plan for currency and banking reform can be found in an article 'Communism versus Mutualism' published in *Socialistic, Mutualistic and Financial Fregments* (Boston: Lee and Shepard, 1875), pp. 24–6 – also in Henry J. Silverman, ed., *American Radical Thought: The Libertarian Tradition* (Lexington: Heath, 1970), pp. 137–41. See also Martin, *Men Against the State*, pp. 125–38.

36.   Greene, 'Communism versus Mutualism . . .,' in Silverman, *American Radical Thought*, p. 139.

37.   Cited in Martin, *Men Against the State*, p. 130.

38.   Greene explains that with Mutual Banks 'there will always be enough Mutual Money for all industrial and commercial needs (due to the flexibility of the issue), there will be no more money panics. . . . As money will be easy to get under the Mutual Banking system, sound enterprises will have no difficulty in getting financed. This will eventually mean the disintegration of monopoly. It will also mean the creation of many more jobs, and consequently competition among employers for workers, resulting in increasingly better conditions of work and pay, until at last the worker will receive the full product of his labor,' in Silverman, *American Radical Thought*, p. 140.

39.   Greenback money was not 'backed' by gold yet it was defined in terms of gold.

40.   Silverman, *American Radical Thought*, p. 139.

41.   On viewing bimetallism as a form of price control, see Murray N. Rothbard, *Power and Market: Government and the Economy* (California: Inst. for Humane Studies, 1970). pp. 19–26.

42.   Cf. Martin, *Men Against the State*, pp. 137–8.

43.   Cited in ibid., p. 106.

44.   The best survey of *Liberty* in terms of its contents, influence and general position within the anarchist movement is in Martin, *Men Against the State*, pp. 202–78. *Liberty* was not the first property anarchist periodical in the United States: Josiah Warren started the *Peaceful Revolutionist* in 1833 to explain how anarchist groups could survive within the jurisdiction of the state. Later Warren started (in 1840) a newspaper called the *Herald of Equity* to propagandize his Time Store philosophy. In the 1870s Heywood published *The Word* to discuss anarchist reform in all its phases. Tucker was on the staff of *The Word* but resigned in 1876 to begin the *Radical Review*, which lasted from 1871 to 1878. Finally in 1881 came *Liberty*, which lasted a record length of time until 1908. After 1908 communist anarchism had eclipsed its cousin and Goldman's *Mother Earth* became America's leading anarchist periodical. The last ten years in the United States have seen a rebirth of property anarchist periodicals. Rothbard's quarterly journal, *Left and Right*, lasted three years (1965–67) until it was superseded by Rothbard's monthly *Libertarian Forum*. An attempt was made to revive the scholarly journal format of *Left and Right* with a magazine called *Libertarian Analysis* but this survived only two years (1970–71). Any attempt to compile a list of all the radical libertarian campus papers would exhaust this page and several others. Rothbard's *Libertarian Forum* is still the dominant medium of this line of intellectual expression.

45.   Though Tucker described the body of anarchist doctrine that he represented as 'scientific anarchism,' he never produced a systematic treatise on the subject. Tucker devoted all of his time instead to the pages of *Liberty*. Tucker did manage to cull a selection of his writings on various topics and publish them in the form of a book. This is still the best single introduction to Tucker's thought and technique of augmentation. Benjamin R. Tucker, *Instead of a Book: by a Man too Busy to Write One* (New York: Haskell House, 1969). First published in 1897. An abridged version of this book was issued by C.L. Swartz under the title *Individual Liberty* (New York: Vanguard Press, 1926). Tucker also issued some less important pamphlets: see Martin's bibliography in *Men Against the State*, p. 299.

46.   In particular, Tucker wanted to steer the European anarchists away from Kropotkin and back to Proudhon. See Martin, *Men Against the State*, pp. 219–33.

47.   Ibid., pp. 258–78.

48. The period between the two World Wars saw the rise of Goldman, Most, and Berkman and their form of communist anarchism. The details of this development are in Schuster, *Native American*, pp. 159–87.

49. Lysander Spooner was, without a doubt, the most prolific of the nineteenth-century anarchists. His entire literary output of over thirty separate pamphlets has been recently published in six volumes with a biographical essay and introductions to each work by Charles Snively under the title *The Collected Works of Lysander Spooner* (Weston, Mass.: M&S Press, 1971). Spooner might have become one of America's most brilliant constitutional lawyers except for the fact that he attacked the document he was supposed to protect. For details on his life and thought see Martin, *Men Against the State*, pp. 167–201.

50. Martin, *Men Against the State*, pp. 167–8.

51. Reprinted in *The Collected Works of Lysander Spooner*, vol. 1.

52. Lysander Spooner, *No Treason: The Constitution of No Authority*, orig. publ. 1870, reprinted along with a *Letter to Thomas F. Bayard*, with intro. by James Martin (Colorado: Pine Trees, 1966). Also in *The Collected Works of Lysander Spooner*, vol. 1.

53. Martin, *Men Against the State*, p. 170.

54. Spooner, *No Treason*, p. 17.

55. See Spooner's *Constitutional Law, Relative Currency and Banking*, 1843 in *The Collected Works*, vol. 5.

56. See esp. Spooner's *The Law of Prices: A Demonstration of the Necessity for an Indefinite Increase of the Quantity of Money*, 1877: reprinted in *The Collected Works*, vol. 6. In this pamphlet Spooner employs an elaborate and tedious numerical example to show that if prices are to remain 'equitable' [i.e., constant] the money supply must increase exponentially over time. The relationship that Spooner depicts assumes that population is growing over time according to some mathematical law. As population proceeds, the division of labor gives rise to greater output and a more diversified output leading to a geometric increase in the volume of transactions. Also, as the population grows the number of intermediary transactions between producers and consumers rises, causing the volume of transactions to rise further still. Permitting P_o and M_o to represent the price level and money supply at some base period, Spooner argues by numerical example that the optimum quantity of money in any period t (M_t^*) is equal to $M_t^* = t\, P_o^{3t}\, M_o/V_t$, where V_t is the velocity of money at any period of time. We can use this formula to present the flavor of Spooner's sometimes abstruse argument. Spooner's point is that if the money supply is not allowed to grow (i.e., $M_t^* = M_o$ for all t), then V_t must grow exponentially if equity is to be maintained in trade. But no community can increase V as rapidly as is required by this formula; thus the money supply must increase by larger and larger absolute amounts to maintain justice in exchange. Whatever the merits or deficiencies of this thinking, he does try to present a 'law of prices' on which to base his case for mutual banking.

57. Spooner, *Universal Wealth Shown to be Easily Attainable*, in *The Collected Works of Lysander Spooner*, vol. 6.

58. Ibid., p. 22.

59. Ibid., p. 18.

60. Ibid., pp. 22–3. See also Spooner, *A Letter to Scientists and Inventors, on the Science of Justice, and their Right of Perpetual Property in Their Discoveries and Inventions*, 1884: reprinted in *The Collected Works of Lysander Spooner*, vol. 3.

61. Rothbard's thought is a unique blend of several long-standing intellectual traditions in Western thought. First, his economic thought is derived largely from the teachings of the later Austrian school and in particular the work of Ludwig von Mises. Second, Rothbard adheres to the natural law tradition of Stoic and later Enlightenment thinking wherein it is held that the wisely directed human mind can arrive at certain fundamental ethical truths concerning what types of interpersonal relationships between men are 'good' and what types are 'bad.' Third, Rothbard's politics stem from the early Conservative movement in the United States which was essentially decentralist domestically and isolationist internationally in its outlook. Unlike the early Conservatives who took their decentralism down to the level of state governments and stopped there, Rothbard takes it to the level of separate individuals – hence, anarchism! Without a state apparatus the question of proper international policy

becomes something of a 'red herring.' Fourth and lastly, his method of history writing is consciously in the tradition of Beard, pointing to the motives behind the actors themselves when analyzing historical events. Rothbard's reappraisal of such American episodes as the Progressive Period, the Wilsonian period, the Hoover New Deal, etc., places him squarely within the ranks of the new breed of revisionist historians. In terms of the breadth of his interests, the quantity of his writings, the scope of his research, and his unwillingness to compromise his interests for temporary academic gain, Rothbard is, in a very fundamental sense, to property anarchism what Karl Marx was to socialism – its most powerful and prolific expositor.

62. Rothbard's major contributions include, *The Panic of 1819: Reactions and Policies* (New York: Columbia Univ., 1962); *Man, Economy, and State*, in two vols (New York: Van Nostrand, 1962); *America's Great Depression* (New Jersey: Van Nostrand, 1963); *Power and Market: Government and the Economy* (California: Instit. for Human Studies, 1971); and most recently *For A New Liberty* (New York: Macmillan, 1973).

63. See Rothbard, 'On Freedom and the Law,' *New Individualist Review* (Winter 1962), pp. 37–40. See also Rothbard, *Man, Economy, and State*, vol. 1, pp. 152–9.

64. Rothbard explains that 'The Law Code of the purely free society would simply enshrine the libertarian axiom: prohibition of any violence against the person or property of another (except in defense of someone's person or property), property to be defined as self-ownership plus the resources that one has found, transformed, or bought or received after such transformation. The task of the Code would be to spell out the implications of this axiom (e.g., the libertarian sections of the law merchant or common law would be co-opted, while the statist accretions would be discarded). The Code would then be applied to specific cases by the free-market judges, who would all pledge themselves to follow it,' *Power and Market*, p. 197.

65. In conversation Rothbard sometimes insists that this requirement is not so radical as it may at first seem. The common law traditions of Western legal practice embody much of this Libertarian Code already and therefore adoption of the Libertarian Code would consist more of chipping away at the encumbrances of Civil Law rather than recreating a new legal tradition from the ground up; also see Bruno Leoni, *Freedom and the Law*, (California, 1972).

66. See discussion, Rothbard, *Power and Market*, pp. 47–56 and *Man, Economy, and State*, vol. 1, pp. 147–51. Rothbard's 'first owner' theory of land titles is criticized by H.E. Frech. III, 'The Public Choice Theory of Murray N. Rothbard, A Modern Anarchist,' *Public Choice* 14 (September 1973), p. 145. Frech insists that the 'principle of first use is not a clear rule', but this criticism overlooks the role Rothbard assigns to common law in filling in the details of what constitutes 'first,' 'use,' etc. Any moral principle can be subjected to this type of criticism; hence the need for courts and judges.

67. Rothbard, 'National Liberation,' *Libertarian Forum* (1 September 1969), pp. 1–2; Rothbard, 'State of Palestine Launched,' *Libertarian* (1 March 1969), p. 3; Stephen P. Halbrook, *Libertarian Forum* (August 1970). pp. 3–4.

68. Rothbard, *Man, Economy, and State*, vol. 1, pp. 67–159.

69. Ibid., p. 156.

70. Rothbard, 'Toward a Reconstruction of Utility and Welfare Economics,' in *On Freedom and Free Enterprise*, Mary Sennholz, ed. (New York: Van Nostrand, 1956), pp. 249–50. I shall return to this point below.

71. Rothbard, *Man, Economy, and State*, pp. vii–xiv.

72. Rothbard admits to a 'tendency' only. This is because he also recognizes the rights of the producers to use their property in any way they choose, either unprofitably or not at all. This explains why Rothbard is cool to the argument that monopoly restriction in a free market represents a net welfare loss to the entire society. By insisting that the welfare of producers also be considered, Rothbard is able to deny that the market price of a commodity is *the* measure of the (relative) worth of the resources incorporated in that commodity; see his *Man, Economy, and State*, vol. 2, pp. 550–660. Frech's criticism of Rothbard's theory of monopoly indicates an unfamiliarity with Rothbard's entire argument; see Frech, 'The Public Choice Theory . . .,' p. 151.

73. Rothbard's theory of interest, embodying aspects of Mises' and Frank Fetter's contributions, is in *Man, Economy, and State*, pp. 313–86.

74. See Rothbard, *America's Great Depression*, p. 1 and *passim*, and *Man, Economy, and State*, vol. 2, pp. 850–79.

75. Rothbard, *What Has Government Done to Our Money?* (Colorado: Pine Tree Press, 1964). This was formerly titled *Money, Free and Unfree*, a more revealing title in terms of Rothbard's intellectual links with his anarchist forebears.

76. Ibid.

77. On the general operation of a commodity standard see, Rothbard, 'The 100% Gold Dollar,' in *In Search of a Monetary Constitution*, ed. by Leland Yeager (Cambridge: Harvard Univ., 1962), pp. 94–135.

78. Rothbard, *Man, Economy, and State*, pp. 832–9 and Rothbard, *Power and Market*, pp. 47–52.

79. Rothbard argues that the present structure of US corporate life operates contrary to the interests of the bulk of the population not because these corporations are large *per se* but because they receive all types of privileges from the state, e.g., patents, tariffs, contracts for munitions, etc. Rothbard traces the growth of the large corporate order to government intervention. His most recent efforts have been devoted to giving a revisionist account of the growth of the corporate economy; see for example his essay 'War Collectivism and World War I,' in *A New History of Leviathan*, ed. by Rothbard and Radosh (New York: Dutton & Co., 1972), pp. 66–110.

80. Rothbard, '100% Gold Dollar.'

81. Rothbard, *Power and Market*, pp. 65–6.

82. Rothbard, *Man, Economy, and State*, p. 880.

83. Rothbard, *Power and Market*, pp. 1–7, and see also *For a New Liberty*, pp. 219–52.

84. Cf. Rothbard, 'Reconstruction . . .', pp. 255–60 and *Man, Economy, and State*, pp. 883–90. Throughout his writings Rothbard stops to consider and criticize various 'classic' arguments for state intervention. Inasmuch as my intention here is solely that of 'placing' Rothbard within the American property anarchist tradition I must pass over many variants of the public goods argument and Rothbard's responses or lack of response to them. One remark on this matter is, however, in order: it is often claimed that Rothbard pays too little attention to the 'free-rider problem' and, by implication, the alleged undersupply of public goods that is produced by the market; see Frech, 'The Public Choice . . .,' p. 146 and *passim*. While I agree that Rothbard does tend to dismiss this line of argument in an entirely unwarranted fashion (especially since the position is consistent with the Austrian approach to economics), I cannot understand why this problem is supposed to seal the theoretical case against property anarchism. It seems to me that within a private court system, contracts could be devised so as to overcome the free-rider problem; see the examples offered by Edwin G. Dolan, *Tanstaafl: An Economic Strategy for Environmental Crisis* (New York, 1969), pp. 40–47.

85. Spencer H. McCallum, *The Art of Community* (California: Institute for Humane Studies, 1961).

86. See for example, Jarret B. Wollstein, *Society without Coercion; A New Concept of Social Organization* (Silver Springs: Society for Rational Individualism, 1969).

87. 'The task of a policy of freedom must therefore be to minimize coercion or its harmful effects, even if if cannot eliminate it completely,' Friedrich Hayek, *The Constitution of Liberty* (Chicago: University of Chicago Press, 1960), p. 12. Unlike Rothbard, Hayek does not consider offensive violence or the threat of offensive violence to be the only types of coercive acts; see ibid., p. 20 and *passim*. Rothbard's definition of 'coercion' in terms of violence is most consistent with Mises' thought; cf. Ludwig von Mises, *Human Action: A Treatise on Economics* (New Haven: Yale University Press, 1963), pp. 149, 281, and 719.

88. My evidence is based entirely on conversations and personal acquaintance. Despite their 'right-wing' backgrounds, many of them are now sympathetic to New Left attitudes. For example, witness their willingness to use the Lockean theory of property in defense of student seizures of public property, etc.; see, for example, Rothbard, 'Massacre at People's Park,' *Libertarian Forum* (15 June 1969), p. 1.

89. See Rothbard, 'Reconstruction . . .' pp. 249–54. 'We are led inexorably, then, to the conclusion that the processes of the free market always lead to a gain in social utility. And we can say this absolute validity as economists, without engaging in ethical judgements,' ibid.,

p. 250; 'Exchanges between persons can take place either voluntarily or under the coercion of violence. There is no third way. If, therefore, free market exchanges always increase social utility, while no coerced exchange or interference can increase social utility, we may conclude that the maintenance of *a free and voluntary market "maximizes" social utility* (provided we do not interpret "maximize" in a cardinal sense).' Ibid., p. 253. (Italics used by author.)

90.   Rothbard, *Power and Market*, p. 170.
91.   We might qualify this by pointing out that the 'person' referred to in the passage is one not accused of a crime, or else we would have to admit that self-defense against aggression lowers social welfare, which Rothbard denies. The possibility of individuals unanimously agreeing to a 'constitution' which specifies the use of coercion as a sanctioning device opens the door to a theory of the state based on voluntarist principles. The conditions under which individuals will voluntarily consent to be coerced does receive some discussion among contemporary authors; see James M. Buchanan and Gordon Tullock, *The Calculus of Consent* (Ann Arbor: Univ. of Michigan, 1965), pp. 43–116. The extent to which this discussion proves damaging to Rothbard's position is discussed in note 92 below.
92.   Frech insists that in the presence of 'costs and transactions . . . individuals may all be made better off by agreeing to be coerced,' 'The Public Choice Theory . . .,' p. 150. While Frech intends to take a position exactly contrary to Rothbard's, the two approaches are not so far apart as may at first seem. Remembering that Rothbard means by 'coercion' the *initiation* of violence between men, he does not mean to exclude the use of coercion to enforce contracts voluntarily entered into. Hence, individuals do not agree to be coerced, as Frech contends, but rather they agree to abide by a constitutional procedure. They are coerced only when they break that agreement.
93.   Rothbard classifies state intervention into two basic categories; 'triangular' and 'binary.' For example, minimum wage controls are an example of the former, while a corporate subsidy is an example of the latter.
94.   Rothbard, *Power and Market*, p. 13.
95.   See above, note 86.
96.   Rothbard nowhere considers the possibility of people 'demonstrating' their preference for one type of coercion over another. The very analysis of the economics of this choice situation might lead to rewarding results. In general, Rothbard is of the opinion that all coercive acts lower at least one person's welfare and that this knowledge alone is sufficient to answer the important questions of political economy.

13. Anarchism and the theory of power*

Warren Samuels

I. INTRODUCTION

The objective of this essay is to provide a sympathetic but critical interpretation of the prospects of anarchism. The interpretation will be undertaken with the aid of a model of choice and power which I have developed and applied to other subjects but which is also relevant here.[1] The procedure will be as follows. Part II will consider the general anarchist position. Part III will examine anarchism in terms of a general model of opportunity sets and interdependence. Part IV will continue the application of the general model of choice and examine anarchism in terms of the theory of power. Part V will present a partial application of the foregoing in a critique of Murray N. Rothbard's *For a New Liberty*.[2]

First, let me state my personal sympathies and the modifying realizations which I feel must be juxtaposed to those sympathies. Together they form my bias. For almost a quarter century I have been deeply inclined to certain views which have seemed to be in sympathy with the spirit of anarchism. These are: (1) a desire for freedom for the individual to do his own thing; (2) a desire for order, for the comfort of predictability and security, so the individual can do his own thing; (3) the market as a mechanism of economic organization to enable freedom with order; and (4) a cynical suspicion, indeed, an antagonism, toward both the state, its officials and pretenders, and the nation-state system, and about the coercion and evils done by and in the names thereof. Given the nature of men to differentiate themselves from each other and to endeavor to impose their own conceptions of rightness and propriety upon others, the nation-state system, which is both the consequence and the reinforcement of those propensities, is the major threat to human welfare and existence. It is rivalled only by mankind's unwillingness to forego self-defeating increases of progeny, also nourished by excessive or misdirected egoism. After Hitler, Stalin, and Viet Nam – yes, after Johnson and especially under Nixon – these

* This paper was first published in *Further Explorations in the Theory of Anarchy*, edited by Gordon Tullock, The Public Choice Society Book and Monograph Series, University Publications, Blacksburg, VA, USA, 1974, pp. 33–57.

feelings about the nation-state system have only intensified. Much of the true *evil* in the world is the product of that profanity, the state.

However, over the last several decades I have also learned that at least some of the sentiments expressed in the preceding paragraph are but the displacement of frustration generated by the human predicament, the discontents of civilization.[3] This has provided perspective but not affection for the state. More specifically, I have learned, first, that freedom exists only within the context of a particular structure of freedom; that the details of the structure of freedom are no less important, in fact are much more important, than any abstract concept of freedom ostensibly characterizing that structure; that freedom is relative to the freedom of others; that freedom is a matter of whose freedom and whose exposure to the freedom of others is involved; that, as Samuelson has argued, freedom is a vector of many components and not a single ordered one-dimensional thing; and that the goal of freedom constitutes a highly complex problem of existential choice. Second, I have learned that order is also complex; that it is a matter of order on whose terms; that security, like freedom, has almost infinite components, including security *from* and security *to* act vis-à-vis others; that there truly is a *problem*[4] of order involving the continuing reconciliation of freedom and control, continuity and change, and hierarchy and equality, and that all solutions to the problem of order are necessarily specific in terms of *some* structure of freedom and power to the exclusion of other structures; that order is less a condition than a process; and that there is a thin and tenuous veneer to what we call order or civilization, that the lion in the streets is never very far away, and that this includes those who preach law and order only against others' crimes and supposed crimes and not their own. Third, I have learned that the market is instrumental to both freedom and order but that it gives effect to the structure of power within which it operates and which conditions the generation and operation of market forces; that the market may be a vehicle or arena for the exercise of private power often just as effective in limiting personal freedom and welfare as the state; and, among other things, that a property system may work to the detriment of a competitive market by abetting monopoly. Fourth, I have learned that we must recognize coercion, domination and aggrandizement, both from the state and from within the private sector; that power will always exist and will always need to be checked; that private power in the market needs to be checked, say, by the state; that the state is capable of abuse of power and of use by the powerful; and that, therefore, the state is not an exogenous factor but an instrument available to those who can control it directly or indirectly, including through the adoption of their theories. In part, I have concluded that there must be a *rebuttable* presumption in favor of the status quo but that any status quo has propriety primarily, albeit not exclusively or conclusively, in proportion to the diffusion of power which it maintains, because it is through the diffusion of power that individual freedom and autonomy is effectively secured, although even this may be destroyed by population growth.

I am sympathetic, then, to the lure of anarchism, but as the following analysis will show, I believe that one must be very careful, indeed extraordinarily skeptical, about its realization. Anarchism, nonetheless, is an approach to the problems of the modern world. Its insight into the human predicament may be formed by attention to the model of choice and power developed and applied below.

II. THE GENERAL ANARCHIST POSITION

Anarchism is most conspicuously, most vigorously, a philosophy of antipathy toward the state: government is antagonistic to individual liberty and is on that account manifestly undesirable. Anarchy, accordingly, would be a system without a state. When one examines the reasoning and, indeed, the soul of the great anarchists – Stirner, Kropotkin, Bakunin, Goldman, Proudhon, Godwin, Malatesta, Tucker, Tolstoy, Warren, and the others, philosophers or propagandists all – it becomes evident that antagonism toward the state is the most conspicuous and direct manifestation of a still deeper vision: anarchism is opposed to *concentrated power*. The state is anathema and abusive by its very nature because it is concentrated power. The emphasis is upon concentrated power in whatever form, upon any system in which the welfare of all individuals is eclipsed or subverted by the welfare of a few.

The literature and philosophy of anarchism manifests a rich and protean diversity and heterogeneity. It thereby presents difficult interpretive problems, for there is a wealth of different and contradictory conceptualizations and positions with regard to means and means–ends relations. Anarchism has indeed 'offered something for everybody.'[5] There is an inevitable tendency, therefore, for analysis to deal with a caricature of the complex and even kaleidoscopic body of ideas that is known as Anarchism. Any statement is bound to be incomplete. An exception probably exists to every general proposition that can be made summarizing anarchist views: in regard to such topics as, for example, violence, large scale industry, private property, materialism, belief in the instant and total transformation of society, and so on.

Nevertheless anarchism is clearly opposed to coercion of the individual; to imperative authority; to *all* authority, command and obedience; to invasions of the individual and his sphere of action and choice; to all repressive, divisive and hierarchical institutions, economic, social, religious, and political; and to class domination. It opposes organized religion; the role of government in feudalism, in western industrial capitalism, and in Russian and other forms of communism; and the availability for and use of the state by all sorts of upper-strata social powers, indeed the state per se. In brief, it opposes all forms of concentrated power as a matter of principle.

Anarchism, conversely, affirms self-government; it rejects both the government of some by others and government by morality-carrying sanctioned obligations. It affirms individual self-expression and development, individual spontaneity, the sovereignty of the individual. The individual should be autonomous: he should not be subject to the will of others, there should be no command, the individual should be free to make his own decisions.[6] This would be true for *all individuals*, not merely a favored few. For *all* individuals there would be extreme freedom of choice, the primacy of individual judgment. It is difficult for me to quarrel with these values.

Anarchists typically do not specify the future form of anarchist society or structure of anarchist social organization. Contrary to the seeming spirit of their doctrines they do not deny that there will be social organization – they insist that it will be something approaching a system of voluntary cooperation for mutual benefit, with the emphasis upon voluntarism and mutualism – but they do insist that the future organization will have to be determined by the people of the anarchical society, the very people who will have to live by it. Above all, it will be organized from below and not imposed from above. Self-determination *is* central to the core of their ideas; they are not master planners. Therefore there is no need for them to provide for mechanisms of organizational or institutional change – a frequent shortcoming of the utopian literature; indeed, various utopias, perhaps even utopianism, is seen by anarchists as rigid, stifling and the very opposite of anarchism.

Anarchists have vehemently opposed the state and organized religion but they have split on private property. The property anarchists – notably Tucker, Warren, Spooner – opposed abusive concentrations of private property (they largely antedated the rise of the corporate system) and affirmed and extolled private property as an institution through which the wide diffusion of ownership and thereby of selfhood and autonomy could be effectuated. Property to them was the mode of individual participation – for all individuals, although not requiring anything like strict equality of holdings or of deserts.

For the more typical, or better known, anarchists, however, private property has been anathema. Differentiating, for the most part, between property for personal use and propertied aggregations of the means of production, they saw in the latter property for power; as with Marx, capital was an economic factor of production but it was also an instrument of class domination and exploitation. For these anarchists, property meant and referred to the power to dominate and exploit others; it meant invasions of the autonomy of others; it meant the role of government supporting concentrated economic and social power; it meant class structure, great inequality, exploitation, repression, elitism. Government, in protecting property, was maintaining the hierarchical structure of the social order; 'protection of property' was the codeword indicating security for the privileged; patriotism meant support of the status quo system of power and privilege, the existing pattern of uses of the state. Property, in short, meant concentrated power and was, accordingly, anathema.

The property anarchist was desirous, then, of reforming property; the anti-property anarchist felt that property *necessarily* meant authority and concentrated power and accordingly had to be replaced. *Both* property and anti-property anarchists opposed centralized collectivism: both capitalist and communist property systems were sensed as highly organized and authoritarian, equally denying the integrity of individual autonomy. Socialism, or central communism, would only mean the substitution of the one exploiter for the many. The state and concentrated property ownership were opposed for the same reason: antagonism toward concentrated power. Especially obnoxious were systems of symbiotic relations between concentrated private economic power and concentrated political power. Anarchists wanted no rulers, neither political nor economic sovereigns; they wanted each individual to be his or her own sovereign; and they wanted this for *all* individuals.

It is not surprising, then, as Gide and Rist[7] and, more recently, Shatz,[8] have pointed out, that anarchism shares both nineteenth-century liberalist and socialist doctrines. With traditional liberalism, anarchism shares an enthusiasm for individual initiative, self-reliance, and self-development; an array of economic criticisms of the state; and the concept of spontaneous economic order. With socialism, anarchism shares, as above, concern tending toward hatred of private property as the source of social evil; and a theory of class domination and exploitation. Yet anarchism departs fundamentally from both. It is no accident, however, that anarchism has appeared to some as liberalist individualism carried to its most extreme extension, nor that Marxism projects the atrophy of the state in the classless society, for the rejection of concentrated power is common to all three systems of doctrine. Practice, suffice it to say, tends to be quite another matter.

It is probably not inapposite to say that anarchism is a psychological as well as a political phenomenon. In both regards it is a posture toward authority and social control. It manifests and expresses the psychology of frustration arising from a sensed loss of autonomy, a sensed inability to influence the conditions affecting one's welfare. It is a response to the class society and class state of the eighteenth, nineteenth and twentieth centuries, as perceived by the anarchists. It is a response to the increasingly powerful state, a state, at least, whose power is increasingly salient. It is a response to increased and urbanized population, and the accompanying pressure of urban social controls. It is a response to the concentration of power not only in the political but also in the economic world, to the plight of the individual as a helpless cog in an industrialized world. It is a response to the replacement of community with society, in

Toennies' phraseology; to the disembedded individual in a system which permitted and abetted his felt victimization.

Anarchist philosophy, and psychology, is clear: it affirms the autonomy of the individual, for all individuals; and it opposes the threat to that autonomy residing in concentrated power, most notably in the form of the state but also in the structure of social, nominally private, power able to use the state.

III.   ANARCHISM: AN OPPORTUNITY-SET ANALYSIS

The purpose of this part is to interpret anarchism in terms of a general model of choice centering upon the interaction of opportunity sets of conflicting individuals. The analysis is continued in Part IV in regard to power.

The basic model[9] involves the following terminology:

Opportunity set: the available alternative lines of action or choice, each with a relative opportunity cost, open to the individual

Power: (1) effective participation in decision making; (2) the means or capacity with which to exercise choice, e.g., rights, position; the first requires the second and the second enables the first

Coercion: the impact of the behavior and choices of others upon the composition of one's opportunity set; nonnormative; is mutual or reciprocal, ergo a system of *mutual coercion*; includes both injuries and benefits visited through the actions or choices of others

Externalities: the substance of mutual coercion (the term *invasions* is found in the anarchist literature; the terms *spillovers* and *neighborhood effects* are found in the economics literature).

In this general model, personal welfare is attained through utility maximization within one's opportunity set, i.e., constrained maximization. The composition of the individual's opportunity set, and by extension the structure of opportunity sets between individuals, is a function of, first, power, and, second, mutual coercion. The individual is able to exercise choice between the alternative opportunities available to him but his opportunity set is a function both of his rights and position and of the impact of the choices of others. Rights, furthermore, are relative: they do not exist in isolation but always vis-à-vis other persons. The right of Alpha enhances his opportunity set; but for Alpha to have a right is for Beta to have an exposure to the impact of the choices made by Alpha on the basis of his right; and vice versa. The power, and the freedom, of Alpha is thus relative to the power and freedom of Beta.

One characteristic of the actual working out of the process described in the model is the selective perception of power, of mutual coercion, of externalities, indeed, of all aspects of the process. Certain choices or behaviors are perceived or identified as beneficent and others as the opposite; certain externalities are seen as resulting from the choices of others, and some are not; some impacts are taken for granted and others not; some manifestations of mutual coercion are perceived as *pejoratively* coercive and others, analytically equivalent, are not; one man's freedom is another man's tyranny; and so on. Where rights are perceived in conjunction with negative externalities or as power over others, they have a different normative connotation or identification, as a rule, than when not so perceived. But power, coercion, and externalities – in the nonnormative, nonpejorative sense – are ubiquitous.

The structure and process of mutual coercion is important; so also are the processes in which rights and position are determined. In particular, the rights determination process helps govern which party in an Alpha–Beta rights conflict will have its interest secured by law (and/or otherwise) vis-à-vis the other. In this process, legal regulation is the functional equivalent of legal rights and rights other than property rights are, or may be, functionally equivalent to property rights in organizing and controlling the decision making process, i.e., in forming opportunity sets and thereby the structure of mutual coercion and, given the substance of individual choice from within extant opportunity sets, the realization of economic welfare. The rights determination process is important, therefore, not only in regard to the foundation of one's opportunity set; it is also important as the basis of control over or formation of others' opportunity sets, through mutual coercion and the generation of externalities – and in the realization of economic welfare.

Several aspects of this analysis deserve to be emphasized. First, the general and ubiquitous character of power, mutual coercion, and externalities (or invasions) must be stressed; they are ineluctable in a world of general interdependence. Second, the phenomenon of selective perception of power, coercion, and externalities is operationally very important: individuals may become aggravated over certain losses imposed by others when there are other and perhaps equally inhibiting invasions not readily (or yet) perceived. Third, from the point of view of social policy making, there is an absolute necessity of moral or valuational choice as to which externalities, or which exercises of mutual coercion, will be acceptable and which will not. Finally, strict or absolute autonomy is impossible: the significant and viable problem is *which* pattern of freedom and of exposure to the freedom of others, or *which* structure of opportunity sets, or *which* pattern of invasions or externalities, is to be desired, promoted, allowed, or inhibited. The individual is 'autonomous' in that he is able to make his own decisions, but he can make them only from his opportunity set from within the total (and dynamic) structure of opportunity sets. In that sense the individual is always, or nearly always, autonomous; but the critical question has to do with the structure of opportunity sets and the factors and forces which govern that structure.

Anarchism stresses, as general propositions, four major relevant interrelated themes: first, meaningful participation by all individuals in decision making; second, localism in the structure of institutions and organizations; third, private or local communal ownership of the means of production; and fourth, some combination of federal (or confederate) and contractual relations between local organizations. Several aspects thereof will be discussed below.

The anarchist *ideal* is that of the spontaneous individual not subject to commands or to exogenously determined limits. A command dictates a decision and thereby forecloses decision by the individual. An invasion, an externality, an exogenously determined limit, forecloses decision by the individual. The anarchist ideal, contemplated in terms of strict or absolute autonomy, is impossible. It is impossible because of the inevitability of the relative character of rights and power (as defined above) and of the processes of mutual coercion. In an interdependent world, autonomy is not possible. The desire for autonomy is bound to be frustrated by the individual's inability to influence the conditions affecting his welfare, for example, forming his opportunity set; some of those conditions will be determined through the choices and behavior of others; the individual largely will have to take his opportunity set as he finds it, formally just as it is under the pre-anarchist society. It is only by defining autonomy in terms of certain excluded invasions, and not others, that one can have autonomy, but then it is selective.

The anarchist program or ideal thus must be reinterpreted. Instead of autonomy, the ideal must be formulated in terms of the structure of power or participation. The anarchist position thus seems to reduce to the following. First, the individual should be able to participate in all (or all 'important' – with the individual himself presumably being the judge) decision making affecting him; which is to say, there should be included within the individual's opportunity set substantive alternatives enabling him to govern the direction and substance, as well as realization, of his own welfare, and he should have influence upon the inclusion of those alternatives. Second, participation may be secured through rights, property or nonproperty, or by positions as the functional equivalent thereto, e.g., as a member of the organization(s) with which his welfare is tied up. Third, the individual should have the options not only to leave an organization and enter another but also to not reenter another. (This is a terribly difficult problem and will be touched upon further below. The fact of leaving, or of entering, creates externalities for others. Moreover, while organizations, even local organizations, can survive the loss of some members, withdrawal (and no reentry) on a large scale can have unintended dysfunctional consequences even for the withdrawing individual and certainly for others. The logic of opportunity-set analysis is inexorable: externalities are ubiquitous. Parallel to the problem of market socialism, wherein the state may or may not be willing to allow the individual enterprise to substitute its own targets for those at the center, is the anarchist's problem of whether a small-unit organization is willing to let a subunit go its own way. Some anarchists would be willing to accept certain consequences and not others; some would be willing to accept all consequences. See Part IV.) Fourth, externality-generating capacity should be limited – not eliminated, which is impossible in an interdependent world, but reduced in scale (see Part IV) – through the wide diffusion of power. In large part this means the absence of concentrations of power; in part, varying among the anarchist thinkers, it means relative equal-ity of power. And fifth, the central principle of organization or institution creation and operation should be localism. With or without private property in the means of production, organization should be in relatively small groups locally developed and administered. In all these respects, the central theme is not absolute autonomy but participation by all individuals in the decision making processes and structures which affect their welfare. The fear of the state, which is part of the general antagonism toward concentrated power, is applied to all large scale organizations insofar as individuals are unable to effectively participate. The key word in the preceding sentence, of course, is effectively: to some anarchists, individuality in large scale organizations is impossible; to others, large scale organization, and its economies, is accept-able, say, so long as it is not conjoined with class structure and individual participation is promoted as far as it can go; and so on. The problem, then, is one of power, to which we now shall turn.

IV.   ANARCHISM AND POWER

From the foregoing at least two themes should stand out: first, that the anar-chist's antagonism against the state is but an example of his more general antipathy toward concentrated power; and second, that the anarchist quest for individual autonomy must be transformed into a search for that power struc-ture which will accommodate individual control, for all individuals, over the conditions governing the realization of their welfare, which is to say, that power structure which will enable individual participation in the processes of decision making governing the realization of one's welfare. The argument of this part is that the anarchists' individualist values may be so congenial and so intoxicating as to obscure the power-based complexities of their realization and thus distort the possibilities and limits of an anarchical society as well as enable misleading conceptualizations and recommendations. The argument will be developed in several steps.

1. The foregoing discussion of the formation of individual opportunity sets indicates the limited, shall we say, partial-equilibrium, character of the general anarchist model. There is more to opportunity-set formation than is given prominence or often acknowledged in anarchist theorizing.

Each theory of anarchy, contrary to its distinctive emotional and intellectual thrust, is in fact a particular theory of the power structure. Each anarchist model does have a place for power, a place for mutual coercion, a place for social control, and a place for either the state as such or the functional equivalent of the state. Each theory of anarchism only posits a different arena, a different form of imposing upon the individual, a different system of the social channeling of individual behavior, and perhaps only a different (safer) group doing the channeling. Anarchists do not find these thoughts congenial and do not like to recognize their import, but the ideas are true and inevitable.

One problem is coercion by society. If the state were in fact absent there would still be social or societal coercion. Anarchism is not really a theory of the absence of power, or the absence of coercion, or the absence of social control, whatever its sentiments thereon and its attractiveness on that account. Anarchism is a theory of reliance upon nonlegal social control, a different power structure, a different structure of mutual coercion. A preference for these does not keep them from being social control, power, and coercion. They continue to affect the composition and structure of opportunity sets. The individual is still subject to forces over which he has no or little control. The individual is still controlled; the new system of control may or may not feel more repressive; the danger of tyranny, by custom if not also by neighbors, remains.[10] Power is always relative and the impact of the exercise of the power of others may be onerous; indeed, where the others are proximate they may be more salient, and the impact of their decisions be more clearly and deeply felt and resented. But power is inevitable; it is only by its selective perception or advocacy that some is acceptable and some is not.

The anarchist thus opts for one system of power and social control as opposed to another. But private or local mutual coercion may have the same deleterious effects on individuals as does legal or centralized social control. To be anti-state does not guarantee safety, freedom or autonomy for the individual – unless it is by a question-begging definition of freedom, such as the nonexistence of the state *or* the absence of change through law *or* the absence of a class state, in each of which cases other components of the vector are neglected. In all such cases, the real problem is not the state but the quality and the structure of power and process of mutual coercion in which the state participates, by whatever name. Every theory or model of anarchy does have a place for power and for the problems of power, which include but transcend the state.

Not only will power exist under anarchy, but most if not all theories of anarchy also have a place for the state although that place is frequently obscured.

If the performance of social control is undertaken by nonlegal social control institutions, it is still a performance; what the state was doing is still being done. Each theory of anarchy is only another approach to the use of the state, by whatever name it is known.

Each theory of anarchy tends to presume the behavior necessary to produce the results intended by the particular theorist. In effect, each theorist is assuming an already functioning and continually reproduced relatively homogeneous socialized or societized man. In each case the socialization pattern is that of the theorist – which raises the question whether this is anarchy or just one person's conception and imposition of his vision and design of social relations, his preferred system of order, his preferred structures of power and freedom. Not all anarchists, to be sure, may be so faulted; typically, indeed, they do not plan the future organization; but they do have in the back of their minds some conception of the socialized character of man that will permit anarchy per se to succeed. The main point is that the critical problems to which the state is addressed in the real world are either presumed to no longer exist *or* to have been solved once and for all time *or* to be solved by nonlegal social control *or* in some black box. In the brave world of anarchy those problems will have to be worked out; the institutions and procedures for working them out will be the functional equivalent to the state; and the solutions achieved, and the procedures of their achievement, likely will seem as onerous and pejoratively coercive to some as they do under the state today and in ages past under the heavy hands of church and custom – unless minds have been desensitized by thought control or drugs.

The problem is not one of state versus no state, nor one of anarchism versus tyranny, nor one of freedom versus control; how simple things would be if that were the case. The problem is, *which* power structure? Concentrating upon the state, and pretending to do away with the state, is wrong and incomplete if not illusory or worse. Even the Marxist, who defines the state as an instrument of class domination and exploitation, holds that in the classless society, in which by definition there will be no state, there will be administrative and conflict-resolution machinery. Aside from the problem of classes, everything, or nearly everything, which most people contemplate as the state will remain. Whatever the terminology, *governance* will remain. Individuals will still have their opportunity sets governed, through mutual coercion, by the power of others.

The inescapable fact is that of public choice interrelated with private choice; and the inescapable problem is that of *whose* choice. That is the existential problem which the anarchist must confront. No individualism can avoid it.

All theories of anarchy have a place for organized social decisional institutions, i.e., for public choice, a place wherein critical problems of interpersonal relations (relative opportunity sets) are resolved as if in a black box. There are institutional arrangements to decide the content and the specificity of application of conflicting working rules, to decide between conflicting rights, to decide when an abuse of power is an abuse of power, and, *inter alia*, to decide which interest shall prevail over which other interests when in conflict. Like it or not, antipathy to the state is partially a function of the fact that the state has the nasty job of serving as that black box in the real world. In a closed society, or to the uninformed, that function is obscured (it is one of the functions of social control to obscure the performance, as well as to rationalize it, in every society); in an open, pluralist society, that function is much more evident, and that saliency leads to frustration. The fact of the black box in the anarchist model means that the anarchist theorist has begged or obscured the central problems of continuing conflict resolution and management of social change; or, if not so much or exactly begged or obscured, only transferred the old battles to a new arena with a new name and under new and perhaps different terms. The problems giving rise to the desire for anarchy are, unfortunately, to be sure, not solved or obviated by anarchy. They are only put into some black-box equivalent – say, into the supposedly simple administration of a simple code. Modern man sees power players with feet of clay (although socialization and wishful thinking often perpetuate or reinstate the old pretenses, the old mysteries, and the old symbols). Men would prefer that the constitution or code be immaculate in conception and administration, but they know that he who administers or interprets code or morality will remake or fashion according to his own lights and that the real power arena is over control of administration and interpretation. Black boxes have a way of being revealed as power structures, and often nasty and brutish power structures at that.

Indeed, modern man is suspect even of anarchist theorizing as being only another play for power. Anarchists may want to install their own power structure, their own commanders. Anarchism is after all another theory of social organization and perforce another theory of power structure. It may only be a substitution phenomenon: a new power structure and elite substituted for the old. Anarchists may only want to extirpate the existing elite. Anarchists may only want to disengage the existing state from changing the structure of social power, thereby reenforcing the status quo structure of power and privilege. At least some recent property anarchism would function to finesse or abort twentieth-century liberalism and its welfare state, i.e., all 'leftist' uses of government, under the pretense of doing away with government. This despite their qualifications and acknowledgements of the illegitimacy of many status quo property rights. Anarchists of both left and right may well have only their own power designs in mind.

2.   What of the anarchist position interpreted as a plea for the wide diffusion of power?

Let me state rather baldly some principles of power that bear on our subject and relate them in a particular way. The principles are offered as positive, neutral, descriptive propositions lacking normative or ideological content and applicable to all decision making situations.

(a)   Decisions are a function of the decision making structure, i.e., of the structures of opportunity sets, power, and mutual coercion.

(b)   Power players attempt to manipulate the decision making structure in order to influence or control the decisions.

(c)   Power is reciprocal: the power of Alpha is checked by the power of Beta, and vice versa, when they are in the same field of power or power situation.

(d)   Institutions represent decision making or power structures and participations in decision making; institutional change means change of or defense against change of the power structure.

Notice that power is not an absolute; power is relative to other power. A change of scale, namely, the diffusion of power, does not obviate the relativity of power. Power is always exposed to other power. Power is ubiquitous. It is nonetheless desirable, of course, to have more rather than less power.

(e)   Power is necessary to accomplish desired ends. By the same token, power is necessary to reach decisions.

(f)   The quest for power is partially derived from the desire for particular ends and from the desire for power per se (e.g., ego fulfillment and/or defense).

Not only is power relative, then, but there is inevitable conflict. The individual is part of a larger conflict situation; he contributes to it and he is exposed to it. Power is necessary; it becomes invested with the presumed nobility of its use, to the point where it is not even seen as power.

(g)   Those with power tend to seek further power.

(h)   The fear of power leads to a desire to use power as a check on the power of others.

Individuals thus fear power but seek power, to accomplish desired ends, to accomplish expanded, power-nourished, ends, and to check the feared or rival power of others.

(i) Power may be used for one purpose or another; in one direction or another; to effectuate one choice or another. Power play is strategic; it affects the size of an individual's future opportunity set and his relations with, including his exposures to, others.

(j) There are different, unequal, and varying perceptions of power, i.e., different persons will have different and changing perceptions as to when 'power' is involved and when not. Incomplete perception of power prevents adequate recognition of past and present power structures, situations, and struggles. Power used to check power is often not seen as 'power', although it is sometimes understood that the power necessary to check another's power may itself require checking.

(k) The checking of the power of Alpha likely means the unchecking of the power of Beta.

(l) The formation of power tends to generate its own rationale for holding and exercising power, its own legitimacy, which is typically formulated in absolutist and exclusivist terms.

(m) Change, particularly institutional or organizational change, tends to be evaluated primarily in terms of probable effects on power structure and/or on the use of power, both intra- and extra-organizationally.

The kaleidoscopic nature of the power situation tends to compel individual concern with the many facets of power. The diffusion of power may be important, but it will tend to be eclipsed by the importance of marginal differences and adjustments in power. Power will continue to be important, albeit in a new and differently structured arena.

(n) Coercive pressure is a function of economic and/or political importance (tested by withholding or threatening to withhold), capacity to organize, and cohesiveness of organization. All are important in the formation of opportunity sets and the exercise of mutual coercion by individuals in the organizational situation in which they find themselves or manage to work their way into.

(o) There are economies of scale in the marshalling of power and, most notably, in the exercise of power. Power being relative, each party or organization has a built-in tendency to seek further power for strategic if for no other reasons.

The anarchist world will be a world of power play. Power built up and nourished from below – the anarchist model – will tend to centralize; in any event it will still be power. The individual will continue to be caught up in the vortexes of power and power play. The individual, after all is said and done, will not be an autonomous decision maker; individual choice will be interrelated with group choice. The power that is diffused will still be power; the individual will still be exposed to the power of others; and the operation of the principles of power (especially under the pressure of population growth – shades of Godwin and Malthus!) will continue to tend to swamp the individual. The diffusion of power will not prevent the operation of the very principles of power which produce the consequences of power so anathema to the anarchist mind. Some of the worst evils of concentrated power may be moderated.

3.   What the foregoing means in part is that even in the absence of the state there is the danger of private concentrations of power. Systems of private power under anarchism, whether ensconced in property or non-property arrangements, can produce onerous, anti-individualist results no less than systems of state power. Indeed, both market and state are what they are in existing systems in large part because of the structure of private power. The anarchist is antagonistic not only to concentrated state power but to concentrated private power as well. The market system is itself coercive and the market gives effect to whenever structure of private power operates through it. The same applies to any anarchical system. The initial distribution of rights, for example, will have profound effects on the course of development of any anarchical system, quite aside from the social control and organizational facets of power discussed above. It will still be worthwhile to have power under anarchy. The ideals of individual autonomy and participation and of diffusion of power can be aborted by private aggregations of power as effectively as by governmental aggregations of power. A system of private government or of private socialism – say, with Howard Hughes as sole or chief capitalist in a nominally property anarchism – can be just as statist as the nominal state.

4.   It must be granted that there is an apparent difference when one considers the state with its monopoly of violence and its ability to compel obedience. But how substantial the difference would be in an anarchical society is open to question. Concentration upon physical violence and obedience is an undue narrowing of the focus upon the full range of mutual coercion. The state or its equivalent will be present, albeit perhaps on a lower level. Social control of whatever is determined to be 'deviant' behavior will be present. Concentrated private power with consequences for opportunity sets and externalities similar to those under extant systems will be present. Opportunities to opt out, to live in other communities, may be no greater than under the modern system. The corvée, or its equivalent, may replace military conscription. Mutual coercion includes much more than physical violence, and obedience in the sense of relatively unconditional acceptance of the decisions of others, whatever their adverse impact upon one's opportunity set, is ineluctable and ubiquitous. It is

only through selective perception of mutual coercion that the anarchist ideal is sensible – and that selectivity begs the critical issues.

5.   Anarchism does suggest, nevertheless, that possibilities exist for creating institutions which will tend toward greatly increasing individual participation, toward defusing the state, and toward producing localism, so that the principles of power and the exercise of mutual coercion will operate on a different level of magnitude and with fewer evil and disheartening consequences. One should neither over- nor under-estimate what can be accomplished by relatively simple, or complex, institutional adjustments. But there are at least two preconditions or requirements that must be met if substantial movement in these directions is to be achieved. First, there must be a universal dismantling of the nation-state system; and second, there must be the universal diffusion of the existing structure of private economic power so that it will not replace the historic state (with which it has been so closely and symbiotically related) with its own system of private government. (This latter includes the prevention of a system of international government through the international corporations – though it is possible to argue that in the existing system the international corporate governing arrangements provide a check upon the nation-states, something which requires much more study.) For only one nation to unilaterally dissolve its concentrated state power is to enhance the relative power of other, rival nations and to invite aggrandizement, in which respect we are prisoners of the system;[11] similarly, for only state power to be defused and dissolved is to allow concentrated private economic governance to rule albeit through another set of devices. The prospects are not too bright but cautious change possibly can improve the lot of man according to anarchist values.

What does the anarchist suggest will make a difference, whatever the improbability of its adoption? General decentralization on all fronts. Greater direct relationships between actual producers and consumers. The dismantling of finance capitalism. Greater worker participation in the governance of industry. Major overhauling of the wage system. The decentralization of industry. The wide diffusion of property, or of position. Greater participation in rule making by those affected thereby in all areas of life. Reliance upon federation and cooperative ventures, through the mode of contract.

Movements can be made in these directions. They should be investigated and some should be pursued. But it must not be forgotten that what will be created will only be a new system of power, a new arena, a new system of mutual coercion. Whether the new regime will be preferable to the existing regime both in the large and in the small will be subjective and not for us to say *a priori*. Greater decentralization may only mean that large masses of population currently having a voice at the center will lose if decentralization means dominance by local minorities. Greater worker participation in the governance of industry may mean even more disregard of consumer interest than under the present regime. And so on. As the anarchists insist, adoption of an anarchical system is not a once-and-for-all-time matter; it is something that will have to be lived with and worked out. That may be their deepest message, however much it is obscured by their rhetoric and values.

Movements in the directions outlined two paragraphs above will not abort the impulse to dominate, the operation of the principles of power, or the process of mutual coercion. But they may facilitate the creation of opportunity-set structures more conducive to the welfare of greater numbers.

Such does not mean equality, whether one likes it or not. There is no equality in a world of kaleidoscopic power structures and power play: power is manipulated (within constraints) by power players along lines and in directions where it will do them the most good. There remains the problem of choosing between maximizing through the number or percentage of people made happy or maximizing through the intensity of happiness of the relatively few made happy.[12] More important, if I understand the anarchist message correctly, is the movement away from or abolition of class domination in at least its major forms and consequences. It does not mean that inequality will no longer swamp the opportunity-set formation of some or many individuals. Will anarchist reform mean that the world as an arena or stage for the power-intoxicated, for megalomania, whatever its psychic origin, will subside? Probably not, but it may make marginal improvements. The danger is that these marginal adjustments will only constitute a restructuring of power, with the world remaining much the same, much as has been historically disliked by the anarchist. That is the existential problem posed but not resolved by anarchism.

V. ROTHBARD'S *FOR A NEW LIBERTY*

Murray Rothbard's recent manifesto proclaims to be written in the essential property or free market anarchist tradition; it asserts the case for a new libertarianism, for 'anarcho-capitalism.'[13] The first and last chapters deal with the 'new libertarian movement' which Rothbard would like to foster. Chapters two and three deal with the theoretical 'libertarian creed' of the movement and chapters four through thirteen survey libertarian applications to such problems as welfare, police protection and the administration of justice, education, ecology, and national defense. For anyone with anarchist sympathies, Rothbard presents an often appealing indictment of the abuse of man by the state. Moreover, the chapters on applications of his doctrine are interesting and suggestive of opportunities not only to rely less upon the state but also to eradicate some grossly inequitable institutional arrangements. In many cases, however, there are solid justifications for state action which Rothbard's analysis cannot incorporate; and in many cases Rothbard's analysis only acknowledges one right from an Alpha–Beta rights conflict and identifies it with autonomy and freedom, to the loss of the other. We shall see below that the recognition is far from random: it is skewed in favor of a propertied elite. Moreover the book is mortally defective in its theoretical basis. The book is a grotesque distortion of anarchism; indeed, it is not anarchism but a cleverly designed and worded surrogate for elitist or aristocratic conservatism.

Rothbard affirms private property and the market; he opposes the state, the welfare state, imperialism, liberalism, laissez faire (as deficient in accepting the state per se), big business (including the military–industrial complex) as a source of statism, and patriotism. He is often very eloquent and appealing, especially his denunciations of state tyranny. He stresses the consistency and rigor with which he maintains his position (denigrating along the way almost every major conservative, free market, laissez faire libertarian writer for not doing the same thing and ending up in his position), including this on the Constitution: 'Furthermore, most libertarians today find the American Constitution (even as originally construed and framed) scarcely a libertarian document. In fact, the Constitution was itself an illegal and statist *coup d'état* against the far more libertarian Articles of Confederation.'[14] But notwithstanding the supposedly innocent shock value of this and similar radical-sounding statements, Rothbard is anything but rigorous and consistent, *except* in the use of property theory to support an elitist oligarchy. Indeed, his consistency is that of *strategic* extremism calculated not out of scholarship but the endeavor to push 'the matrix of day-to-day action further and further in his direction.'[15] As with so many other anarchist writers, we are dealing more with the propagandist and less with the philosopher, or with the propagandist in philosopher's trappings. But Rothbard is very candid on this, to his credit; he is deliberately producing a manifesto for the faithful, the content determined upon the basis of likely actionable consequences.

Rothbard argues that the central core of the libertarian creed is given by the axiom: 'no man or group of men have the right to aggress against the person or property of anyone else.'[16] This he calls the 'nonaggression axiom,' and says that aggression 'is defined as the initiation of the use or threat of physical violence against the person or property of someone else. Aggression is therefore synonymous with "invasion".'[17] The result is that 'If no man may aggress against – invade – the person or property of another, this means that every man is free to do whatever he wishes, except commit such aggression.'[18] To the extent that this approximates anarchism, it is deficient; yet it is not anarchism. Both themes will be developed in the following critique.

1. My first two points may be stated without immediate elaboration. First, Rothbard advances the typical conservative–libertarian argument that a ubiquity of markets is possible. Second, he advances the *a priori* propriety of the results of markets, i.e., of whatever market or market-like arrangements evolve, regardless of other alternative institutions' arrangements and criteria: justice, and any other criterion for that matter, is only what comes out of markets. The first is phantasmagorical; the second is presumptuous. I have criticized the former elsewhere;[19] the latter will be amplified below. What Rothbard's analysis amounts to, however, is not affirmation of the market per se; rather the argument in favor of markets operates to sweeten, and obscure, the economic elitism which is the major result of his analysis.

2. The central axiom is severely deficient in a number of important respects. It formally begs the question of the process whereby one's person and property are identified and the latter assigned. It is misleading and selective with regard to 'invasions.' It can only pretend to abolish invasions and coercion by selectively admitting them, i.e., it abolishes only certain invasions and coercion. Invasion is only another name for externality in the foregoing analysis, and it is impossible to eliminate all externalities. Rothbard's system would permit the operation of mutual coercion in the market, but he does not see it as pejoratively or analytically coercion.[20] In other words, he would abolish only the coercion he is willing to acknowledge. His conception of voluntarism and freedom is similarly incomplete and selective: where they are not advocated only in the abstract, thus begging the matter of details,[21] they are specified only in terms of market exchange. There is more to coercion, to voluntarism, and to freedom than Rothbard's system admits. Autonomy exists only within the existing structure of power, and there would be a structure of power in Rothbard's system, only he declines to acknowledge its existence except in one regard: in Rothbard's system the social welfare function is generated only by wealth and thus is weighted in favor of the haves, i.e., it is a system in which only wealth counts.[22] (See below.)

3. Rothbard's theory of property rights, offered in partial theoretical–ideological support for his axiom and system, is also deficient. He rejects the emotivist and utilitarian theories of property and adopts a natural rights theory, specifically the Lockean labor application theory. Locke deserves better treatment. Rothbard neglects to include Locke's fundamental distinction between property in the state of nature and in civil society; Locke's fundamental qualifications in the state of nature, namely, that there is enough and as good left in common for others and that one appropriates only as much as can be made use of; and Locke's emphasis that the introduction of money means inequality (although this latter is not uncongenial to Rothbard).

4.   Rothbard endeavors to resonate with radical ideas by rejecting status quo titles to property as being derived from the repugnant existing state. He says that a theory of justice in property is necessary in order to determine legitimate owners.[23] Rothbard's solution to the problem, however, is grossly inadequate. The allocation of titles would be in accordance with Locke's labor application theory.[24] This is, of course, a difficult formula to administer in the modern world; more important is that it is no answer at all to the problem of status quo titles once the existing government is rejected. (It must be remembered that Rothbard is not trying to explain anything; he is only trying to legitimize.) In addition, Rothbard attempts a subtle transformation of the labor application rule. He begins by asserting, 'The central core of the libertarian creed, then, is to establish the absolute right to private property of every man: first, in his own body, and second, in the previously unused natural resources which he first transforms by his labor.'[25] Here the emphasis is upon 'the previously unused natural resources which he first transforms by his labor.' (It is in connection with this statement that Rothbard argues the corollary right to give away or exchange property titles and from which 'stems the basic justification for free contract and for the free-market economy,'[26] and advances the proposition that 'Freedom and unrestricted property right go hand in hand.')[27] Apropos the 'previously unused natural resources,' a few pages later Rothbard jumps to 'material objects . . . voluntarily acquired,'[28] and thirty pages later he conjoins material resources found and transformed with titles received in exchange.[29] The simple labor appropriation theory is transformed into a market-exchange theory; as has been stressed by MacPherson and Hundert, this means that laboring and appropriating have become separable and the doctrine has shifted from laboring to appropriating and with it the denouement wherein labor, hitherto a convenient rationalization, is now eclipsed.[30]

5.   The problem of the determination (identification and assignment) of property rights pervades Rothbard's discussion. How is it, or through what agency is it, that one's property rights are to be ascertained, particularly in the case of unanticipated rights conflicts? Property is more than titles; property is bundles of relative rights. In the case of externalities, how are the relative-rights conflicts to be worked out? Rothbard gives no answer to the problem of status quo titles (and if he did accept redistribution of inequitable titles, who would determine inequity and proper distribution?); his answer to the problem of continuing rights determination is inadequate and misleading. He continually talks about unrestricted property rights, when the very nature of rights is that the right of Alpha is limited by the right of Beta and vice versa. It is only by the sleight-of-hand of narrowly contemplating externalities, or invasions, that a semblance of reasonableness is attained. But the result is spurious; rights have to be determined. So Rothbard asserts that 'discovering and identifying

the property rights involved will resolve any apparent conflicts of rights that may crop up.'[31] (This statement is in a discussion of how human rights and civil rights are best thought of as property rights – I would say that all three need to be thought of as *rights* for analytical purposes, but Rothbard's is an exercise of legitimation of *property* rights.) But notice that Rothbard expects rights conflicts to be the exceptional thing – 'any apparent conflicts of rights that may crop up' – and not only exceptional but likely misconstrued. (He reminds me of Bastiat's tautology that all legitimate rights are in harmony.) He is wrong or naive here; not that rights conflicts cannot be and are not resolved in this way but, first, that this is the exceptional thing, and second, that rights remain unrestricted (and undamaged)[32] in the process.

6. Even more damaging to the Rothbardian analysis is the answer to the query, *who* is to identify property rights and resolve property rights conflicts? This is the same question posed at the beginning of (4), *supra*. The answer, of course, is the state, whatever it happens to be called in his system. As Frech, among others, has argued, Rothbard provides for 'society,' that is, for a black box, which 'meets the definition of a government,' such that whatever else may said of the Rothbardian system, 'it is not a model of a *stateless* society.'[33] There will be a Libertarian Code and its administration and enforcement will constitute the state. The Code will insist upon the no-aggression principle, define property rights, establish rules of evidence, and establish maximum punishment for particular crimes.[34] It may not look like contemporary states and it may not have all of their obnoxious capabilities, but it will be doing, in regard to rights and the organization and control of economic life, very much what the contemporary state does. Among other things, it will determine which externalities (invasions) to 'correct' and which not, i.e., it will be determining the resolution of Alpha–Beta rights conflicts. It also will be a distinctive state, however, as we shall now see.

7. Rothbard does not fudge on the question of inequality: he admits to being a rightist libertarian not opposed to inequality. Indeed, he accepts Michels' Iron Law of Oligarchy not only as a descriptive proposition but as a principle of policy, i.e., as a normative proposition. Rothbard's individualism is not egalitarian; in his system, 'leadership in the activity will inevitably be assumed by a relative handful of the most able and energetic, while the remaining majority will form themselves into rank-and-file followers.'[35] I admire Rothbard's candor here but I insist that this is not what the traditional anarchists – property or communal – had in mind. What Rothbard wants is his own oligarchical system. Rothbard's is here quite clearly only another system for the control of the human labor force.[36] Rothbard is much more authoritarian than his clever language makes him appear at first unreflective glance.

8.   Rothbard's manifesto, then, is a plea for elitist or aristocratic conservatism. He acknowledges, indeed stresses, the rule of an oligarchy. His
approach to property rights functions basically to legitimize existing property
rights, this despite his disclaimer about the repugnance of the state under
which they were developed. The strategy is unveiled when Rothbard, after
calling for the abolition of the state, says he is willing to settle for less: 'if
abolition cannot be achieved, at the least there should be a relentless whittling
down of governmental power and activity.'[37] This can only mean the protection of the status quo system of power; we are back to government protecting
property – against leftist social change. Rothbard would only abort the state
from doing things and producing changes which he does not like, for there is,
as we have seen, a state in his system, a state which would be the instrument
of the ruling political and economic oligarchy – this is what Rothbard's 'new
liberty' amounts to. Hardly anarchy, and hardly freedom – except for the
rulers. Rothbard is the self-appointed spokesman for the existing propertied
who would rule, directly or indirectly, in his 'new' system or under a whittled-
down state, in either case a state which would serve propertied interests and
not others.[38]

9.   I cannot fault Rothbard for writing a tract in an endeavor to entice the
unhappy or naive new left into an ostensible new right. Because it is a manifesto with a strategic purpose, it cannot claim attention as a work of serious
scholarship. (My own prejudice should be clear: I do not like ideology
although I must stress its social function. In addition, unlike anarchism in
general, Rothbard's is a closed and dogmatic system.) Indeed, that is true of
most of the traditional anarchist literature: as an exploration of values, yes;
as knowledge, no, although there is much to learn from the book, albeit not
what Rothbard would have us learn. One lesson is that anarchism – property or communal – is not science; it is a normative or speculative approach
to the problem of organization and control. We do need positive analyses of
the economic role of government; but beware the pseudo-science of anarchy or anything else that tends to yield normative conclusions tautological
with normative premises. It may be objected that science and positive
analysis is not the presently important thing; that anarchism, e.g.,
Rothbard's book, is an endeavor in value clarification. I cannot fault that;
it is an important part of what life is all about. But I would stress that to
argue that is to agree with a main thrust of the early parts of this paper,
namely, that anarchism is like all metaphysical systems, unrealistic with
regard to the complexities of the real world; that anarchism is an emotional
quest for the impossible. In the case of Rothbard's book, however, what
would pass as anarchism is in reality a doctrine quite the opposite of traditional anarchism.

10. One lesson from Rothbard's book is this: both positive and normative analysis must beware of a fixation with the state that neglects the origins of the state's activity in its use by people. The state – government – is not exogenous; it is used by those who can control it. Rothbard's play with words, the pretense of statelessness, only functions to mislead. Whether Rothbard wants to admit it or not, 'Every demand for a right by any person or group is, directly or indirectly, a demand for government.'[39] Moreover, Rothbard's state is the instrument of concentrated power. Rothbard's state – his Libertarian Code and its administrative and interpretive apparatus – is the instrument of the plutocracy, who are the plutocracy largely because of their capture of the state.[40] Rothbard's is only a narrow and elitist solution to the problem of order. One prefers the conservative Thomas Nixon Carver's argument that

> However, it seems that we cannot trust implicitly to either the money getter or the vote getter in these matters, but must play one against the other, and in the tug of war between the two the rest of us plain people may manage to get what we want . . . In other words, government control of prices is the control exercised by the vote getters, because government in a democracy is a government of vote getters. This method of playing the vote getter against the money getter is, frankly, an awkward method, but it is the best there is.[41]

The problem, of course, is the development of symbiotic relations between money getters and vote getters; and that, or the equivalent, is precisely what would develop under Rothbard's system – and with his oligarchic blessings. But Carver was not as rigorous or consistent as Rothbard; hardly! The difference is that Carver was frank about serious social problems; Rothbard is frank about his strategic venture – his word games with statelessness are only grist for that mill. If the subject were not so serious, it would be funny. If the conservative or radical disaffected want to read, let them study Frank Knight. Better yet, let them read Tolstoy if they are anarchistically inclined.

Rothbard has his own state, with its own agenda. But Rothbard is not alone in neglecting the inevitability of mutual coercion. That Rothbard has his own ideal system of concentrated power should not obscure the general difficulty with anarchist thought notwithstanding their usual attempt to control concentrated power. Anarchism fails to resolve the very problems of power which it set out to conquer.

VI. CONCLUSION

The conclusion which I would urge based upon all of the foregoing is the utter necessity of careful and discriminating analysis of the details and nuances of power, coercion, and externalities in society. Normative systems, as attractive as they may be, tend to melt when confronted with contradictions of the very principles on which they are presumably erected. *All* coercions, *all* powers, and *all* externalities should be included within analysis. I urge that procedure for positive study. But I urge it also for more informed normative choice. Perhaps, upon the merits of Rothbard's norms, given the positive study of the real world of coercion, his system would be compelling. He might overcome my own preference for *all* individuals rather than for *some*. Ah, were it only possible that anarchism could become 'the great liberator of man from the phantoms that have held him captive' and could 'rescue the self-respect and independence of the individual from all restraint and invasion by authority.'[42] That is a vision whose advocacy may be intentionally or non-intentionally deceptive; it is certainly illusory. Power and coercion cannot be eliminated by verbal manipulations. But power and coercion can be deliberately, objectively, and completely studied, perhaps to the improvement of normative choice. No ideology can satisfactorily preempt that approach to the existential burden of man: coming to grips with power.

NOTES

1. See W.J. Samuels, 'Welfare Economics, Power, and Property,' in G. Wunderlich and W.L. Gibson, Jr, eds, *Perspectives of Property* (University Park: Institute for Research on Land and Water Resources, Pennsylvania State University, 1972), pp. 61–148; 'Interrelations Between Legal and Economic Processes,' *Journal of Law and Economics*, vol. 14 (1971), pp. 435–50; 'In Defense of a Positive Approach to Government as an Economic Variable,' *idem*, vol. 15 (1972), pp. 453–60; 'The Coase Theorem and the Study of Law and Economics,' *Natural Resources Journal*, vol. 14 (1974), pp. 1–34; and 'Some Notes on Government as an Economic Variable' and 'Legal Change and Compensation,' both mimeographed.
2. New York: Macmillan, 1973.
3. S. Freud, *Civilization and its Discontents* (New York: Norton, 1962).
4. J.J. Spengler, 'The Problem of Order in Economic Affairs,' *Southern Economic Journal*, vol. 15 (1949), pp. 1–29.
5. D.E. Apter and J. Joll, *Anarchism Today* (Garden City: Doubleday, 1972), p. 248.
6. R.P. Wolff, *In Defense of Anarchism* (New York: Harper & Row, 1970), pp. 14–15.
7. C. Gide and C. Rist, *A History of Economic Doctrines* (Boston: Heath, n.d.), pp. 614ff.
8. M.S. Shatz, ed., *The Essential Works of Anarchism* (New York: Bantam, 1971), pp. xivff.
9. The model is elaborated and applied in the references given in note 1, *supra*, and in W.J. Samuels, 'Public Utilities and the Theory of Power,' in M. Russell, ed., *Perspectives in Public Regulation* (Carbondale: Southern Illinois University Press, 1973), pp. 1–27. See also W.J. Samuels, 'The Economy as a System of Power and Its Legal Bases: The Legal-Economics of Robert Lee Hale,' *University of Miami Law Review*, vol. 27 (1973), pp. 261–371.
10. Shatz, *Essential Works of Anarchism*, pp. xxvii–xxviii; and G. Woodcock, *Anarchism* (Cleveland: World, 1962), p. 25.
11. This is a problem on which Rothbard is very unsatisfactory, particularly in regard to his view that the Soviet Union would not aggress a stateless society in what is now the United States. See Rothbard, *For a New Liberty*, chapter 13. See also the Book Review by Walter Grinder, in *Books for Libertarians*, April 1973, p. 1.
12. O.H. Taylor, *A History of Economic Thought* (New York: McGraw-Hill, 1960), p. 134.

13. Rothbard, *For a New Liberty*, p. 18.
14. Ibid., p. 14; cf. p. 308.
15. Ibid., pp. 306ff.
16. Ibid., p. 8.
17. Ibid.
18. Ibid.
19. See Samuels, 'The Coase Theorem and the Study of Law and Economics.'
20. Rothbard tries to limit coercion to violence but he is not, and probably cannot be, consistent on this. Cf. Rothbard, *For a New Liberty*, p. 49 and *passim.*
21. M. Kominsky, Book Review, *Annals*, vol. 412 (March 1974), p. 166.
22. A number of the papers in G. Tullock, ed., *Explorations in the Theory of Anarchy* (Blacksburg: Center for the Study of Public Choice, 1972) deal with the emergence and operation of a property anarchy system, especially with the formation and operation of the power structure. See W.J. Samuels, Book Review, *Public Choice*, vol. 16 (1973), pp. 94–7, for a characterization and summary of power play within the property anarchist system.
23. Rothbard, *For a New Liberty*, pp. 28–9.
24. Ibid., pp. 30–37.
25. Ibid., p. 40.
26. Ibid.
27. Ibid., p. 43. Rothbard can write about 'unrestricted' property rights and absolute freedom only because the limits have been hidden away in his black box serving as the state. See below.
28. Ibid., p. 47.
29. Ibid., p. 77.
30. E.J. Hundert, 'The Making of *Homo Faber*: John Locke Between Ideology and History,' *Journal of the History of Ideas*, vol. 33 (1972), pp. 14–15.
31. Rothbard, *For a New Liberty*, p. 45.
32. See Samuels, 'Legal Change and Compensation,' *supra*, note 1.
33. H.E. Frech III, 'The Public Choice Theory of Murray N. Rothbard, A Modern Anarchist,' *Public Choice*, vol. 14 (1973), p. 145.
34. Rothbard, *For a New Liberty*, p. 235. Compare Rothbard's ambiguous common-law Libertarian Code with historical criticisms of civil codes by common-law lawyers: codes are deemed more statist and authoritarian and less attuned to the practices and customs of the people.
35. Ibid., p. 53.
36. 'Whoever does not wish to render history incomprehensible by departmentalizing it – political, economic, social – would perhaps take the view that it is in essence a battle of dominant wills, fighting in every way they can for the material which is common to everything they construct: the human labor force.' (Bertrand de Jouvenel, *On Power* (Boston: Beacon Press, 1962), p. 177.) On how statism and the free market can serve as substitute instruments whereby dominant classes can oppress and exploit the underlying population, see R.B. Seidman, 'Contract Law, the Free Market, and State Intervention,' *Journal of Economic Issues*, vol. 7 (1973), pp. 553–75. The de Jouvenel and Seldman arguments beautifully serve to place Rothbard's analysis in perspective.
37. Rothbard, *For a New Liberty*, p. 18.
38. Rothbard's system is only a modern version of Nicholas Murray Butler's *True and False Democracy* (New York: Scribner's, 1940).
39. Herman Finer, *Road to Reaction* (Chicago: Quadrangle Books, 1963), p. xii.
40. See W.J. Samuels, 'Adam Smith and the Economy as a System of Power,' *Review of Social Economy*, vol. 31 (1973), pp. 123–37; and *Pareto on Policy* (New York: American Elsevier, 1974).
41. Thomas Nixon Carver, 'Government Price Regulation: Discussion,' *American Economic Review, Supplement*, vol. 3 (1913), p. 137.
42. Emma Goldman, *Anarchism and Other Essays* (New York: Dover, 1969), pp. 52–61.

14. Polycentrism and power: a reply to Warren Samuels

Scott Beaulier

I. INTRODUCTION

There is no doubt that the anarcho-capitalist faces challenges from all sides. Leftist anarchists tend to agree with anarcho-capitalists as to the source of problems in political economy essentially stemming from state, but they argue that anarcho-capitalists are mistaken in their defense of private property. Instead of turning to the rather traditional institution of private property, some argue that communal living with fully participatory democracy ought to replace the current capitalist regime.[1] By contrast, many libertarians are critical of anarcho-capitalism for its lack of stability, the lack of historical examples of its success, or a belief that some goods must necessarily be provided by the government due to network effects.[2] But there is another group among the critics that raises a challenge regarding the kind of governance that should be expected to exist and/or emerge out of an anarcho-capitalist utopia. Among this last group of eclectic scholars, whom we can try to generalize under the heading of public economists, one of the most sophisticated challenges to anarcho-capitalists has been raised by Warren Samuels.

Throughout his career, Samuels has repeatedly raised the question to political economists: 'Who is to hold the power in a particular social system?' Whether a social system is a concentrated dictatorial nation or is instead a cluster of privately organized condominium associations, somebody is going to have the guns and control of the rules of the game in any social system. Therefore, the political economist is guilty of naiveté if she fails to appreciate this essentially axiomatic element of any society.

There are few places where Samuels makes himself more clear regarding the significance of power in political economy than in his 'Anarchism and the Theory of Power' (1974). Perhaps this is in large part due to the fact that in this essay Samuels not only derives his theory of power, but he also puts it to work in mounting heated criticism upon anarcho-capitalism – particularly that strand of anarcho-capitalism advocated by Murray N. Rothbard. In addition to the most serious criticism that will be discussed later, Samuels raised the following charges against Rothbard's anarcho-capitalist vision:

1. Murray Rothbard's manifesto is a plea for elitist or aristocratic conservatism (Samuels, 1974: 54).
2. John Locke deserves better treatment. Rothbard neglects to include Locke's fundamental distinction between property in the state of nature and in civil society (ibid.: 52–3).
3. Rothbard has a misconstrued notion of justice in which justice is only what comes out of markets (ibid.: 51).
4. Rothbard's society is not a model of a stateless society. There will be Libertarian Code and its administration and enforcement will constitute the state (ibid.: 54–5).[3]

For Samuels, then, Rothbard has not even come close in attempting to provide an adequate defense for anarcho-capitalism that addresses many of the 'messy details' involved in any form of social organization.

In another piece (Beaulier, 2004), I argued that, in large part, Samuels is asking too much of anarcho-capitalists. I argued that Samuels seems to be suggesting that anarcho-capitalists have a faith that power will be eliminated from their system of social organization. However, any smart anarcho-capitalist would not be making such a claim. Instead, Samuels should be asking two questions: (1) what system of social organization keeps the owners of the guns from doing the least harm?; and (2) what system of social organization provides diverse individuals with the level of power they desire? If these are indeed the relevant questions to be asking, then the burden of proof falls on Samuels to show why an anarcho-capitalist system is less efficient at reaching these two goals.

In this piece we will instead examine whether Rothbard's system of anarcho-capitalism can be defended against Samuels's charge that it fails to address the problem of power. Such an inquiry forces us to go inside Samuels's model of power. Therefore, the next section will provide a detailed discussion of Samuels's theory of power. In Section III we will then return to the particular criticisms that Samuels raises against Rothbard in his 'Anarchism and the Theory of Power'. After highlighting the charges raised against Rothbard, Section IV will attempt to defend Rothbard based on more contemporary market process and anarcho-capitalist insights. Section V concludes.

II.   SAMUELS'S THEORY OF POWER

Throughout his career, Warren Samuels has offered successively refined versions of his theory of power (Samuels, 1971, 1972a, 1972b). At approximately the same time that Samuels was originally laying out his theory, political implications of his thinking were unraveling in a private correspondence he was engaged in with James Buchanan (Buchanan and Samuels, 1992). In these correspondences, Samuels repeatedly drove home two fundamental points to Buchanan: (1) all state action is inherently non-neutral; and (2) all economic action is embedded in a deeper socio-cultural, political and legal nexus.[4] As Boettke (2001: 208) notes, from these two points, Samuels leads us 'to dispassionately recognize that government is omnipresent as the basic framework against which all economic activity takes place'. Furthermore, 'it is never the case that the choice is between government or no government, intervention or laissez-faire. Laissez-faire, in a fundamental sense, is conceptually bankrupt.' In order for us to understand how Samuels can reach such conclusions, we need to briefly digress into a summary of his theory of power.

For Samuels (1974: 38), power involves two conditions: '(1) effective participation in decision making'; and '(2) the means or capacity with which to exercise choice, e.g., rights, position; the first requires the second and the second enables the first.' From these conditions, Samuels's theory of power is deduced. In order to do so, Samuels turns many of the questions of constrained maximization on their head; rather than focus on the location of the tangency of one's opportunity set, Samuels instead asks the important questions:

> But what determines the opportunity set of the individual? What factors and forces govern the available alternatives and their respective costs? What is the larger process of choice out of which is generated the actual (and changing) structure of opportunity sets which comprise the economic decision-making process of any point of time and over time? (1972b: 64)

He goes on to argue that an economic system is not as simple as a choice among alternatives for individuals enjoying a constant opportunity set, but, rather, a system of *mutual coercion* (Samuels, 1974: 39), where one's decisions in the economic and legal nexus necessarily impact other individuals in the nexus. *Injuries* (which today would be deemed negative externalities) are reductions in the range of alternatives; *benefits* (positive externalities) are an increase in this range.

As Samuels sees it, power is a necessary consequence of choice. Therefore, power is present when an individual engages in volitionally powerful acts, but it is also present (and perhaps as strong) when the individual makes choices that she did not even know were exercises of power – in this latter case, the power of human action's unintended consequences can be even stronger than purposeful exercises of power. For Samuels, then, power is an inescapable aspect of any economic, political and legal web.

Let us now return to Boettke's claim that 'Laissez-faire, in a fundamental sense, is conceptually bankrupt'. As Samuels states:

[S]trict or absolute autonomy is impossible: the significant and viable problem is *which* pattern of freedom and of exposure to the freedom of others, or *which* structure of opportunity sets, or *which* pattern of invasions or externalities, is to be desired, promoted, allowed, or inhibited. The individual is 'autonomous' in that he is able to make his own decisions, but he can make them only from his opportunity set from within the total (and dynamic) structure of opportunity sets. In that sense the individual is always, or nearly always, autonomous; but the critical question has to do with the structure of opportunity sets and the factors and forces which govern that structure. (Ibid.: 40)

Samuels grants that the individual does indeed enjoy *some* autonomy under any system of social organization. The individual can autonomously choose from his opportunity set, and in this sense the individual is indeed free. However, the nature of an individual's opportunity set at any given time is something that is much more out of his control. Here the 'conceptual bankruptcy of laissez-faire' presents itself: do we have any reason to believe that 'autonomous' individuals in a laissez-faire regime will be less subject to changing forces (powers), which are largely outside of their control, than in alternative regimes? For Samuels, there is no clear reason to believe that laissez-faire will overcome this problem.

As he sees it, even in an anarcho-capitalist utopia, there will be power nodes dispersed throughout the decentralized system. Though it is a system of voluntary transactions, some individuals will inevitably be dissatisfied. In addition, individuals will be subject to the forces described above that are largely out of their control. According to Samuels, to therefore argue that the anarcho-capitalist social system overcomes problems of power because it is the result of voluntary exchange is to miss the point. Unless all individuals are completely satisfied with a system of voluntary exchange, all of its possible outcomes, and all of the effects anarcho-capitalism might have on the individual's opportunity sets, then the problem of the interests of some coercing those of others is not overcome.

This challenge is a very serious one. It is one that is germane not only for the few anarcho-capitalists of the world, but for any Austrian or public choice economist who is attempting to argue the benefits of certain institutional arrangements.[5] In one sense, Samuels's theory of power accommodates many dynamic aspects of Austrian economics. It offers us a story of embedded social beings who are not free-floating automata maximizing utility independent of their social condition,[6] but, rather, social agents who bring their history, family background and culture to the table when making decisions.

Samuels's theory of power also offers a more dynamic story of choice. The individual is not maximizing subject to a constant opportunity set, but is instead doing the best he can given constantly changing relative prices and power positions in society. While Neoclassicals could suggest that their theory of choice, with constant parameters, is a picture of an infinitesimally small time period within Samuels's theory, Samuels's theory seems to shed more light on the dynamic nature of the process of exchange. These contributions are undoubtedly with value-added to the establishment of a more rich, humanistic economic science. But, what are we to make of Samuels's theory of power and its relation to many Austrian arguments for political individualism? In order to answer this, let us first turn to an examination of the former.

III.   SAMUELS'S 'ANARCHISM AND THE THEORY OF POWER'

Samuels begins his article by expressing his sympathies for the anarchist position, but he then proceeds to discuss how he is much less certain in arguments for complete freedom because of the 'human predicament' (1974: 34). Samuels claims that he has reached this conviction for the following reasons:

1.   Freedom exists only within the context of a particular structure of freedom. The details of this structure of freedom are far more important than any abstract concept of freedom that characterizes this structure. (Ibid.)
2.   Order is also a complex term; it is a matter of order *on whose terms*. At some level, order is a vacuous notion that has an infinitude of components. (Ibid.)
3.   The market is instrumental to freedom and order, but it gives effect to the structure of power within which it operates and which conditions the generation and operation of market forces. The market may be the arena for the operation of private power that is often as effective as the state in limiting personal freedom and welfare. (Ibid.: 34–5)
4.   We must recognize coercion, domination and aggrandizement, both within the state and from within the private sector. Power will always exist and always need to be checked. (Ibid.: 35)

He concludes that he is therefore 'sympathetic to the lure of anarchism, but . . . skeptical about its realization' (ibid.).

Samuels then proceeds to offer a summary of anarchism generally and the position of the 'property anarchist' in particular. He concludes by defining the anarchist philosophy as a philosophy, and psychology, which affirms 'the autonomy of the individual, for all individuals; and it opposes the threat to that autonomy residing in concentrated power, most notably in the form of the state but also in the structure of social, nominally private power to use the state' (ibid.: 37–8).

From there Samuels turns to a discussion of his aforementioned theory of power before finally using this theory to attempt to point out the illegitimacy of Rothbard's version of anarcho-capitalism. Samuels begins (ibid.: 42) to develop his argument by suggesting that the 'anarchists' individualist values may be so congenial and so intoxicating as to obscure the power-based complexities of their realization and thus distort the possibilities and limits of an anarchical society as well as enable misleading conceptualizations and recommendations'. He goes on to offer a lengthy attack of Rothbard's anarcho-capitalism that can be summarized as follows (numbers in parentheses are page numbers in the 1974 article):

1. Each theory of anarchy has a place for power, but each posits a different arena and different group doing the channeling of power. One form of this is social or societal coercion. Anarchism relies on nonlegal social control, a different power structure. The anarchist thus opts for one system of social control over another (42–3).
2. Each theory of anarchy tends to presume the behavior necessary to produce the results intended by the particular theorist. All anarchists have a particular preconception of socialized man that permits anarchy per se to succeed. The critical problems to which the state is addressed in the real world are either presumed to no longer exist *or* to have been solved once and for all in some black box (43–4).
3. The problem is not state versus no state, nor anarchism versus tyranny. The problem is instead *which* power structure. The inescapable fact is that of public choice interrelated with private choice; and the inescapable problem is that of *whose* choice. That is the existential problem which the anarchist must confront. No individualism can avoid it (44).
4. Anarchism might just be a new power structure and elite substituted for the old (45).
5. The anarchist world will be a world of power play. Power built up and nourished from below – the anarchist model – will tend to centralize; in any event it will still be power. Individual choice will ultimately be interrelated with group choice. The diffusion of power will not prevent the very operation of the principles of power which produce the consequences of power so anathema to the anarchist mind (47).
6. The ideals of private autonomy and participation and of diffusion of power can be aborted by private aggregations of power as effectively as by governmental aggregations of power (47).
7. The state with its monopoly on violence and its ability to compel obedience might not be that different than what will result in an anarchical society – some form of social control of 'deviant' behavior will have to be present. In addition, opportunities to opt out, to live in other communities might be no greater than under the modern system (47–8).

8. The anarchist vision requires a universal, world-wide dismantling of the nation-state. For only one nation to unilaterally dissolve its concentrated state power is to enhance the relative power of all other nations (48).
9. Will anarchist reform mean that the world as an arena or stage for the power-intoxicated, for megalomania, whatever its psychic origin, will subside? Probably not! (49)

As these nine arguments against anarco-capitalism suggest, Samuels has many reasons to be suspicious about the legitimacy, efficacy and sustainability of an anarcho-capitalist system.

After raising these concerns, he finally turns to a direct attack on Murray Rothbard's (1973) *For a New Liberty*. Samuels surmises that Rothbard's work is 'a grotesque distortion of anarchism; indeed, it is not anarchism but a cleverly designed and worded surrogate for elitism or aristocratic conservatism' (50). Samuels argues that while Rothbard's 'propagandist' argument is appealing, tremendous problems arise when we move from the realm of vision to analysis. Just a few of the problems that Rothbard's analysis runs into include: how the just provision and identification of one's property rights is to be determined, how are relative-rights conflicts going to be worked out, and how are we going to deal with status quo titles (51–3)? Serious limitations in Rothbard's analysis lead Samuels to conclude that:

> Rothbard has his own state, with its own agenda. But Rothbard is not alone in neglecting the inevitability of mutual coercion. That Rothbard has his own ideal system of concentrated power should not obscure the general difficulty with anarchist thought notwithstanding their usual attempt to control concentrated power. Anarchism fails to resolve the very problems of power which it set out to conquer. (56)

IV. ROTHBARD ON ECONOMIC AND POLITICAL POWER

The previous section has shown that Samuels has many reasonable reservations and challenges to the anarcho-capitalists' position. Some of these challenges, particularly the question of 'who is to choose?', are concerns that no longer remain in the realm of positive economics. It is a normative judgment made by anarcho-capitalists that the best mechanism for 'public choice' is the use of an organizational head who has been *voluntarily* granted authority by a collection of private individuals. At some essentialist level, the legitimacy of this position does indeed rest on a value judgment. This value judgment is that individual choice and voluntary transactions are our absolute good. It is fair for Samuels to question this essentialist position, but let us put this problematical aspect of the anarcho-capitalists' position aside for the remainder of this chapter.

Besides problems related to the positive–normative dichotomy, can Rothbard's particular strand of anarcho-capitalism be defended against the charges Samuels has raised? First, let us be clear that there are two distinct problems of power that Samuels seems to be addressing. The first problem is some kind of Nietzschian human nature claim that man has a 'will to power'. Therefore, no matter how our social system is designed, there is no way to change this blemish of man's nature. The other problem of power that Samuels raises relates to the decision mechanism used in any social arrangement. It is this aspect of Samuels's theory of power where our attention should be concentrated; not only is it the more germane question for political economy, but pursuing this question helps us formulate a reasonable response to man's 'will to power' claim.

Samuels's theory of power is essentially claiming that even in the best anarcho-capitalist arrangement, there will be some decision mechanism where the interests of some individuals are trumped by the interests of a more powerful group of individuals. For example, what are we to do when members of a condominium association in an anarcho-capitalist utopia are in a dispute over what to do with a vacant lot? Two Muslims in this community would like to see a mosque built; five Yuppies would like to see a swimming pool constructed; and two environmentalists would like to see it remain 'as is'. Now, certainly, a willingness to pay is one criterion in determining which project should be pursued, but the interests of some are inevitably going to conflict with those of others. Suppose the swimming pool project is voted on and passed by condominium association members. Then, at least to some extent, those who were opposed to the swimming pool project are unsatisfied.

This is where Samuels sees the anarcho-capitalist vision as a fundamentally flawed form of social organization. So long as private property rights are not completely divisible, we run into the same kind of public-good problem as that which arises under modern welfare state regimes. There are two options for individuals living under these arrangements: either find ways for a logrolling mechanism to emerge which allows them at least to get the particular private goods with 'publicness' characteristics that they most desire, or exit.

Samuels sees the latter as a much more unstable and unlikely option than the anarcho-capitalists make it out to be. Samuels's central concern is that this exit option is not something that promises stability in the anarcho-capitalist arrangement of private communities. As there is exit from one society because of discontent over the public goods being chosen, the individuals who remain bear a larger brunt of the costs for the community. In other words, *ceteris* is far from *paribus* when it comes to these dynamic issues within the anarcho-capitalist vision.

So, can the anarcho-capitalists in general, and Murray Rothbard in particular, answer Samuels's criticism? If we take an approach that asks the question,

'As compared to what?', perhaps the anarcho-capitalists' position can still be defended. To a large extent, Samuels seems to be raising a criticism that anarcho-capitalism would not be able to reach some kind of ideal state where there are no social problems that emerge from conflicts over private use of goods with 'publicness' features. This is an unattainable possibility for any social arrangement, and there is no doubt that Samuels should realize this.

The point that he seems to be missing in his criticism of Murray Rothbard relates to the question he is asking.[7] For Samuels, the fundamental problem is that there will always be power. For Rothbard and other anarcho-capitalists, however, the problem is not so much that power will always be present – this should be treated as a given – but rather that some social arrangements do better than others at guaranteeing that individuals can get around or out of power nodes that they cannot tolerate. A market process approach emphasizes the fact that individuals can always work their way around any set of rules. Therefore, perhaps an ideal institutional arrangement is one which attempts to minimize the costs of obstructive rules.

When we see the problem in this light, we also get insight into the first power problem Samuels raises – that related to man's 'will to power'. If individuals are indeed the kind of knaves that Samuels seems to suggest, then the Hayekian/Humean/Smithean (and, as we will see, Rothbardian) proviso is to construct a form of social organization where our chief concern is:

> [N]ot so much with what man might occasionally achieve when he was at his best but that he should have as little opportunity as possible to do harm when he was at his worst. It would scarcely be too much to claim that the main merit of the individualism which he (Smith) and his contemporaries advocated is that it is a system under which bad men can do least harm. It is a social system which does not depend for its functioning on our finding good men for running it, or on all men becoming better than they now are, but which makes use of men in all their given variety and complexity, sometimes good and sometimes bad, sometimes intelligent and more often stupid. (Hayek, 1980: 11–12)

What Samuels might have missed in his scathing review of Rothbard's *For a New Liberty* is that Rothbard is part of the same tradition as Hayek, Hume and Smith. For Rothbard, anarcho-capitalism is not a story of best-case theorizing, but, rather, one institutional arrangement that might be capable of meeting the above criterion of keeping 'bad and stupid men from doing least harm'.

This is not some kind of ridiculous claim, for there is definitely evidence that Rothbard was serious about taking man as he is (perhaps even a man whose nature contains a 'will to power') and finding a form of social organization that can minimize the potential harm. One point that Samuels most certainly overlooks in Rothbard (1973) is Rothbard's assumptions about man. The following captures the seriousness of Rothbard's position and the very pessimistic assumptions the anarcho-capitalist makes regarding the nature of man:

In the deepest sense, then, the libertarian doctrine is not utopian but eminently realistic, because *it is the only theory* that is really consistent with the nature of man and the world. The libertarian does not deny the variety and diversity of man, he glorifies in it and seeks to give that diversity full expression in a world of complete freedom.

The libertarian believes that, in the ultimate analysis, every individual has free will and moulds himself; it is therefore folly to put one's hope in a uniform and drastic change in people brought about by the projected New Order. The libertarian would *like* to see a moral improvement in everyone, although his moral goals scarcely coincide with those of the socialists. He would, for example, be overjoyed to see all desire for aggression by one man against another disappear from the face of the earth. But he is far too much of a realist to put his trust in this sort of change. Instead, the libertarian system is one that will at once be far more moral and work much better than any other, *given* any existing human values and attitudes. (Ibid.: 303–4)

Clearly, then, Rothbard was trying to offer us an alternative institutional regime where man is taken 'as is', rather than as he could be under some ideal. Is it any coincidence that the political individualism that he derives in the form of anarcho-capitalism is in a similar vein to Hayekian, Humean and Smithian arguments for the minimal state? What makes Rothbard, who claims to be making a contribution in political economy by offering us a realistic picture of man, an 'aristocratic elitist', but keeps the likes of Hayek, Hume and Smith insulated from this charge?

Warren Samuels has made a career of discussing the messy process of actually 'working things out' among agents in a market economy. What he seems to have misunderstood in the argument for anarcho-capitalism is that, when taken seriously, this is an argument for cleaning up and reducing some of the messy properties of the economic, legal and social nexus. When at its best, the argument for anarcho-capitalism is something that derives not only from moral presuppositions, but also from a rich commitment to market process notions of information, uncertainty and ignorance. A good deal of the blame for Samuels's misunderstanding could certainly lie in Rothbard's rhetorical style and emphasis on natural rights, but this work, coupled with contemporary contributions in the anarcho-capitalist literature, has attempted to both reconcile Rothbard and make the case for anarcho-capitalism an even more legitimate one.

One can make arguments in favor of anarcho-capitalism in addition to moral ones. Benson (1988, 1990), Friedman (1979, 1989), and Klein (1997) have managed to go further than Rothbard (1973) by illuminating how voluntary organization led to better economic results *and* a more orderly, moral environment. This kind of rich anarcho-capitalism argues for private enforcement and voluntarism not only because it is right, but also because of the good outcomes that result. Perhaps Samuels's position would change in light of these advances, for they all show how problems of power can be (and actually are) managed – or, worked around – in voluntary arrangements in history.

V.   CONCLUSIONS

In one sense, Samuels might have been way ahead of his time. Some of the most recent criticisms of the reputation model that the anarcho-capitalists' case so firmly rests upon argue that there are two major factors that might produce instability in private self-governance: (1) a heterogeneous population;[8] and (2) private goods with 'publicness' characteristics. We have already discussed how, if the latter is present, certain conflicts seem inevitable in our anarcho-capitalist ideal. This chapter has attempted to get around this issue by making a 'compared to what?' argument where it is hard to think of a better alternative that provides agents in society with a way around these conflicts. But this argument alone suffers from serious limitations. What the Samuels challenge, coupled with recent game-theoretic critiques of the reputation model, calls for is a more serious inquiry by the likes of Benson, Klein, Stringham, and Caplan and Stringham – who each in their own way rest their case for private self-governance on the reputation model.

This chapter has attempted to show that *even if* we treat power as a given which will be as omnipresent in an anarcho-capitalist utopia as it is today under a massive welfare state regime, our central concern should remain focused on whether one institutional regime is more effective than another at assuring that individuals can get around and away from powers they dislike. While this is certainly in part a moral proposition based on a strong belief in individual autonomy, there is tremendous economic support for regimes that promise greater openness and greater variety of governance to individuals. It is ultimately this question which proves to be *the fundamental question* in all of political economy. Samuels was on the right track in recognizing that power is an important element of the framework, but Rothbard, the Austrians and anarcho-capitalist contemporaries were/are part of the group of political economists who recognize(d) that it was not power *per se*, but instead power in relation to individuals' options that is our chief concern.

There is no doubt that Samuels would agree with this as the key issue of political economy. It is unfortunate that he did not view Rothbard's work in anarcho-capitalism as work in the same vein as other classic Austrian contributions. Perhaps Samuels is correct about Rothbard being confusing as to whether he is arguing for anarcho-capitalism economically or morally. If this is an isolated problem related only to Murray Rothbard, then Samuels's position should be subject to change in light of recent work. If anarcho-capitalism remains a suspect argument for Samuels, then perhaps it is time he gave us an update as to exactly why this is still the case.

NOTES

1. Perhaps the leading proponent of this leftist anarchism and an advocate for 'libertarian municipalism' is Bookchin (1971 and 1989).
2. There is a vast literature of libertarian criticisms against the anarcho-capitalist vision. Nozick (1974) remains the classic 'invisible hand story' as to how state courts and police authority are the result of an evolutionary, efficient market process. More recently, Cowen (1992) has criticized anarcho-capitalism's inherent instability and the network externalities of the legal system. For a response to Cowen's criticisms, see Caplan and Stringham (2003).
3. See also Frech (1973: 145).
4. For some of Samuels's most recent work on embeddedness and the emergence of norms, see Samuels (1999 and 2000). For a favorable review of Samuels's recent work on norms, see Beaulier and Boettke (2000).
5. Interestingly, in the Buchanan–Samuels correspondences, Buchanan was charged with having an unfair bias for the status quo.
6. Even some of the better New Institutionalists, such as Hodgson (1999), fail to recognize the social aspect of methodological individualism. For example, Hodgson offers a rather common straw-man attack on Austrian economists when he states:

   > Generally, if contract and trade are always the best ways of organizing matters, then many functions that are traditionally organized in a different manner should become commercialized . . . Pushed to the limit, market individualism implies the commercialization of sex and the abolition of the family. A consistent market individualist cannot be a devotee of 'family values' . . . They cannot in one breath argue that the market is the best way of ordering all socio-economic activities, and then deny it in another. If they cherish family values then they have to recognize the practical and moral limits of the market imperatives and pecuniary exchange. (Ibid.: 99)

7. Beaulier (2004) makes a similar claim. However, in that analysis, the emphasis is on the implications of power when we take a subjectivist approach to its logical conclusion. Here, the argument will suggest that the point of these power analyses is not to design a social system that will overcome the problem of power, but rather offer a system that allows individuals the greatest amount of freedom to get around power problems.
8. This argument has been advanced by several different economists (Alesina and Drazen, 1991; Alesina and Spolaore, 1997; and Shleifer and Vishny, 1993).

REFERENCES

Alesina, Alberto and Drazen, Allen (1991), 'Why are Stabilizations Delayed?', *American Economic Review*, **85**: 465–90.

Alesina, Alberto and Spolaore, Enrico (1997), 'On the Number and Size of Nations', *Quarterly Journal of Economics*, **112**: 1027–56.

Beaulier, Scott (2004), 'In Pursuit of the Relevant Question: An Appraisal of Warren Samuels's "Powerful" Challenge to Proponents of the Free Society', Working Paper, Mercer University School of Business and Economics.

Beaulier, Scott and Boettke, Peter (2000), 'Of Norms, Rules, and Markets: A Comment on Samuels', *Journal des Economistes et des Etudes Humaines*, **10**: 547–52.

Benson, Bruce (1988), 'Legal Evolution in Primitive Societies', *Journal of Institutional and Theoretical Economics*, **144**: 772–88.

Benson, Bruce (1990), *The Enterprise of Law: Justice Without the State*, San Francisco, CA: Pacific Research Institute for Public Policy.

Boettke, Peter (2001), 'Putting the Political Back into Political Economy', in J.E. Biddle, J.B. Davis and S.G. Medema (eds), *Economics Broadly Considered: Essays in Honor of Warren J. Samuels*, New York: Routledge, pp. 204–16.

Bookchin, Murray (1971), *Post-Scarcity Anarchism*, Montreal: Black Rose Books.

Bookchin, Murray (1989), *Remaking Society*, Montreal: Black Rose Books.

Buchanan, James and Samuels, Warren (1992), 'On Some Fundamental Issues in Political Economy: An Exchange of Correspondence', in Warren Samuels (ed.), *Essays on the Methodology and Discourse of Economics*, New York: New York University Press, pp. 201–30.

Caplan, Bryan and Stringham, Edward (2003), 'Networks, Law, and the Paradox of Cooperation', *Review of Austrian Economics*, **16**: 309–26.

Cowen, Tyler (1992), 'Law as a Public Good: The Economics of Anarchy', *Economics and Philosophy*, **8**: 249–67.

Frech, H.E. (1973), 'The Public Choice of Murray N. Rothbard, A Modern Anarchist', *Public Choice*, **14**: 143–54.

Friedman, David (1979), 'Private Creation and Enforcement of Law – A Historical Case', *Journal of Legal Studies*, **8**: 399–415.

Friedman, David (1989) [1995], *The Machinery of Freedom*, La Salle, IL: Open Court.

Hayek, F.A. (1980), *Individualism and Economic Order*, Chicago, IL: University of Chicago Press.

Hodgson, Geoffrey (1999), *Economics and Utopia*, New York: Routledge.

Klein, Daniel (1997), *Reputation: Studies in the Voluntary Elicitation of Good Conduct*, Ann Arbor, MI: University of Michigan Press.

Nozick, Robert (1974), *Anarchy, State and Utopia*, New York: Basic Books.

Rothbard, Murray (1973/1996), *For a New Liberty: Libertarian Manifesto*, San Francisco, CA: Fox & Wilkes.

Samuels, Warren (1971), 'Interrelations Between Legal and Economic Processes', *Journal of Law and Economics*, **14**: 435–50.

Samuels, Warren (1972a), 'Defense of a Positive Approach to Government as an Economic Variable', *Journal of Law and Economics*, **15**: 453–60.

Samuels, Warren (1972b), 'Welfare Economics, Power and Property', in G. Wunderlich and W.L. Gibson, Jr (eds), *Perspectives of Property*, University Park, PA: Institute for Research on Land and Water Resources, Pennsylvania State University, pp. 61–148.

Samuels, Warren (1974), 'Anarchism and the Theory of Power', in G. Tullock (ed.), *Further Explorations in the Theory of Anarchy*, The Public Choice Society Book and Monograph Series, Blacksburg, VA: University Publications, pp. 33–57.

Samuels, Warren (1999), 'Hayek from the Perspective of an Institutionalist Historian of Economic Thought: An Interpretive Essay', *Journal des Economistes et des Etudes Humaines*, **9**: 279–90.

Samuels, Warren (2000), 'An Essay on the Unmagic of Norms and Rules and of Markets', *Journal des Economistes et des Etudes Humaines*, **10**: 391–7.

Shleifer, Andrei and Vishny, Robert (1993), 'Corruption', *Quarterly Journal of Economics*, **108**: 599–617.

15. Reflections after three decades

James M. Buchanan

It is interesting that the new papers here are devoted to a critical re-examination and re-evaluation of seminar papers written in the early 1970s – papers that represented responses to the turbulent events of the 1960s. For those of us in the academies, the institutions of order seemed to be crumbling about us, and those institutions that seemed able and willing to resist the sheer will toward destruction by the anarchists – a proper descriptive term – were few and far between. One of the institutions that did resist was VPI, now renamed Virginia Tech (Virginia Polytechnic and State University). Under the leadership of Marshall Hahn, this university had little time for the anarchists, who, as they folded their tents, again demonstrated their relative weakness of will against even the slightest of genuine opposition.

The seminar papers, as published in the small volumes edited by Gordon Tullock (1972, 1974a), as well as Tullock's book, *The Social Dilemma* (1974b) and my own book, *The Limits of Liberty* (1975), should, at least in part, be interpreted as reactions to the times written by those of us who were, ourselves, relatively cozy in our own private cocoon of academia and able to observe the outside world. Stimulated more or less directly by Winston Bush, we found explorations into the properties of anarchist equilibria to be fascinating in their own right, as well as indirectly topical in the extreme.

These works, along with my earlier book with Devletoglou, *Academia in Anarchy* (1970), implicitly interpreted, were more pessimistic about prospects in the academy and beyond than the subsequent history we experienced. Despite permanent damage to the social fabric within the academies and without, order of sorts was restored in the 1970s, although generalized respect for rules, including those involving ordinary manners and courtesy, vanished from the 1960s on, perhaps never to be restored. The 1960s were, indeed, a watershed decade, the effects of which really cannot be appreciated by those who were not living participants in the turmoil.

The published materials discussed in the papers here stand on their own, independent of their inspiration and origins. And my remarks are not intended to make excuses for their inadequacies and inaccuracies. My suggestion is only that the works can be understood more fully by some appreciation of the times and the setting of their composition.

The anarchists of the 1960s, and perhaps also the Russian anarchists of the nineteenth century, were enemies of order, as such, rather than proponents of any alternative organizational structure. They sought, for themselves, unprincipled liberty unbound by any sense of equal liberty for other than themselves. Indeed, the campus radicals of the 1960s were the meritoriously selected elite, as proven to their own satisfaction by their exemption from the compulsion of the military draft and the consequent risk of death – exemption not granted their more ordinary generational peers.

Their rebellion against the surprisingly easy targets of the academy was prompted, in part, by their conviction, often quite genuine, that, if given their liberties, they could remake the world to the benefit of the great unwashed as well as their own. If, however, the elites could escape from order, from rules, from law, how could others not claim like privilege? How could the modern Hobbesian anarchy be far behind? At least the anarchy research program at Virginia Tech in the early 1970s was, relatively, focused in its ultimate intent. What would things be like if the institutions of order did indeed collapse? Surely this question was worthy of examination.

The world today is quite a different place. The USA, and Western civil order more generally, faces a categorically different threat. The terrorists of this new century seek to destroy *our* whole civil order. And they do have an alternative order to impose on us after our whole structure of interaction collapses. We do not need further examination of what internal anarchy might produce. We do need, and desperately, hard-headed analysis of what terrorism might produce and how it might be fought by persons in a society that respects personal liberties. Perhaps the primary modern usefulness of the re-examination and extension of the earlier analyses of anarchy lies in an appreciation of its obvious linkage to the events of its time. The earlier program reflected academic *responsibility* at its best. A modern emulation of the spirit of that program would involve the launching of a comparable effort directed toward diagnoses and analyses of terrorism. Such an effort might, indeed, involve predictions that the soft-headed among us do not enjoy making or even reading.

The America of the 1970s did not live out the hard-headed predictions of those of us who analyzed anarchy. Yet, would it not be nice to think that the arguments that contained those predictions had at least some small part to play in forestalling the worst?

REFERENCES

Buchanan, James M. (1975), *The Limits of Liberty: Between Anarchy and Leviathan*, Chicago, IL: University of Chicago.

Buchanan, James M. and Devletoglou, Nicos E. (1970), *Academia in Anarchy: An Economic Diagnosis*, New York: Basic Books.

Tullock, Gordon (ed.) (1972), *Explorations in the Theory of Anarchy*, Blacksburg, VA: Center for the Study of Public Choice.

Tullock, Gordon (ed.) (1974a), *Further Explorations in the Theory of Anarchy*, Blacksburg, VA: University Publications.

Tullock, Gordon (1974b), *The Social Dilemma: The Economics of War and Revolution*, Blacksburg, VA: University Publications.

16. Anarchy

Gordon Tullock

Anarchy originally developed in Europe as a sort of offshoot of Christianity. Non-violence was regarded as morally good and European anarchists normally thought that by arguments they could convince everyone and hence end war. Anarchy was usually closely associated with socialism. This movement has almost entirely died out. There was another kind of anarchism essentially invented in the USA by Spooner. This, like the European brand, proposed to abolish the state, but thought that the market would carry out all the desirable functions of the state. Although they did not advocate war, these anarchists believed that force would be needed to defend both against ordinary criminals and possibly foreign countries. The force was to be provided privately rather than through the government. Although this brand of anarchism is mainly found in the USA, it has recently spread to Europe. On both continents, and in the few other parts of the world where it has at least a few disciples, it is a very much a minority point of view.

There were a few experiments in anarchy in communities along the western border of white settlement in the USA in the nineteenth century. They all failed quickly or developed religiously based local governments. Some religiously based, and in practice although not in theory, autonomous local communities of this sort still exist in the West, in Canada and in Paraguay. The theoretical anarchists discussed in the previous paragraph do not seem interested in them. On a more unfortunate note, some of the modern terrorist organizations are theoretically anarchists. They fit the normal definition of 'anarchy' as a state of violence and confusion, but I do not think one can argue that this is a natural development of anarchy. Before the Spanish Civil War there was a powerful anarchist party in Spain. Although anarchist in its ideology, in practice it was the most totalitarian party in that country. It provided troops for the government during the Civil War and was eliminated afterwards.

The bulk of anarchists today, and that bulk is rather small, do not attempt to set up a government, but confine themselves to writing and arguing for anarchy without trying it experimentally. Even full-blooded anarchy seems to be on the wane. Both Friedman and Benson have said that some kind of military defense would be necessary. In both cases, however, this is simply a passing sentence in their books showing how, in their opinion, anarchy would work.

Most of the history we read about in books is a history of war. Countries are conquered, governments overthrown and occasionally whole peoples exterminated. Israel had the misfortune of attracting the attention of the Assyrians. As a result most of the Jews disappeared from history. Only a small outlying state survived, and this only because of an accident in which the plague struck Jerusalem. Massive conquests in which whole peoples disappeared are not uncommon. The fall of the Western Roman Empire set back civilization for many generations. Babur, limping Timur, Genghis Khan and his descendants cleared whole areas of their population. The Spanish conquest of the Americas was almost equally devastating. Anarchists almost never discuss how they will defend without large armies.

Military activity is subject to very significant economies of scale. It is not always true, but, normally, big armies beat small ones. Further, professional troops who devote most of their attention to training when not at war seem to have a decided advantage over amateur soldiers. In the nineteenth and early twentieth centuries conscripts with little training dominated the battlefields of Europe, but this was mainly because they could be thrown into the Army without much cost and hence heavily outnumbered the professionals. Today, when the Army needs complex equipment which amateurs would have trouble operating unless they were given long periods of training, the situation has changed. The Afghan war was not a good model for main line battles, but very small numbers of professionals beat a large collection of more or less amateur troops. The possibility of nuclear war should always be kept in mind. It does not require large bodies of troops for victory.

In the late nineteenth and early twentieth centuries slavery and piracy were eliminated by the military forces maintained by such countries as England and the USA. Since World War II both have returned, largely because it is no longer thought fashionable to use military forces to suppress them. Suppression would require only very small forces, as it did formerly.[1] There is another area where force or violence is used with general public approval. This is the domestic peace forces such as the police, and here again numbers and training pay off. It should be said, however, that there are many private police forces in the USA and other westernized countries, but they are always dominated by government-organized forces. In the USA, for example, although there are private police companies, detectives, mediators who may settle cases, and prisons, they are always subordinated to government forces. They cannot arrest, try and imprison people on their own. If I am correct, the modern anarchists think that they should be permitted to do so because they want to get rid of the regular government.

We have considerable historical experience in this matter. When the

Western Roman Empire collapsed, various local entrepreneurs took over the provision of police activity and, of course, the collection of taxes. At first they pretended to be part of the Empire and took titles from the Roman Army. Duke, viscount and count are all derived from ranks in the Roman Army but eventually became hereditary titles of nobility. We call the result feudalism and it guaranteed Europe a disorderly and poverty-stricken society for 1000 years. It is interesting that even as late as the time Gibbon wrote, the best roads in Europe were still the remnants of those built by the Romans.

This outcome was just about inevitable, granted the need for some protection against simple criminals and the economies of scale and training in combat. There were of course various nongovernmental activities such as the Church and the fairs which, under the shelter of feudal military organizations, carried on various activities of their own. For some reason the dusty foot courts have attracted attention from modern anarchists. They met in various fairs and other commercial centers, but they depended on the men-at-arms of the feudal lords for defense against violent bands of armed men who were in plentiful supply in the forests which covered much of Europe. Some records of the dusty foot courts survived, but the brief skirmishes between bandit gangs and the local lords were not recorded. Boycott might be a useful method against a merchant, but not against a bandit chief. Today all countries have learned the lesson and maintain police forces under government control. Occasionally citizens provide some reinforcement, but usually the professional police forces object to such amateur intervention.

All this is far from optimal, but what can be done to replace it? Occasionally one will find private arbitration not enforced by the courts, but it is rare. Normally arbitration or mediation is simply incorporated into the regular court system. Today many contracts in the USA provide for arbitration if there's a dispute. However, the arbitrator depends on the use of force to carry out his decisions if one of the parties objects. The court orders the parties to proceed to arbitration and then orders them to obey the arbitrator. If they don't, the judge will call out the sheriff or whatever other police forces are available to use force. He does not rely on boycotts or public opinion.

Although the use and control of force is a primary function of government, it normally has others. In some cases this is just a mistake, leading to retaining activities that earlier had sensible motives. In other cases, however, it is hard to see how the activity could be provided privately. An obvious case is quarantine; another is control of the electromagnetic spectrum. In neither case is government activity ideal, but in both cases we are better off with than without, and it's very hard to see how a private arrangement could be enforced without the use or implied threat of the police force.

Transportation rights of way are mainly provided by the government. This was not always so. There were many toll roads and in the USA and England there were privately owned railroads which provided the bulk of long-distance transportation. In England there were also many privately owned canals. There does not seem to be any reason we should not experiment further with them. I should emphasize, however, that they would be experiments. There is no guarantee of success. When I talk to modern American anarchists about roads I invariably get into disagreements about trespass on privately owned property. A privately owned road, railroad or canal is not only a means of transportation; it is a long thin strip of private property which under the ordinary laws of trespass cannot be crossed without permission of the owner. If he was permitted to charge a fee for this permission, the possibility of the country being broken up into a large number of small pieces between roads would not be zero.

All governments have dealt with this problem by requiring the owner of the long thin strip, whether a railroad, a canal, or a road, to provide permission, subject to reasonable conditions, for people to cross, build a crossing railroad or road (in a few cases canals). To repeat, anarchists frequently object to this, I think mainly because it is a government making these laws. Conversations with them produce the most fantastic ideas about building bridges over the road or digging a tunnel under it. In current law these are as much trespasses as simply walking across. There is of course no reason why the law could not be changed to permit them, but allowing direct crossing on the surface with appropriate regulation seems far more sensible. This anarchist argument seems foolish, but I have heard it offered many times. It is true that without a government, roads, canals and railroads could be used as barriers to transportation as well as means of transportation, depending on perspective. Thus we need a government for this very minor but necessary activity.

Many questions connected with short-range activities near houses or other private property require regulation. This has traditionally been done by governments under local control, but much can also be contracted out. Normally, however, these contracts relate to more than one household. In Arizona there are many private fire departments. They sell a combination of fire protection and fire insurance and thus are like the early privately sponsored fire departments in places such as Philadelphia. Fire, however, is no respecter of property. A fire in one house can easily spread to others; thus if the houses are close together these companies will normally not sell policies to only one house in the row. The condominium I once lived in arranged insurance itself, although householders were individually billed. Whether the condominium should be regarded as private or governmental is a subject upon which there can be disagreement, but is of little importance to anybody except the theoretical anarchists. I must admit I do not know what their solution to this question is. In any event, small communities, whether condominiums or villages, are in competition with each other, and the Tiebout effect provides most of the advantages of freedom through the ability to move and it provides most of the advantages of economies of scale in various activities carried on by a central organization.

As the reader may know, I have spent much time in China. Traditional China was a monarchy with a strong central government. Local government, however, was carried out, in general, by a rather democratic set of local governments. In the countryside these were villages, but in the city they were formally organized neighborhoods. They had their own little governmental council and maintained police forces and engaged in other activities which in the USA are considered governmental. I would be in favor of adopting the same system here. Indeed, I have the last few years always lived in condominiums which differ from local governments in only minor ways. Once again I do not know what the American anarchists think about this. I suspect they regard it as an example of anarchy rather than local government.

Finally, I turn to common nuisances. Suppose I want to practice the trumpet at three in the morning. My neighbors would certainly object and today they would turn to the police force to stop me. I do not know what the anarchist solution to this problem is. However, it is true that what I do on my property may be an inconvenience to others. The condominium in which I lived in Tucson had very complicated rules about the external appearance of the houses and for that matter their gardens. This was intended to, and no doubt did, increase the sale value of the houses. It is a little difficult to see what the anarchist solution to this matter would be. Of course we had purchased our houses with contracts, making us members of the condominiums' association. Thus we had agreed to obey its orders. But people who had not made any agreement, heirs after death for example, were also bound.[2]

I suspect that the anarchists would agree to being so bound, although not to a government agency to enforce the agreement. If you permit people to be bound by their ancestors or predecessors in title's agreement, then it can be argued that all of us are so bound by the agreement made in Philadelphia and the innumerable minor agreements which have been made since then by our ancestors or predecessors in title. Thus such agreements are inconsistent with anarchy. Spooner dealt with this problem by saying that agreements by our ancestors or predecessors in title do not bind us. Logically this is perfectly possible, but it means that my neighbor, a recent arrival, can play the trumpet at any time. I doubt that this is satisfactory.

This concludes my very brief explanation of why neither I nor any other sensible person actually favors anarchy. I anticipate a vigorous but not very well-reasoned response. As a follower of Popper, I think discussion is the best way of reaching the truth. So let the discussion continue.

NOTES

1. Burnett (2002) gives an excited but basically accurate account of this new piracy.
2. My father left me a piece of real estate subject to a 99-year lease.

REFERENCE

Burnett, John S. (2002), *Dangerous Waters: Modern Piracy and Terror on the High Seas*, New York: E.P. Dutton.

17. Tullock on anarchy

Jeffrey Rogers Hummel

Gordon Tullock's rebuttal offers up a muddle of both profoundly serious and amazingly silly objections to a stateless society. Many of them rest on a common but unreflective identification of government with law. Concerns about private roadways, quarantine for disease, the electromagnetic spectrum, the spread of fires, other frequent nuisances, and above all ultimate enforcement fall into this category. In all these cases, Tullock refuses to come to grips with one of the libertarian anarchist's central insights: a monopoly state is not a necessary precondition for uniform law to prevail.

Consider the USA, Canada and the UK. An intricate legal network peacefully resolves disputes not only between those three countries but also between their respective residents, and has done so since 1816, without any world government enforcing the decisions. International anarchy does not always produce such happy results, a point upon which Tullock pounces and to which I shall return. The frequency of civil wars, however, attests that a government is no absolute guarantee of legal peace either.

Few libertarian anarchists have ever questioned that protecting property and upholding contracts sometimes requires force. But they deny that such force must emanate from a coercive monopoly. Competing private agencies will suffice. Tullock's first paragraph acknowledges the anarcho-capitalist belief that 'force would be needed to defend both against ordinary criminals and possibly foreign countries' so long as it is 'provided privately rather than through government'. Yet this recognition mysteriously slips Tullock's mind when he gets to concretes. Suddenly anarchists are placing all their hopes on 'boycotts or public opinion'.

The basis of Tullock's disregard for even the possibility of law without monopoly enforcement is difficult to discern. He does observe that existing private protection and arbitration services 'are always subordinated to government forces'. Granted; so what? This is the anarchist complaint exactly. That the state by its nature monopolizes coercion is alone no argument for such a monopoly.

Tullock might, of course, follow the course set by Robert Nozick and semantically evade the debate by defining any society where protection agencies resolve their disagreements without open warfare as having a state – or having, if he prefers Nozick's term, a 'dominant protection agency'. But such a tautology will hardly convince most residents of North America and the British Isles that they all live under one overarching government.

Tullock could dispute the relevance of the previous international analogy. Law prevails between the USA, Canada and Britain, he might argue, only because each of those three countries has a government. Notice, however, that if he takes this approach, Tullock implies that competing states tend to be more peaceful than competing private agencies would be. This runs counter to his grave worries about foreign conquest, and since private protection agencies would lack any power to tax and conscript, they would seem to share every incentive that governments have to avoid war plus a few more.

Perhaps Tullock's account of Rome's collapse is meant to suggest that private agencies invariably degenerate into governments. Even if true, this thesis says less about government's desirability than about its persistence. Moreover, it ignores the remarkable internal stability of several past stateless legal regimes. Medieval Iceland flourished without government for 300 years. Indeed, humans for most of their existence on this planet have lived under the non-state laws of primitive hunter–gatherers.

The most glaring manifestation of Tullock's equivocation between law and government is his hint that private homeowners' associations become governments when they impose contractually agreed-upon rules. Would Tullock say the same about landlords who impose rules on their tenants or employers who impose rules on their employees? Admittedly the precise dividing line (like all dividing lines) between a private owner and a government can raise thorny philosophical issues. With sufficient intellectual ingenuity, one can portray even Stalinist Russia as a market economy with a peculiar structure of property rights.

But such definitional quibbles need not confuse us about the distinction between a society subject to a monopoly state and a society where customers can choose among competing agencies that enforce law. If a private protection agency apprehends and punishes a criminal against his will, it would be doing something that the state sometimes does. So would a private agency that delivers mail. That does not convert United Parcel Service and Federal Express into governments.

Once we stop conflating law and government, Tullock's objections often either vanish or become no trickier for a stateless society to handle than for government. The noise pollution from Tullock's trumpet at 3:00 a.m. could be equally actionable and preventable under either arrangement. Government itself appears to be the major obstacle to the ingenious market solutions that economists have devised for these assorted externalities. Tullock's favorite hobby-horse, private roads that cordon people off, leaves the impression that he has never heard of an easement. Many a private right of way in the past definitely did *not* treat crossing over as trespass. The bundle of rights we call land, as with other kinds of property, can be and has been divided up and traded separately – if demand warrants. I fail to understand why the market should be unable to deal with such jointly owned resources when it smoothly deals with the complex, jointly owned firms we call corporations and partnerships.

Nor does Lysander Spooner, properly and sympathetically read, contradict these kinds of flexible expedients. Spooner wrote that our ancestors cannot bind us with respect to our own services and property, but that does not prevent them from disposing of what is solely theirs. A father could sell his buggy, horses and cows without his children's consent, and Spooner nowhere implied that such alienable property would revert to the children upon the father's death. The leaseholder who shares in some of the property rights to Tullock's inherited land is presumably another living person, not the deceased ancestor who first transferred the lease. There are major differences between Spooner's ideas and those of modern libertarian anarchists but this is not one of them.

The far more difficult problem that Tullock raises is national defense, which he correctly points out has troubled even such anarchist thinkers as David Friedman.[1] But when Tullock states that 'anarchists almost never discuss' the problem, he goes too far. I myself have contributed to an extended anarchist literature on this very question.[2] In all fairness, this writing has appeared mostly in obscure libertarian publications, which probably explains why Tullock has not investigated it.

Just as government is not a *necessary* condition for rule of law, it is equally obvious that government is not a *sufficient* condition for effective defense against invasion. Tullock makes much, as we have seen, of the fall of the Western Roman Empire, but the last time I checked, it had a government when it collapsed, whereas many of the invaders arguably did not. Ancient Israel was also blessed with one when taken over by the Assyrians; the Russian Principalities were similarly blessed when ravaged by Genghis Khan, as were the Aztec and Inca Empires of the New World when succumbing to Spanish conquistadors.

To be sure, primitive stateless societies have crumbled before conquest as well. Although the Indians of North America, usually without governments, were not subdued so quickly and easily as the far more numerous Incas and Aztecs, and were able to sustain a protracted resistance over several centuries, they were eventually dispossessed or exterminated. The fact that assorted states have now successfully carved up the entire inhabitable globe does pose an inconvenient empirical outcome for those anarchists, like myself, who believe that government defense is unnecessary.

Since this is a challenge that I have tried to answer in a recent, longer article (Hummel, 2001), I will not go into detail here. What I will say is that history does not support some of Tullock's glib generalizations. For not only is government far from a flawless defense against foreign invasion, but also conquest is not invariably and totally a bad thing. Tullock intimates as much with his reference to European suppression of slavery and piracy. Others might assert that the German people would have been far better off if the Nazi regime had simply surrendered to the Western Allies. Adding to the list would bog us down in interminable arguments about historical details, but nearly every reader will be able to come up with at least one government whose wartime extinction has made the world a better place.

National defense, according Tullock's rendition, is a service that government provides to its subjects. The state allegedly protects their lives, liberty and property from foreign governments. The reality, however, is that people often sacrifice their lives, liberty and property to protect the state and its territorial claims. The country in which Tullock and I live is already conquered by a brutal, thuggish government calling itself the USA. Yes, other governments in the world are much worse. But when our standard of comparison is Adolf Hitler, Josef Stalin and Mao Tse-tung, how much is that saying?

If liberty is really the goal, whether the capital city is located in Washington, Moscow, Tokyo, or Baghdad makes no intrinsic difference. What should concern us is the resulting tax rate – or more precisely, the total level of government oppression. The automatic assumption behind the nationalistic model of defense is that a foreign government can duplicate within a conquered country the approximate political, social, or economic conditions that prevail within the conqueror's home. But this is historical nonsense, as the USA is rediscovering in Iraq and Afghanistan. Brute military force is not some magical talisman with which George Bush or anyone else can bend the world to his will. Reality is far more complicated.

The amount of liberty that people enjoy, as well as the legal code under which they live, results from an incompletely understood interaction of myriad factors. One of the most important, if not the most, is ideas. For, as I have written elsewhere, ideas determine in which direction people point their guns, or whether they point them at all. Americans have been among the freest people in history not because they have been uniquely blessed with benevolent rulers. Their freedom stems from deeper, more resilient ideological dynamics and social structures that would persist even if somehow a living Saddam Hussein instantly replaced George Bush as US president.

Protection from a foreign government is thus a subset of a more general service: protection from *any* government, whether we label it foreign or domestic. As Tullock insists, numbers do matter too. An anarchist in Luxembourg would be quite vulnerable to a militarized Germany or militarized France, but the same would apply to a militarized Luxembourg. This just reflects the unfortunate truth that how much liberty I enjoy depends on what my neighbors think. Even with privately owned nuclear weapons I would be unable to reduce my taxes down to Tullock's optimum, let alone to zero, which simply goes to show that the policy question of providing defense without a state and the strategic question of how to reduce state power go hand in hand. Only solving the latter will allow us to solve the former. Both hinge on ideological transformations.

Do not mistake this emphasis on ideas for the total pacifism of the old Christian anarchists to whom Tullock alludes. Libertarian anarchists need no more eschew military force than legal force. But in both cases, the efficacy of force depends on more fundamental determinants. An unpopular law can become impossible to enforce, and an unpopular war can become impossible to win. Violent revolution or military action may sometimes be the appropriate way to overthrow a state and the best way to prevent foreign conquest. Yet precisely when such recourses are appropriate, best, or even possible is a function of the underlying ideological, social and institutional framework.

We can now understand why most anarchists, in Tullock's puzzling aside, 'confine themselves to writing and arguing for anarchy without trying it experimentally'. The reason no doubt parallels Tullock's own for confining himself to writing in favor of lower taxes rather than trying to lower them unilaterally. And libertarian anarchists may ultimately prove no more successful in their persuasive endeavors than Tullock has proven in his. This brings us back to national defense, an issue that insinuates a subtle but significant shift into the discussion. Tullock's other arguments try to demonstrate that government is desirable. But the salient thrust of his litany of conquests, however unintentional, is that government is inevitable, an altogether distinct proposition.

Sadly, this pessimistic assessment could be right. To paraphrase what I have written elsewhere: the human species may be unable to rid the earth of macroparasitic states. But this carries no more normative weight than the fact that we may never eliminate all microparasitic pathogens. The possibility that disease is inevitable would never be accepted as an adequate justification for abandoning the efforts of medicine against this scourge. The possibility that we may never completely curb the criminality of monopoly governments is scarcely a worthy reason to dismiss those who are convinced a more just world is possible and are striving to achieve it.

NOTES

1. David D. Friedman questions whether a stateless society can provide effective national defense in *The Machinery of Freedom: Guide to a Radical Capitalism* (1989: 135–43).
2. My most recent article on this subject is Hummel (2001). My other contributions include Hummel (1981, 1984, 1985, 1986, 1990), and Hummel and Lavoie (1990). See also Rothbard (1978: 263–94 and 2000: 115–32); Wollstein (1969: 35–8); Tannehill and Tannehill (1970:

126–35) and Hoppe (1998). Although Rand (1973) believed that national defense was a proper government function, she held that it should be funded voluntarily. One of her followers who agrees is Machan (1982).

REFERENCES

Friedman, David (1989) [1973], *The Machinery of Freedom: Guide to a Radical Capitalism*, La Salle, IL: Open Court.

Hoppe, Hans-Hermann (1998), 'The Private Production of Defense', *Journal of Libertarian Studies*, **14**: 27–54.

Hummel, Jeffrey Rogers (1981), 'Deterrence vs. Disarmament', *Caliber*, **9**: 8–10.

Hummel, Jeffrey Rogers (1984), 'On Defense', *Free World Chronicle*, **2**: 18–23.

Hummel, Jeffrey Rogers (1985), 'The Great Libertarian Defense Debate', *Nomos*, **3** (May/June): 19–25; (July/August): 21–30.

Hummel, Jeffrey Rogers (1986), 'A Practical Case for Denationalizing Defense', *The Pragmatist*, **3** (April): 1, 8–10 and (June): 3–4.

Hummel, Jeffrey Rogers (1990), 'National Goods Versus Public Goods: Defense, Disarmament, and Free Riders', *Review of Austrian Economics*, **4**: 88–122.

Hummel, Jeffrey Rogers (2001), 'The Will to Be Free: The Role of Ideology in National Defense', *Independent Review*, **5**: 523–37.

Hummel, Jeffrey Rogers and Lavoie, Don (1990), 'National Defense and the Public-Goods Problem', in Robert Higgs (ed.), *Arms, Politics, and the Economy: Historical and Contemporary Perspectives*, New York: Holmes & Meier.

Machan, Tibor R. (1982), 'Dissolving the Problem of Public Goods', in T. Machan (ed.), *The Libertarian Reader*, Totowa, NJ: Rowman and Littlefield.

Rand, Ayn (1973), 'Government Financing in a Free Society', in E.S. Phelps (ed.), *Economic Justice*, Baltimore: Penguin Books, pp. 363–7.

Rothbard, Murray N. (1978), *For a New Liberty: The Libertarian Manifesto*, rev. edn, New York: Macmillan.

Rothbard, Murray N. (2000), *Egalitarianism as a Revolt against Human Nature: And Other Essays*, Auburn, AL: Mises.

Tannehill, Morris and Tannehill, Linda (1970), *The Market for Liberty*, Lansing, MI: Tannehill.

Wollstein, Jarret B. (1969), *Society Without Coercion: A New Concept of Social Organization*, Silver Springs, MD: Society for Individual Liberty.

18. Anarchism as a progressive research program in political economy*

Peter J. Boettke

Economic theory, since its first systemic treatment in Adam Smith's *An Inquiry into the Nature and Causes of the Wealth of Nations*, has clearly stressed the mutual benefits of voluntary trade. By specializing in production and offering the goods and services for exchange with others, both individuals and society will be made better off. The source of wealth is not the natural resources that lie in the land, or the conquests of foreign lands, but an expanding division of labor driven by voluntary exchange. Smith had established a presumption toward voluntarism in human interaction on consequentialist grounds. Individual liberty was not only right from a moral perspective, but would yield greater social benefits as well. However, from the beginning of economics it was argued that these benefits of voluntary exchange could only be realized if the presumption toward voluntarism was suspended in order to create the governmental institutions required to provide the framework within which voluntary exchange can be realized.[1]

Precisely how much the presumption toward voluntarism would need to be suspended in order to provide the framework for voluntary exchange has been one of the most contested issues in economics since the late nineteenth century. The theory of public goods, monopoly and market failure all contributed to expanding the acceptance of coercion and qualifying the presumption toward voluntarism among mainstream economists. It is important to remember that each of these arguments for qualifying the presumption have been met with counter-arguments by economists that have demonstrated that so-called public goods can actually be privately provided, monopoly is not a natural outgrowth of voluntary exchange but the result of government intervention, and that market failures are themselves at root

* Earlier versions of this paper were given to the Hayek Society at Oxford University and as part of my Hayek Visiting Fellow lectures at the London School of Economics. I appreciate the critical feedback I received from these seminar participants and also from Edward Stringham, Peter Leeson, Chris Coyne, Gene Callahan, Jennifer Dirmeyer and Dan Klein. Financial assistance from the Mercatus Center and the Hayek Visiting Fellowship at the London School of Economics is gratefully acknowledged. The usual caveat applies.

caused by legal failures and not the consequence of unfettered exchange. Although a dominant line of research has pushed against the presumption of voluntarism, another line of research suggests that the presumption should be upheld more consistently if peaceful and prosperous social order is to be achieved.

It is this alternative line of research that I want to emphasize in my comments here. As I will explain, my emphasis will be on what I will call 'positive analytical anarchism' and the evolutionary potential of these ideas as a progressive research program in political economy in the contemporary setting of social science.

ANARCHISM AS A HISTORICAL IDEA IN POLITICAL ECONOMY

The idea that the voluntary presumption should be held in a consistent and unwavering manner has not been absent in political economy. It has, however, been consistently argued by the mainstream of political and economic thought to be an impractical ideal. In *Leviathan*, Thomas Hobbes argued that social order in the absence of an effective government would devolve into a war of all against all and life would be nasty, brutish and short. John Locke was not so pessimistic in his judgment of society without a state, but he argued that such a natural state would not be as effectively organized as a society governed justly. As we have already seen, Adam Smith argued that commerce and manufacturing could not flourish outside of a state of just government, and while David Hume argued that we should model all politicians as if they were knaves, he still insisted that an effective government was required to realize the system of 'property, contract and consent'.

In histories of political and economic thought we often pass over the anarchist writers too quickly. There are, however, some good reasons for this. Anarchist writers have always been minority figures, and anarchist writers have often waxed lyrical about worlds of post-scarcity and populated by transformed human spirits. But not every anarchist thinker in the history of political economy should be so easily dismissed. The historical anarchist discussion can be divided into three major categories:

1. Utopian – following in the tradition of William Godwin's *An Enquiry Concerning Political Justice* (1793).
2. Revolutionary – following in the tradition of Mikhail Bakunin and the First International, 1864–76.
3. Analytical – in the tradition of Murray Rothbard's *For a New Liberty* (1973) and David Friedman's *The Machinery of Freedom* (1973).

For my present purposes I will limit my discussion to analytical anarchism.[2] The reasons for this are straightforward. However historically important utopian and revolutionary anarchism may be, both traditions are decidedly devoid of economic content, whereas analytical anarchism is grounded in economic reasoning.

Thomas Carlyle described nineteenth-century *laissez faire* as 'anarchism with a constable'. Rothbard and Friedman were the first modern economists to ask whether the services of the constable needed to come from a monopoly provider. Unlike previous anarchist authors, Rothbard and Friedman avoided slipping in assumptions of post-scarcity or the benevolent transformation of the human spirit.[3] Instead, in a world of scarcity, populated by self-interested actors, Rothbard and Friedman reasoned that not only could social order be achieved in a world without a government-supplied constable, but, in fact, peace and prosperity would be achieved as well.

The challenge that Rothbard and Friedman represented to the mainstream of political philosophy and public economics did not attract the attention it deserved, but it was recognized by two major figures – Robert Nozick in political philosophy, and James Buchanan in public economics.[4] Nozick (1974) argued, using the invisible-hand style of reasoning that is closely associated with the discipline of economics, that if one starts in a world of anarchism one can derive a minimal state without violating the rights of individuals due to the natural monopoly character of law and order. Nozick, in a fundamental sense, harked back to Locke's argument and argued that civil society was possible absent the state, but that certain goods and services required for a more prosperous social order could only be provided by a monopoly supplier.[5] Buchanan (1975), on the other hand, relied on social contract theory to escape from the anarchist state of nature and in so doing explicitly harked back to Hobbes's argument that absent a sovereign the social order would be meager at best.

The discussion of analytical anarchism in the academic literature tailed off after Nozick and Buchanan.[6] Nozick's argument on the logical inevitability of a minimal state via an invisible-hand process was taken as proof of the failure of the argument of Rothbard and Friedman concerning anarcho-capitalism. The academic discussion in political philosophy moved from the justification of a minimal state to whether Nozick's arguments against distributive justice worked as an argument against the dominant Rawlsian notions of just distribution. The vast majority of political philosophers sided with Rawls on this issue, but even for those who sided with Nozick the question remained whether he had established appropriate limits on the redistributive state.[7] Buchanan's work, as it relates to this discussion, had its greatest impact in the effort to provide an analytical argument for the constraint of the growth of government. Buchanan distinguished between the protective state, the productive state, and the redistributive state. The argument against Rothbard and Friedman made by Buchanan was intended to establish the necessity of the protective state (court system, and domestic and national security) and the desirability of the productive state (public goods such as roads and libraries). But Buchanan warned of the expansion of the state via rent-seeking through the redistributive state. The puzzle in Buchanan's work moved from escaping from anarchism to effectively constructing constitutional-level constraints in government so that the protective and productive state could be established without unleashing the destructive rent-seeking tendencies of the redistributive state.[8] How can a minimal state be kept in check and not evolve into a maximum state? Anarchism represents one side of the social dilemma, with Leviathan representing the other.

Researchers in the field of political economy have sought to provide an answer to the paradox of government as put by Buchanan. The most notable attempt is probably in the work of Barry Weingast (1995) on what he terms 'market-preserving federalism'. Weingast argues that the paradox of governance can be solved through a federalist structure where political authority is decentralized, economic regulation is limited to the local level, and competition between the different levels of government is ensured. In such a political structure, a common market, Weingast reasons, is cultivated and the expansion of the markets (and with that the corresponding division of labor) results. The political institutions of constitutional constraint and the organization of federalism, where the political ambition of some is pitted against the ambition of others through structural design, leads to the economic growth and development of nations. When this structure breaks down, and the ambitions of some are realized at the expense of others (e.g. the rent-seeking phenomena of concentrated benefits on the well-organized and well-informed, and dispersed costs on the unorganized and ill-informed), economic growth is retarded. Weingast's work, while making a compelling case for the importance of fiscal federalism and a constitutional structure of limited government as responsible for the tremendous growth experienced among western democracies, also suggests that this organizational structure is fleeting at best and will break down in times of crisis. Market-preserving federalism breaks down as delineated authority is violated and economic regulation becomes centralized.[9] The ties that bind the rulers' hands are broken, and the limits on government give way to an increase in both the scale and scope of government. State power, rather than restrained, is now unleashed.

There is no doubt that governmental structure matters for economic interaction. A state structure which aligns incentives to minimize predation economically outperforms one that provides incentives for the predation by the powerful over the weak. But it is also the case that government by its very nature is predatory and thus will be used by some to exploit others wherever and whenever the coercive power of the government is established. In a fundamental sense government can only be constrained if the people the government is established to govern can coordinate around norms of governance which are self-enforcing.[10] This is the power behind the idea that a free society works best where the need for a policeman is least. No bonds are strong enough to tie a ruler's hands, at least not for any length of time. A government that is strong enough to tie its own hands is almost by definition strong enough to break those bonds any time its rulers deem it necessary. The quest for constitutional constraints that will forever bind rulers is in vain, though it might be an example of a noble lie.

The discussion in constitutional political economy is abstract and normative in intent. The ideal of a limited government that cultivates a market economy is a normative benchmark against which real-world political economies are judged. This normative exercise emerged as practically relevant in the wake of the collapse of communism in East and Central Europe and the former Soviet Union in the late 1980s and early 1990s. The original stage of transformation began with the recognition that socialist economies were shortage economies and thus the first policy moves had to be focused on *getting the prices right*. Freedom of contract had to become the rule for economic interactions so that market prices could adjust to coordinate buyers and sellers. But getting the prices right proved to be more difficult than simply freeing up the trading process. In order for a market economy to operate, the rules providing security to market participants must be instantiated. The transformation discussion moved to a focus on *getting the institutions right*. Institutions were defined as both the *de facto* and *de jure* rules and their enforcement. But since the *de jure* rules are much easier to identify and manipulate, the focus in the literature was mainly on the official sector such as the judicial system or the regulatory apparatus. This was unfortunate because in practice the acceptance of the *de jure* rules is constrained by the *de facto* norms and conventions that govern everyday life in any given society. The difficulty of getting institutions to 'stick' in the transforming societies proved to be much more difficult than merely manipulating formal institutions of governance. For rules to stick they must be to a considerable extent self-enforcing. Thus, we have entered the current stage of discussion in transition analysis, where the focus is on *getting the culture right*. The discussions surrounding social capital, trust and civil society all relate to the idea that you need some underlying set of shared values that reside in the everyday morality of the people which legitimate certain institutional structures and patterns of social intercourse and ultimately enable the gains from peaceful cooperation to be realized.[11]

This quick detour through the past 15 years of transition political economy demonstrates that we have moved from the normative ideal to the description of the underlying conditions necessary to realize that ideal. The social world is not so malleable that we can impose whatever social order we desire wherever and whenever we want.[12] But there is another side to this evolution of intellectual interests. Precisely because our ability to impose exogenously the institutional structure that will effectively govern society has proven to be so weak, we must open up our analysis to the evolution of rules from games of conflict to games of cooperation. Instead of designing ideal institutional settings that we can exogenously impose on the system and thus provide the 'correct' institutional environment within which commerce and manufacturing can flourish, we have to examine the *endogenous* creation of the rules by social participants themselves. The science and art of association is one of self-governance and not necessarily one of constitutional craftsmanship. And herein lies the contribution that contemporary research on anarchism can make to modern political economy.

THE POSITIVE POLITICAL ECONOMY OF ANARCHISM

The focus on endogenous rule creation in commercial societies started to receive serious attention during the late 1980s. For our purposes the most important studies were conducted by Bruce Benson (1990) and Avner Greif (1989). Benson provided an examination of the law merchant and how a body of law governing the commercial transactions of traders in an international setting had developed spontaneously to provide the security for the expansion of trade. The development of international trade and the expansion of the division of labor did not require governmental institutions, but instead developed on the basis of endogenous rule creation by commercial parties as they sought to minimize conflicts and realize the gains from exchange. Greif's work explained how trading partners functioned in medieval Europe without the sanctity of government enforcement of contracts. Greif provides a detailed historical account and uses the analytical lens of modern game theory to analyze how reputation mechanisms facilitate cooperation among traders outside of state enforcement. Benson's argument is one where self-interest drives the development of a body of non-state law that parties agree to so that they can realize the gains from exchange even among socially distant individuals. Greif, on the other hand, shows how reputation mechanisms can serve to ensure cooperation among traders who are socially near. Greif's work is not as optimistic as Benson's about the ability of self-interest to generate endogenously rules of social intercourse once we move beyond small group settings where reputation mechanisms are effective.[13]

Benson and Greif are but two prominent examples of a literature that seemed to explode on issues of self-governance in the late 1980s and 1990s. Janet Landa's (1995) study of trading networks, Lisa Bernstein's (1992) study of the extra-legal rules governing trade in the diamond industry, and Robert Ellickson's (1991) examination of the resolution of conflicts between ranchers and farmers in Shasta County, CA all point to a growing recognition among social scientists that advanced cooperation without command can indeed occur and does occur in a variety of social settings. Social order is not necessarily a product of governmental institutions; instead, peace and prosperity can emerge outside of the structure of state enforcement.

It might be useful to remind ourselves of the original puzzle with which we started this chapter. Economics from its founding has demonstrated that wealth and the harmony of interests in society are realized through voluntary exchange. However, the main line of thinking has been caught in a quandary because in order to realize the gains from exchange, notions of mine and thine had to be strictly defined and enforced by state agencies which required the use of coercion to secure the funds necessary to provide these services.[14] The literature I pointed to above demonstrates that main-line thinking makes an error of overpessimism with regard to the ability of rules of good conduct to emerge naturally through social intercourse.

Of course, we can also make an error of overoptimism and assume that social order will emerge in the absence of any rules whatsoever. But we do not live in a world where the majority of individuals are atomistic and devoid of social feelings and desires for cooperative belonging.[15] Instead, we are social creatures finding our way in the world by relying on family networks and then more extended networks. As Adam Smith put the puzzle, man 'stands at all times in need of the cooperation and assistance of great multitudes, while his whole life is scarce sufficient to gain the friendship of a few persons' (1776: 18). This cooperation among anonymous actors provides the central mystery in economics from its classical to contemporary incarnation.[16]

In addition to the theoretical puzzle of how cooperation among strangers can emerge, there is the practical issue that in many different settings the assumption of a given institutional structure of workable governance is simply inaccurate.[17] To discuss these issues I shall focus on three contributors to this volume whose work on self-governance directly touches on the themes that I highlighted as characteristic of anarchism as a progressive research program in political economy. In this regard I will discuss the work of Edward Stringham (2002), Peter Leeson (2005), and Christopher Coyne (2005).[18]

EXCLUSION, INCLUSION AND THE ELICITATION OF COOPERATION OUT OF CONFLICT

Realizing cooperation among strangers is one of the core mysteries that economics has sought to explain since the discipline's founding. In fact, the

Greek word meaning exchange – Katallaxy – has another meaning which translates as the bringing of a stranger into friendship. The historical and anthropological record is full of examples of how exchange relationships between warring factions can emerge to improve the situation of these previous enemies, and often result in enemies becoming allies. Of course, we also have examples where warring strangers fail to cooperate with one another for centuries and are therefore unable to realize the cooperative benefits that would be realized if they could get past their distrust for the 'other'.

At some level we can argue that the realization of social cooperation is the result of a delicate balancing act.[19] Most economists postulate that this balancing act is accomplished by effective government to protect against predatory behavior. Yes, human nature includes a propensity to 'truck, barter and exchange', but it also includes an opportunistic side which when pursued uninhibitedly leads to the 'rape, pillage and plunder' that define much of human history. Governmental institutions, it is argued, exogenously impose order on what otherwise would be a chaotic situation. Law and order enable us to curb our opportunistic nature and realize our cooperative nature. But this solution is unsatisfactory for a variety of reasons. First, governmental institutions did not historically emerge as a consequence of a social contract, but instead through revolution and conquest. Government, in short, is not an institution that appeals to our cooperative side, but to the opportunistic side of our nature. Second, we know that the cooperation in anonymity that defines the modern division of labor resulted in the absence of government and not because of government. Trade between individuals in domestic and foreign settings does not require government oversight to emerge and develop. Third, in the pressing situations of the late twentieth century with regard to the collapse of communism in East and Central Europe and the former Soviet Union, the failure of development planning in Africa and Latin America, and the post-conflict situation of the countries of the Middle East, we cannot assume a functioning state.

The work of Stringham, Leeson and Coyne addresses these situations each in its own way. Stringham's work focuses on the development of complicated financial arrangements such as stock exchanges in the absence of government control. He examines both historical episodes in Amsterdam and London, as well as contemporary situations such as the Czech Republic. Stock markets are an excellent case to study to highlight the issues of self-governance. Traders are asked to commit capital to an investment that will pay off only in the future, so the level of trust required is much higher than would be required to swap current goods for currency in a street market. For our present purposes, what is important is the mechanism that Stringham discovered which made these historical episodes work to elicit cooperation among strangers in the absence of government control. He postulates that in situations of dealing with strangers, a series of 'club-like' arrangements emerge that seek to identify different characteristics and employ *exclusion tactics* to eliminate potential and real dishonest dealers. The self-governance of complicated financial arrangements, in other words, is possible because the organization adopts 'Stringham mechanisms' to exclude cheaters. By postulating a situation where a variety of traders enter the marketplace, but by examining the 'exclusion' criteria adopted by the trading 'club', Stringham highlights how only those traders who can be trusted will in fact pass the criteria threshold and be accepted. If we go back to the claim that the key idea in realizing social cooperation is somehow to get institutions that make individuals treat strangers as if they were honorary friends, then what Stringham does is show how in situations of anonymous traders, trading organizations will adopt rules that restrict membership so that traders are less anonymous, and thus reputation and multilateral punishment will suffice to ensure cooperation rather than opportunism.

Peter Leeson's work looks at this process from the other way around. He does not address questions of trading clubs, such as stock exchanges, but focuses instead on how complete strangers signal to potential trading partners that it is worth their while to accept them into trading relationships. Stringham looked at the behavior of those accepting new trading partners; Leeson looks at the behavior of those wanting to join the circle of trading.[20] In this regard, 'Leeson mechanisms' focus on inclusion, rather than exclusion. The norm for dealing with strangers is distrust and thus exclusion, so new traders must signal to others that they possess characteristics which overcome this natural distance. We are different enough that the gains from trade are significant, but similar enough so that trust can be assured in the interaction – promises will be made and kept. Leeson's work comes in both theoretical exercises exploring signaling and commitment, and also historical narratives discussing the law merchant, trade in pre-colonial Africa, and modern international trade. In the absence of any defined government, Leeson shows that social cooperation is indeed possible and voluntarism can flourish.

Chris Coyne's work is different from that of either Stringham or Leeson, and focuses instead on situations of what I shall call 'practical anarchy'. His focus is on war-torn areas where conflict is the norm, and the question is: how do they move from conflict to cooperation and realize peace and prosperity?[21] He examines US military interventions in the post-World War II era and judges the success or failure from the intervener's point of view. He finds that self-sustaining social order is, in fact, quite elusive. One of the important insights from Coyne's work is the recognition of the 'dark side' of cooperation as well as the 'bright side'. The stock of social capital may indeed provide us with the background trust required to realize the gains from exchange with others. But social capital can also bind us together in groups which attempt to exploit others for our private gain. In sorting out precisely when social capital is productive, when it is destructive, and how to move along a spectrum from conflict to cooperation, Coyne is advancing our understanding of the social conditions required to realize a peaceful and prosperous order in the face of dysfunctional, or complete absence of, government rule.

All three of these researchers are advancing the existing body of literature on the nature and significance of anarchism as a starting point for research in political economy. Their work invites others to explore the political economy of stateless orders and how social cooperation through the division of labor can be realized through rules of self-governance rather than state government. The art of voluntary association moves from ideological wishful thinking to the focus of a scientific research program and in so doing harks back to the central puzzle of political economy since its founding.

CONCLUSION

I have argued that political economy was born out of a mystery and a puzzle. The mystery is, how did a complex division of labor among socially distant individuals emerge and serve as the basis of the wealth of modern civilization? In exploring this mystery economists came to highlight the mutual benefits of voluntary exchange and its self-reinforcing nature. However, this raised a serious puzzle for economists. There was a presumption toward voluntarism in human affairs, but in recognition that our nature is divided between a cooperative nature and an opportunistic nature we must figure out a way to curb our opportunistic side if we hope to realize the fruits of our cooperative side. While our cooperative nature is reflected in our propensity to truck, barter and exchange (which no other species actually exhibits), our opportunistic side is revealed in the warring nature witnessed throughout human history. Political economy solved the puzzle by suggesting that we could sacrifice in a small way the presumption of voluntarism in order to create a government which will curb our opportunistic side and enable our cooperative side to flourish. Thus was born the argument for limited, but effective, government that was the core of classical liberal thought from John Locke, David Hume and Adam Smith to more contemporary writers such as Frank Knight, Ludwig von Mises, F.A. Hayek, Milton Friedman and James Buchanan.

This solution, I have argued, must be found wanting for a variety of reasons. Instead, the sort of explorations in this book must be encouraged by scholars who understand the central mystery of economic life and are more optimistic that the puzzle of governance can be solved in a voluntaristic manner, rather than by the coercive nature of the state. Work along these lines in not only valuable at a fundamental theoretical level, but also of practical significance as well, as we attempt to wrestle with the great social transformations of our era.

NOTES

1. As Adam Smith wrote in *The Wealth of Nations*: 'Commerce and manufacturing can seldom flourish long in any state which does not enjoy a regular administration of justice. . . . in which the faith in contracts is not supported by the law, and in which the authority of the state is not supposed to be regularly employed to enforce the payment of debts from all those who are able to pay. Commerce and manufacturing, in short, can seldom flourish in any state in which there is not a certain degree of confidence in the justice of government' (1776: 445).
2. Rothbard and Friedman did not emerge out of nothing and there are several precursors to their position found in the history of classical liberalism and the individualist anarchist movement of the late nineteenth century. An excellent resource for those interested in studying the rich history of anarchism is provided by Bryan Caplan and can be found at: http://www.gmu.edu/departments/economics/bcaplan/anarfaq.htm.
3. The differences between Rothbard and Friedman are significant, but not crucial to my discussion here. Rothbard relied on economic reasoning to explain the operation of the free society, but he drew normative justification from natural rights theory. Friedman, on the other hand, did not resort to rights-based reasoning, but instead presents his work as a utilitarian defense of anarchism. What I am focusing on is the economic reasoning behind each thinker, not the normative thrust of their writings.
4. The timing of these works is significant, as is the fact that they emerged in the USA rather than in the UK or elsewhere. The rise of the welfare/warfare state in the USA of the late 1960s and early 1970s provided the historical background. In the hands of Rothbard and Friedman, anarchism was a viable alternative to Vietnam War era statism. Buchanan and Nozick sought to provide an argument for the necessity of the state, but one that could be effectively constrained to minimize the coercion introduced into the social order by the state.
5. In the terms of the modern literature of public economics, Nozick argued that law and order represented a network externality. Tyler Cowen (1992) and Cowen and Dan Sutter (1999) use this network externality argument to suggest that anarchism could only work if it mimicked the state as a natural monopoly provider of law and order, and therefore would cease to be 'anarchy'. Cowen, and Cowen and Sutter provide a new twist on Nozick's invisible-hand theory of the emergence of the state which challenges the radical libertarian conclusions of Rothbard and Friedman. However, Caplan and Stringham (2003) provide a counter-argument to Cowen, and Cowen and Sutter.
6. A small libertarian following continued to work in the framework of Rothbard and Friedman, but its influence in professional discussions was limited. The arguments by Nozick and Buchanan, on the other hand, attracted considerable attention in the mainstream literatures of philosophy, politics and economics. Nozick's *Anarchy, State and Utopia* actually won the 1975 National Book Award for Philosophy and Religion, and Buchanan was awarded the 1986 Nobel Prize in Economic Science.
7. Not enough work, in my opinion, was done to follow up on the last section of *Anarchy, State and Utopia*. However, see Boettke (1993: 106–31), where Nozick's discussion of decentralized communities is employed to examine the restructuring of post-communist societies.
8. This volume is dedicated to addressing the effectiveness of Buchanan and his colleagues' effort to provide the lead out of anarchy, and the papers can be divided into two camps. The first camp challenges the proposition that the anarchist state would be as undesirable as Buchanan and his colleagues describe. The second camp argues that the effort by Buchanan and his colleagues to escape from anarchism is not as solid as was concluded at the time these works first appeared. I am emphasizing a slightly different path forward for research on anarchy than either challenging the Hobbesian description or the effectiveness of the

constitutional contract, though my intellectual sympathies lie with these challenges. I first discussed this in my student days (Boettke, 1987) while commenting on Buchanan's contribution to political economy and Austrian economics in celebration of my teacher winning the Nobel Prize.

9. One of the most candid essays I have ever read in the academic literature was written by Robert Higgs and is entitled 'Can the Constitution Protect Private Property Rights During National Emergencies?' The answer, Higgs states, 'is no. The historical record is quite clear; and in regard to this question there is no reason to suppose the future will differ from the past' (1988: 369).

10. This coordination aspect of constitutional governance is explored in Russell Hardin's *Liberalism, Constitutionalism and Democracy* (1999).

11. Another significant literature that has emerged is the one on state-building and in particular the idea of the governing capacity of a society. This literature is summarized in Fukuyama (2004). This literature fits into my description between getting the institutions right and getting the culture right. It is an attempt to clarify what is required of the apparatus of public administration in transition and less developed economies to achieve success while leaving the question of the underlying morality aside. In the end of the analysis, however, the underlying morality of the people under examination is recognized to be the constraint that ultimately determines success or failure in the effort at state-building.

12. See Boettke (2002: 248–65).

13. However, see Klein (1997), where a collection of articles across disciplines and in a variety of circumstances demonstrates that reputation and other social customs emerge to elicit good conduct among individuals even in the absence of governmental rules to protect against fraud and theft.

14. However, see David Schmidtz's *The Limits of Government: An Essay on the Public Goods Argument* (1991), where this standard public-goods defense of government coercion is challenged.

15. Experimental work in economics has repeatedly demonstrated that we get higher degrees of cooperation among anonymous traders than what strict rationality as assumed in game theory would predict. See Smith (2003) for an overview of this work. Of course, our sense of belonging can also be a curse as well as a blessing. This is the great tension that Hayek highlighted in his later work (e.g. 1979), where we are hardwired biologically for cooperation in small bands and thus have a natural tendency toward atavistic morality whereas to live and thrive in modern society we have to take a less atavistic approach toward our interaction with others. Developing a morality for the modern commercial society is actually one of the more challenging tasks in political philosophy.

16. See Seabright (2004) for a discussion of this central mystery of economic life and how research in economics and other disciplines is improving our understanding of the mediating institutions which enable us to realize the gains from division of labor and exchange through our cooperation with complete strangers and yet ward off complete ruin through opportunism.

17. Rajan (2004) discusses this with regard to underdeveloped countries and argues that standard economic models are poor guides to public policy precisely because of this. He calls for research that assumes anarchy as the starting state and then explains how social cooperation can emerge in such a setting. Francis Fukuyama (2004) also argues that standard economic models fail on the ground of assuming what they must prove in his discussion of the building of state institutions and improving their operation. Both Rajan and Fukuyama can be seen as establishing the research ground for 'practical anarchism', but the question of whether a working government is required to realize the benefits of an advanced network of exchange relations must remain open.

18. There is no substitute for reading the original, so the reader is encouraged to read these works rather than rely on the superficial summary provided here, as I focus on certain aspects of their work rather than on the entire complex story that these authors weave. My purpose here is only to look at their work as an invitation to others to follow their analytical lead and do theoretical and empirical research on the elicitation of cooperation in the absence of a recognized government and under a situation of anonymity. Let me be clear

about my terminology before proceeding. First, by progressive I do not mean merely empirical progress, but a much broader notion which is meant to capture the idea that a research idea stimulates others to do work on the same topic. If a research program is progressive, it will, for example, generate ten papers by different scholars for every core paper written on the topic. It will lead others to explore the empirical world to see the mechanism in operation, or it will motivate others to examine the logical foundations of the mechanisms specified. Second, by absence of government I mean both the absence of governmental institutions, and also situations where there is no clearly recognized monopoly of coercion. Situations with competing governments are anarchical, just as situations where there is no government to speak of. Third, the social dilemma will be limited to situations of large group settings with socially distant individuals (strangers) and we will not examine the situation of how social cooperation can emerge among family members or close kin. In other words, we have to examine the question of cooperation in anonymity. The answer seems to lie in mechanisms to make situations of anonymity appear as situations of kinship. Fourth, by social cooperation I do not mean the complete absence of violence or dishonest behavior, but rather that social interaction is primarily cooperative and that effective mechanisms emerge that penalize anti-social behavior so that a cooperative norm rather than a conflict norm dominates social intercourse.

19.   The idea that our social order is a delicate balancing act is explored in Seabright (2004). As he puts it: 'Nature knows no other examples of such complex mutual dependence among strangers.' The complex division of labor that defines modern society must be protected against our opportunistic nature. Our institutions must make it possible for us to treat complete strangers as if they were honorary friends. There is a delicate balancing act between our opportunistic and cooperative natures, but we need robust institutions that ward off our opportunistic side and encourage our cooperative side. 'In other words, participants need to be able to trust each other – especially those they do not know. Social cooperation depends on institutions that have exactly such a property of robustness' (2004: 2; 5).

20.   Leeson has focused his research on those situations where a strict meaning of reputation and multilateral punishment would not suffice because the trading group is too large and anonymous, and yet cooperation is elicited through the process of signaling and commitment.

21.   In this regard Coyne (2005) is taking seriously the admonition from Rajan (2004) that economists stop assuming the functioning background of respected property rights enforced by the courts and developed markets. Instead, Coyne is examining the 'mechanisms' by which, starting in a conflict-torn area, cooperation can emerge through the choices of individuals, and the difficulties confronted by outside actors (e.g. foreign military intervention) to impose a cooperative order.

REFERENCES

Benson, B. (1990), *The Enterprise of Law*, San Francisco, CA: Pacific Research Institute for Public Policy.

Bernstein, L. (1992), 'Opting Out of the Legal System', *Journal of Legal Studies*, **21**: 145–53.

Boettke, P. (1987), 'Virginia Political Economy: A View from Vienna', reprinted in *The Market Process: Essays in Contemporary Austrian Economics*, Aldershot, UK and Brookfield, USA: Edward Elgar Publishing.

Boettke, P. (1993), *Why Perestroika Failed: The Politics and Economics of Socialist Transformation*, New York: Routledge.

Boettke, P. (2002), *Calculation and Coordination: Essays on Socialism and Transitional Political Economy*, New York: Routledge.

Buchanan, J. (1975), *The Limits of Liberty: Between Anarchy and Leviathan*, Chicago, IL: University of Chicago Press.

Caplan, B. and E. Stringham (2003), 'Networks, Law, and the Paradox of Cooperation', *Review of Austrian Economics*, **16**(4): 309–26.

Cowen, T. (1992), 'Law as a Public Good', *Economics & Philosophy*, **8**: 249–67.

Cowen, T. and D. Sutter (1999), 'The Costs of Cooperation', *Review of Austrian Economics*, **12**(2): 161–73.

Coyne, C. (2005), 'After War: Essays on the Mechanism for Successful Post-War Reconstruction and Social Change', PhD thesis, Department of Economics, George Mason University.

Ellickson, R. (1991), *Order Without Law*, Cambridge, MA: Harvard University Press.

Friedman, D. (1973), *The Machinery of Freedom*, New York: Harper & Row.

Fukuyama, F. (2004), *State-Building*, Ithaca, NY: Cornell University Press.

Greif, A. (1989), 'Reputation and Coalitions in Medieval Trade', *Journal of Economic History*, **49**: 857–82.

Hardin, R. (1999), *Liberalism, Constitutionalism and Democracy*, New York: Oxford University Press.

Hayek, F.A. (1979), *Law, Legislation and Liberty*, Vol. 3, Chicago, IL: University of Chicago Press.

Higgs, R. (1988), 'Can the Constitution Protect Private Property Rights During National Emergencies?', in James Gwartney and Richard Wagner (eds), *Public Choice and Constitutional Economics*, Greenwich, CT: JAI, pp. 369–86.

Klein, D. (ed.) (1997), *Reputation*, Ann Arbor, MI: University of Michigan Press.

Landa, J. (1995), *Trust, Ethnicity and Identity*, Ann Arbor, MI: University of Michigan Press.

Leeson, P. (2005), 'Cooperation and Conflict: Self-Enforcing Exchange Among Socially Heterogeneous Agents', PhD thesis, Department of Economics, George Mason University.

Nozick, R. (1974), *Anarchy, State and Utopia*, New York: Basic Books.

Rajan, R. (2004), 'Assume Anarchy?', *Finance & Development*, **41**(3): 56–7.

Rothbard, M. (1973), *For a New Liberty*, New York: Macmillan.

Schmidtz, D. (1991), *The Limits of Government: An Essay on the Public Goods Argument*, Boulder, CO: Westview.

Seabright, P. (2004), *Company of Strangers*, Princeton, NJ: Princeton University Press.

Smith, A. (1776), *An Inquiry into the Nature and Causes of the Wealth of Nations*, Chicago, IL: University of Chicago Press, 1976.

Smith, V. (2003), 'Constructivist and Ecological Rationality', *American Economic Review*, **93**(3): 465–508.

Stringham, E. (2002), 'Essays on Self-Policing Networks in Financial Markets', PhD thesis, Department of Economics, George Mason University.

Weingast, B. (1995), 'The Economic Role of Political Institutions', *Journal of Law, Economics and Organization*, **11**: 1–31.

Index

Printed in Great Britain
by Amazon